LEGACY OF INJUSTICE

THE UNTOLD STORY OF ASHARAM BAPU

ASHISH KUMAR

Made with ♥ on the Notion Press Platform
www.notionpress.com

Contents

Legacy of Injustice: The Untold Story of Asharam Bapu book is written for the mature reader. Its purpose is not to hurt anyone's feelings. Neither is it in favor or opposition to any person, society, gender, creed, nation, or religion.

These are the author's own views.

Hope that by reading this book, you will try to understand and appreciate the author's point of view.

It is merely an attempt to portray social reality. The aim of the book is to shed light on the untold story of Asharam Bapu, advocate for justice, judiciary reformation, and highlight the dual face of kangaroo media. Moreover, it aims to promote peace, non-violence, tolerance, friendship, unity, prosperity, happiness, and integrity.

Thank you for your understanding and cooperation.

I would like to express my deepest gratitude to all those who have contributed to the creation of this book. Firstly, I extend my heartfelt thanks to the divine presence of Asharam Bapu, whose life journey has inspired countless souls towards enlightenment and truth.

I am indebted to the unwavering support and encouragement of my family and friends, whose love and belief in me have been a guiding light throughout this endeavor. Their patience, understanding, and encouragement have been invaluable.

I am immensely grateful to the legal experts and researchers who provided invaluable insights and assistance in unraveling the complexities of the legal aspects surrounding the case. Their expertise and dedication have been instrumental in shedding light on the intricacies of the legal proceedings.

I also extend my sincere appreciation to the countless individuals who have tirelessly advocated for justice and fairness, seeking to uphold the principles of truth and integrity in the face of adversity.

Last but not least, I acknowledge the readers whose curiosity and quest for knowledge have driven the exploration of this narrative. May this journey inspire reflection, dialogue, and a deeper understanding of the pursuit of truth and justice.

With Humility and Gratitude

As a psychologist, it's fascinating to see how Ashish Kumar's book, "*Legacy of Injustice: The Untold Story of Asharam Bapu,*" sheds light on the intersection of spirituality, psychology, and societal dynamics. The portrayal of Asharam Bapu's life journey, particularly in the context of Maslow's hierarchy of needs, underscores the significance of his purported attainment of self-actualization.

The narrative also brings to the forefront the alarming prevalence of media sensationalism and the detrimental impact of biased media trials. The fabrication of facts by the media, coupled with the absence of fair treatment such as bail and parole, highlights the systemic injustices faced by an elderly saint of 85 years, Asharam Bapu. It's distressing to note that despite equivalent cases receiving bail and parole, he has languished in jail for over 11 years.

As a neutral observer and psychology professional, it's imperative to acknowledge the importance of objective analysis and the pursuit of justice. Ashish Kumar's book serves as a crucial testament to the complexities of human behavior, societal prejudices, and the urgent need for reform within our justice system.

In conclusion, "*Legacy of Injustice*" by Ashish Kumar offers a thought-provoking exploration of spirituality, the justice system in India, and media bias. As psychologist Carl Jung once said, "*Knowing your own darkness is the best method for dealing with the darknesses of other people.*" Through this lens, Kumar's work challenges us to confront societal injustices and strive for a fairer, more compassionate world.

Shilpa Agarwal

Best Regards,
Shilpa Agrawal
Clinical Psychologist (Licensed by the Rehabilitation Council of India)

"*Legacy of Injustice: The Untold Story of Asharam Bapu*" This is an enlightening book authored by Ashish Kumar as it gives deep insights into the true facts of Ashram Bapu's case. An unfortunate troublesome case of the decade, which was sensationalised by the media & actual facts were brushed under the carpet. As an advocate I can put it very straight that the case was not dealt properly, the media got swayed away by the high profile nature of the case & no one bothered for the real facts. The entire events which unfolded raises serious doubts & queries. Even I had gone through the case papers a year back and spoken in detail about how the case story it itself absurd and improbable on my YouTube Channel - "*Fight for your Right by Shri R.M.Mishra & Adv Kirti*". I have also spoken in my videos that this injustice which has been done in Asharam Bapu Case by the trial courts, if not set aside by higher courts, will become an authority/citation in future and any friend of yours will appear after 20 years and claim that I have been sexually assaulted by this person 20 years back! Therefore, not only people who are connected with Asharam Bapu should challenge the judgements of Asharam Bapu in Higher Courts, but all lawyers and jurists connected with the justice dispension system should speak up about the strange judgements of jodhpur and ahmedabad trial courts in Asharam Bapu case. The author in this book has done an incredible job by answering various unfilled gaps and queries which were never touched by any media. I recommend everyone to read this book.

Kirti

KIRTI AHUJA
Advocate
Supreme Court of India, Manager (Fight for your right)

Very pleased to have a glimpse of the wonderful book by Ashish Kumar entitled **Legacy of Injustice**, which comprises the untold story of the inhuman, unbelievable acts of citizen Honourable Asharam Bapuji, revered sant. It is a surprise and an eye-opener for all the people in the world that not even a remand is granted to the great sant, on whose feet many prostrate. Sometimes in his career, even great personalities like Bharat Ratna Atal Bihari Vajpayee Ji, Bharat Ratna Lal Krishna Advani Ji, R.S.S. Chief, numerous Cabinet Ministers, and many National Presidents have paid respects. Yet, in the hard waters that followed, no one is there even to consider a genuine grievance. Not even a single day's parole was granted to him. Meanwhile, murderers of honorable Prime Minister Mr. Rajeev Gandhi are roaming freely on the roads. Even though the Supreme Court passed death sentences and life imprisonments on the culprits, they are not behind bars or on parole, they are freely moving around. But this facility is not available for Asharam Bapuji. What a joke it is! It is surprising. Where are we heading? Are we heading towards **Ram Raj or Rome Raj?** All these conspiracies were caused because he was a barrier to the large-scale conversion of Hindu core beliefs. However, my blessings are for Ashish Kumar, who ventured to cover this truly untold story, which deserves to be filmed, similar to the Kashmir stories & Kerala Stories – what is happening and how it is happening? Are terrorists involved in the murder of former Prime Minister Rajiv Gandhi less harmful? And is Asharam Bapu more harmful? What a world we are living in, revealing these shocking affairs! Ashish Kumar has done a tremendous service to Sanatan Dharma, to the Indian nation, and to all those who respect revered sants. I'm highly hopeful for a bright career for him in the field of reading and writing.

Suvrat Tripathi

Suvrat Tripathi, DG (Retired) IPS-RR 1977

It is a great fortune if you are in contact with Sant Asharam Bapu! Not writing this casually.. there are profound reasons behind it! Personally while researching his case and witnessing more than many social service activities guided through him, in various parts of India & abroad, has left me in awe! From the very beginning, I have been astonished by the extensive support Sant Asharam Bapu has received from Prominent Lawyers, Renowned Personalities, and even from Many other Sants. The millions of disciples of Bapu come from diverse backgrounds including scientists, engineers, doctors, lawyers, bureaucrats, businessmen, and people from all walks of life. Such a diverse and educated following cannot be easily misled solely based on faith or religious beliefs. Can a multitude of millions stand behind a wrongdoer!!? Somehow it indicates that there might have been injustices against him that the society at large is not fully aware of.

Therefore, my first gratitude goes to Sant Asharam Bapu. The author, Ashish, has been able to write this book so effectively for this very reason!! Congratulations! :)

Being in academics and research, I comprehend the critical importance of having the guidance of an exemplary Sant in today's ever-evolving world, particularly for the youth. Having been part of university environment for more than many years, I have closely observed the youth of today.

For India to become a world leader, it is essential for today's youth to be equipped with self-confidence, a deep understanding of religion, a commitment to service, and the ability to find solutions to problems, make wise decisions, and bring about positive changes for the Nation. However, attaining these qualities necessitates young individuals to nurture their inner capabilities alongside their formal education. They should have the opportunity to be mentored by revered Sants and Sages too who can offer them not only spiritual but ethical guidance too. Unfortunately, the incarceration of such Ideal Sants is a tragedy that deprives the country, religion, and its youth of the right guidance they deserve Rectifying the damage caused to the country and religion as a result of this situation is a formidable challenge!

I am delighted that people like Ashish continue to strive to bring truth to society despite facing diverse challenges! This book is highly recommended for its ability to present facts objectively, uphold justice in the face of injustice, and dispel misunderstandings and distances between People and Great Sants. Congratulations to Ashish Kumar and I wish for widespread readership of this valuable book both nationally and internationally!

Vasudha Vashisht

Dr. Vasudha Vashisht
Associate Professor
(Academician & Researcher)
Amity University

In the intricate tapestry of human history, there are narratives that compel us to reflect on the complexities of justice, faith, and the human spirit. "Legacy of Injustice" by Ashish Kumar is one such narrative that delves into the life and trials of a figure enshrined in the hearts of many as a beacon of spiritual guidance, Asharam Bapu.

The book navigates through the labyrinth of events that have led to the revered sant's current circumstances, juxtaposing his revered status with the legal challenges he faces. It raises poignant questions about the scales of justice, the support of followers, and the role of influential leaders in times of adversity.

Ashish Kumar's work is not just a chronicle of events; it is a mirror reflecting the societal and cultural undercurrents that influence the perception of justice. It is a bold exploration of the dichotomy between the reverence of a spiritual leader and the allegations that have led to his incarceration. The narrative is a catalyst for dialogue and introspection, urging readers to ponder the delicate balance between respect for religious figures and the pursuit of legal truth.

May this book serve as a bridge between differing perspectives, fostering understanding in a world where justice and compassion must walk hand in hand.

As a counselor and writer, I commend Ashish Kumar for his dedication to bringing forth this untold story. It is a narrative that deserves attention, discussion, and reflection. May his journey through the realms of reading and writing continue to illuminate the many facets of truth and belief that shape our world.

Rekha Rani

Dr. Rekha Rani
Counselor and Writer

Do you know why Sant Shri Asaram Bapu has been imprisoned? It is because he liberated thousands from addiction, converted thousands of Christians to Hinduism, and facilitated the return of thousands of Muslims to their ancestral faith. As a result, today he languishes in jail. This seems to be the rule in our India. A person who walks the path of righteousness will find thousands ready to pull him down, and this is not a new phenomenon. It has been the norm since time immemorial. In our country, if a Sant shows the right path, thousands are ready to point fingers at him. Whether it be Tulsidas Ji, Raidas Ji, or Kabirdas Ji. When Tulsidas Ji wrote the Ramcharitmanas, thousands opposed it, and today, the same Ramcharitmanas is pervasive among the populace. There is no Sant like Asaram Bapu in the present times across the whole world.

Ashish Kumar's book, 'Legacy of Injustice: The Untold Story of Asharam Bapu,' is a message for all humanity that 'India will no longer tolerate atrocities against Sants.' I am very pleased that today's youth stand with the Sants and are raising their voices for them.

My best wishes to Ashish Kumar for this book.

Radhe Radhe!!!

Anmol

- Anmol Ji Maharaj
Shree Dhaam Vrindavan

CHAPTER ONE

Early Life To Marriage

INTRODUCTION

Sants are the true treasures of any nation. Their lives serve as exemplary guides for the people of their time. One esteemed Sant has even stated that it's more beneficial to hear about a Sant's life than to witness the divine presence first-hand. Throughout history, the Lord has manifested Himself in the form of Sants to uphold the principles of righteousness suitable for each era.

Among the Sants of our time, Sant Asharam Bapu stands out as a beacon of spiritual wisdom. He is not only a Master of Yoga but also deeply knowledgeable about the Vedas. Revered Bapu's spiritual state is beyond description; attempting to capture it in words is akin to comparing a dim lamp to the brilliance of the midday sun.

Nevertheless, out of reverence and love, we humbly endeavour to present a brief account of Bapu's life, a living embodiment of the esoteric science of Brahman.

Sant Asharam Bapu's journey began with a deep longing for spiritual fulfilment. From a young age, he exhibited a natural inclination towards meditation and self-reflection. His unwavering dedication to spiritual practices led him to attain profound insights into the nature of existence.

Bapu's teachings emphasize the importance of leading a righteous life, rooted in compassion and selflessness. He tirelessly worked to uplift society by imparting spiritual knowledge and guiding individuals on the path of righteousness.

Despite facing numerous challenges and obstacles, Bapu remained steadfast in his commitment to truth and justice. His life exemplifies the power of faith and resilience in overcoming adversity.

Throughout his life, Bapu has touched the hearts of millions with his wisdom and compassion. His discourses and writings continue to inspire people from all walks of life to lead meaningful and virtuous lives.

Sant Asharam Bapu's life is a testament to the transformative power of spirituality. His teachings resonate with simplicity and depth, offering invaluable guidance to seekers on their spiritual journey. May his legacy continue to illuminate the path of truth for generations to come.

BORN

Sant Asharam Bapu was born on April 17, 1937, (Vikram Samvat 1994) in the village of Berani, situated along the Sindhu River in the Nawabshah district of Sindh province, India. His birth name was Asumal, and he was born into the household of Nagar Seth Shri Thaumal Sirumalaniji and mother Mahangiba.

Asumal's family included his parents and siblings, consisting of an elder brother and three elder sisters. From a tender age, his mother instilled Vedic cultural values in him, fostering a deep sense of devotion and spirituality. Early each morning, it was customary for Asumal to awaken and engage in worship and meditation, a practice that continued to nurture his spiritual growth as he matured.

Despite his young age, Asumal's commitment to spiritual practices only intensified over time, guided by the teachings and values imparted by his mother. These foundational principles laid the groundwork for his profound spiritual journey, shaping his character and guiding his actions.

As Asumal grew older, his devotion to spiritual pursuits remained unwavering, influencing every aspect of his life. His humble beginnings and early exposure to Vedic traditions laid the foundation for the remarkable spiritual leader he would later become, inspiring countless individuals to embark on their own paths of self-discovery and self-realization.

Through simplicity and sincerity, Sant Asharam Bapu's story serves as a testament to the transformative power of spirituality and the enduring influence of a mother's love and guidance.

CHILDHOOD

Since His early years, there was a unique radiance about Him, and His eyes shone with a special brilliance. His family's Guru had foreseen that this child would one day become a revered Sant and uplift humanity. Today, that prophecy is unfolding before our eyes. At the tender age of eleven, He began to demonstrate extraordinary abilities, though perhaps unaware of their significance. His innate kindness and compassion guided His actions, touching the lives of those around Him. It was as if a divine light illuminated His path, leading Him towards a greater purpose. This journey, rooted in simplicity and humility, would eventually transform countless lives.

EDUCATION

The revered Sant began his education in Sindhi Language and later joined Jai Hind High School in Mani Nagar, Ahmedabad, at the tender age of 7. Despite His young age, His remarkable memory allowed Him to effortlessly recite songs, poems, and other materials word for word after hearing them just once from His teachers. During breaks, instead of indulging in play or gossip like other children, young Asumal would seek solitude under a tree, deep in meditation on God.

Despite His early devotion to God, He continued His worldly education up to the third standard. It's worth noting that today, intellectuals ranging from those holding M.A. and Ph.D. degrees to high-ranking government officials such as IAS officers, as well as millions of learned professionals including leaders, doctors, and lawyers, have become His disciples.

This account highlights the Sant's humble beginnings and His unwavering dedication to spirituality from childhood. It portrays His simplicity and deep connection with the divine, which ultimately led Him to become a revered figure with followers from various walks of life, all inspired by His teachings and wisdom.

DISCERNMENT-DETACHMENT

Asumal's profound intellect discerned the emptiness of worldly pursuits, realizing that the ultimate essence worth seeking is the Supreme Being. With a fervent desire for God-realization, a detachment from worldly attachments ignited within him. Despite his family's intentions to marry him off, Asumal, driven by his dispassion, chose a different path. Eight days prior to the planned wedding, he quietly departed from home. After an extensive search, his family eventually located him in an ashram in Bharuch.

Asumal's deep understanding led him to prioritize spiritual pursuits over worldly entanglements. His decision to leave home in pursuit of a higher truth reflects his unwavering commitment to spiritual growth. This incident marks the beginning of Asumal's journey towards Self-realization, guided by his discernment and detachment from material distractions. Through his humble yet profound actions, Asumal exemplifies the essence of simplicity and spiritual devotion, inspiring others to seek a similar path of inner fulfilment and realization.

MARRIAGE

The marriage was arranged, and due to familial pressures and the course of destiny, it was solemnized. Yet, he remained committed to his spiritual path. He convinced his wife, Lakshmi Devi, to join him in a life of celibacy until he achieved self-realization. Embracing his ideals, Lakshmi Devi also chose a life of austerity and spiritual practice alongside her revered husband.

Their decision stemmed from a deep sense of devotion and dedication to their spiritual journey. Despite the societal expectations and familial obligations, they remained steadfast in their resolve. Their commitment to each other was not based on conventional norms but on a shared aspiration for spiritual growth and enlightenment.

Their union exemplified a rare blend of love and devotion transcending earthly desires and attachments. Together, they embarked on a journey of self-discovery and inner transformation, supporting and inspiring each other along the way.

Their story serves as a testament to the power of spiritual partnership and the pursuit of higher truths. It reminds us that true fulfilment lies not in worldly pursuits but in the pursuit of the divine within oneself.

During societal pressures and expectations, they chose a path less travelled, guided by the light of their inner wisdom and devotion. Theirs was a union blessed by the divine, bound not by earthly ties but by a shared commitment to spiritual evolution and enlightenment.

CHAPTER TWO

Left Home & Had A Meeting With Satguru

FORSAKED HOME AND MET WITH SATGURU

On the auspicious day of February 23, 1964, Asumal embarked on a profound journey, leaving behind the comforts of home to seek the ultimate truth. With a heart full of determination and a spirit unburdened by worldly attachments, he ventured forth into the unknown, guided solely by the inner calling of his soul.

His path was not easy. Through rugged caves and dense forests, across snow-covered mountains and thorny terrains, Asumal pressed on, undeterred by the challenges that lay ahead. Nights spent on rocky beds and days filled with the trials of solitude tested his resolve, yet his faith remained unwavering.

After a long and arduous journey, Asumal found himself amidst the tranquil woods of Nainital, where he awaited the meeting with his destined guide, Sai Shri Leelashahji Maharaj. For forty days, he waited patiently, his heart filled with anticipation and longing for the wisdom that awaited him.

When the moment finally arrived, Asumal approached his guru with humility and reverence, ready to receive the teachings that would shape his spiritual path. Under the guidance of Sai Shri Leelashahji Maharaj, he underwent rigorous tests and trials, each one serving to strengthen his resolve and deepen his understanding of the divine.

Through moments of struggle and moments of grace, Asumal remained steadfast in his commitment to the path of self-realization. His dedication and sincerity earned him the blessings of his guru, who entrusted him with the sacred practices of meditation and worship.

For seventy days, Asumal immersed himself in the teachings of his guru, practicing diligently and surrendering himself completely to the journey of inner transformation. With each passing day, he felt his heart expand with love and his mind awaken to the infinite possibilities of spiritual growth.

And then, as instructed by his guru, Asumal prepared to return home, carrying with him the light of wisdom and the blessings of divine grace. Though his physical journey had come to an end, his spiritual journey had only just begun, as he embarked on the path of service and compassion, guided by the timeless truths imparted to him by his beloved guru.

In the quiet moments of reflection, Asumal would often think back to the days of his journey, remembering the trials and tribulations that had shaped him into the person he had become. And with a heart full of gratitude and a spirit filled with humility, he would offer thanks to the universe for the gift of guidance and the blessing of spiritual awakening.

PERIOD OF SADHANA

After spending 13 days at home, he reached the banks of the river Narmada at Moti Koral and resumed his intense spiritual practices. Here, he embarked on a 40-day-long period of deep devotion and austerity, known as an Anushthan. During this time, his focus on divine love was so intense that he paid little attention to his physical well-being or daily diet. He would often lose himself in states of profound meditation, remaining absorbed for hours on end.

One night, while he was meditating on the bank of the river Narmada, a violent storm suddenly arose. Seeking shelter, he moved to the veranda of a house located in Chanod Karnali. However, his presence there caused alarm among the locals, and a fisherman mistook him for a thief or a bandit. This led to a commotion, with people from the entire area gathering with weapons such as cudgels, spears, knives, daggers, and swords, ready to confront him.

Despite the tumult, his deep state of inner peace remained unshaken. The disturbance eventually roused him from his meditative trance. With love and compassion, he looked upon the gathered crowd and calmly walked out, passing through them without any confrontation. Later, when the truth became clear to everyone, they realized their mistake and earnestly sought his forgiveness.

In this incident, we witness the Sant's unwavering tranquillity and compassion even in the face of misunderstanding and potential harm. His ability to maintain inner peace amidst external chaos serves as a powerful example of spiritual strength and resilience.

Through this narrative, we learn the importance of remaining centred and grounded, especially during challenging circumstances. The Sant's forgiveness towards those who misunderstood him reflects his deep understanding of human nature and his commitment to love and compassion.

This story not only highlights the Sant's remarkable spiritual journey but also offers valuable lessons for all seekers on the path of inner awakening and self-discovery. It reminds us that true strength lies not in wielding external weapons but in cultivating the inner qualities of love, forgiveness, and peace.

INCREDIBLE MOMENTS OF SELF- REALIZATION

Just before the completion of his Anushthan, Lord Shiva inspired him to meet his Guru for God-realisation. After completing the spiritual ritual, Asumal departed from Moti Koral and journeyed to Vajreshwari in Mumbai, where his revered spiritual guide, Param Pujya Sai Shri Leelashahji Maharaj, had arrived for a period of solitude. Witnessing Asumal's profound dedication to spiritual practice, the compassionate heart of his guru overflowed with joy. Showering affection upon his devoted disciple, Gurudeva expressed, "*My dear child, I am immensely pleased to witness your fervent desire for realization of the Divine.*"

The boundless grace emanating from Gurudeva's heart fulfilled all the spiritual practices of the aspirant. The Supreme Guru bestowed upon his disciple the exalted state of Absolute Gurudom, wherein Asumal attained the realization of his True Self and the Supreme Self. This divine revelation occurred at 2:30 p.m. on Wednesday, the 2nd lunar day of the bright fortnight of the Ashwina month in Samvat 2021 (7th October, 1964), marking the emergence of Sant Asharam Maharaj from Asumal.

The momentous occasion encapsulated the culmination of Asumal's spiritual journey, as he transitioned from a seeker to a Self-realized master under the benevolent guidance of his guru. The significance of this event reverberates through the annals of spiritual history, symbolizing the timeless bond between the guru and the disciple, and the transformative power of divine grace.

It was not merely a personal revelation for Asumal; rather, it signified a profound shift in consciousness that rippled through the fabric of existence, illuminating the path for countless seekers of truth. The simplicity of his demeanour belied the depth of his spiritual attainment, as Asumal, now known as Sant Asharam Maharaj, radiated a serene aura of wisdom and compassion.

The words exchanged between guru and disciple echoed the eternal truths of the spiritual journey – the unwavering faith, the relentless pursuit of self-realization, and the boundless grace that guides the seeker along the path. In the presence of his guru, Asumal experienced the destruction of the ego (Dissolution of the ego happens in Yoga samadhi (Nirvikalpa samadhi) because the ego emerges again after samadhi state is gone. In Jnana samadhi, the ego is destroyed forever), the unveiling of divine knowledge, and the ultimate union with the Supreme.

The legacy of this sacred moment endures as a beacon of hope for all who tread the path of spirituality, reminding humanity of its inherent potential for transcendence and transformation. Through the simple yet profound teachings of Sant Asharam Maharaj, seekers continue to find solace, inspiration, and guidance on their quest for spiritual fulfilment.

In essence, the incredible moment of self-realization represents the pinnacle of Asumal's spiritual odyssey – a journey marked by unwavering devotion, profound insight, and boundless grace. It is a testament to the transformative power of divine love and the eternal bond between guru and disciple, transcending time and space to illuminate the path of truth for generations to come.

IN THE DEPTH OF YOG

For seven years, Asharam immersed himself in the absolute brahman, spending time at the Deesa ashram and the Nala cave of Mount Abu. Recognizing his disciple's ripe state of spiritual Jivanmukti, Pujya Shri Leelashahji Bapu acknowledged his disciple's mastery. He expressed that Asharam had nurtured the seed of knowledge given to him into a fully grown tree or Brahmanishtha.

Observing Asharam complete prowess in uplifting others spiritually, Pujya Shri Leelashahji Bapu instructed him to transition into a householder's life. He urged Asharam to share the spiritual bliss he had attained with those engulfed in worldly flames of sins, agony, grief, tension, animosity, rebellion, ego, and unrest. The command was clear: to assist others in awakening to their true selves.

Asharam accepted this noble task with humility and determination. He understood the importance of simplicity in spreading spiritual teachings. He committed himself to communicate in a language that even a child could comprehend, avoiding the complexities of abstruse philosophy. His mission was to reach out to people from all walks of life, irrespective of their educational background or intellectual capacity.

With a compassionate heart and a clear purpose, Asharam embarked on his journey as a householder. He travelled far and wide, sharing the message of spiritual awakening and inner peace. Through simple yet profound teachings, he guided people towards realizing their true nature and breaking free from the shackles of ignorance and suffering.

Asharam's approach was rooted in love, empathy, and humility. He met people where they were, offering them practical tools and techniques to navigate life's challenges with grace and resilience. His teachings emphasized the importance of self-reflection, mindfulness, and compassion towards oneself and others.

As Asharam continued his mission, he witnessed countless transformations. People from all walks of life found solace and inspiration in his words. They experienced profound shifts in their consciousness, leading to greater harmony, clarity, and fulfilment in their lives.

In every interaction, Asharam radiated love and kindness. His presence alone was enough to uplift spirits and ignite a sense of hope and possibility. Through his simple yet profound teachings, he touched the lives of many, leaving behind a legacy of love, wisdom, and compassion.

In essence, Asharam's journey exemplified the power of humility, simplicity, and service in spreading the light of spiritual awakening. His dedication to sharing the timeless wisdom of Vedanta & Yoga transcended language barriers and touched the hearts of people around the world.

THE FEARLESS LIGHT

In a bold test of his unwavering connection to the divine, Asharam ventured deliberately into a settlement teeming with unruly drunkards. Two inebriated individuals, their senses clouded by alcohol, spotted him amidst their midst. One of them, brandishing a weapon resembling a scythe fixed at one end of a long staff, menacingly positioned it at his neck, challenging him with a sinister proposition: "*Shall I sever your throat?*"

With serene fearlessness, He responded, "*Let Your will prevail.*" His words echoed with a quiet assurance, drawing upon an inner strength that transcended mortal fears. Witnessing His unshakable resolve and spiritual grandeur, both men were seized by a sudden wave of awe and reverence. In an instant, their bravado crumbled, replaced by a profound humility as they prostrated themselves at His feet, imploring for forgiveness.

Even amidst periods of solitary contemplation, Asharam remained steadfast in His commitment to uplifting others and guiding them towards the path of righteousness. His altruistic endeavours extended far beyond the confines of seclusion, as He tirelessly worked to liberate individuals from the shackles of addiction, urging them to forsake harmful habits such as the consumption of alcohol, non-vegetarianism, and other vices.

Through His compassionate actions and unwavering dedication, He illuminated the hearts of countless souls, offering them solace and hope amidst the darkness of their struggles. His teachings resonated with simplicity and clarity, accessible to all, regardless of their background or level of understanding. He exemplified humility and compassion, embodying the timeless virtues of love and forgiveness.

In His presence, the boundaries of fear dissolved, replaced by an overwhelming sense of peace and serenity. His radiant aura cast a luminous glow, dispelling the shadows of doubt and uncertainty that plagued the minds of those who crossed His path. Each encounter with Him was a profound reminder of the transformative power of faith and the boundless potential of the human spirit.

As His legacy continues to endure, His teachings serve as a guiding light, illuminating the path towards spiritual awakening and inner fulfilment. His life stands as a testament to the triumph of the human spirit over adversity, inspiring generations to embrace the light of truth and walk fearlessly towards enlightenment.

One day, Asharam decided to leave, Deesa, and journey towards Nareshwar. He went deep into a dense forest near the Narmada riverbank, a place where hardly anyone went. He found a quiet spot under a tree and started to meditate on himself and the higher power. He was so engrossed in his meditation that he didn't realize the night had passed.

When the sun rose, he felt hungry and thirsty. But instead of searching for food, he decided to stay put. He thought to himself,

(Socha main na kahin jaunga, Yahin baithhkar ab khaunga Jisko garaj hogi aayega, Srishti karta khud layega)

"I won't go anywhere. I'll sit here and wait for someone to bring food for me if he needs to feed me. The Creator of the universe will take care"

As he sat there, two farmers suddenly appeared with milk and fruits. They told Asharam that they were guided by a dream to bring him food. Despite his initial refusal, they insisted, and eventually, he accepted their kind fruit and milk from them when they told him God appeared in their dream, ordered them to bring food for a sadhu, and showed the path to this place.

After eating, Asharam continued his journey. He visited caves in Abu, remote forests, and even the Himalayan region.

Asharam's story teaches us about faith and humility. Despite facing hunger and thirst, he trusted that the universe would provide for him. He also showed kindness by accepting the farmers' offer, even though he initially refused.

Through his simple yet profound actions, Asharam inspires us to trust in the divine and remain humble on our own spiritual journeys. His story reminds us that sometimes, the answers we seek come when we least expect them, guided by forces beyond our understanding.

The establishment of the Ahmedabad Ashram marks a pivotal moment in the spiritual journey guided by the revered Sat Gurudev Swami Sai Shri Leelashahji Maharaj. After a hiatus of nearly seven years, Pujya Shree returned to Ahmedabad on the auspicious occasion of Guru Purnima in Samvat 2028, which fell on Thursday, 8th July 1971. This return was not only in compliance with the ardent insistence of Sat Gurudev but also to fulfil a promise made to his mother.

The humble beginnings of the ashram date back to 29th January 1972 when devotees came together to erect a temporary hut in a rugged and uneven valley along the Sabarmati River. The surrounding terrain was fraught with thorny bushes and dense forests, instilling fear in the hearts of people who dared not venture into the area even during daylight, wary of encounters with drunkards and robbers. However, with the establishment of the ashram, a remarkable transformation unfolded, dispelling the atmosphere of fear and hostility.

Today, the branches of this magnificent tree of spirituality have not only spread across the nation but have also reached distant shores of foreign lands. What began as a modest cottage along the Sabarmati River has blossomed into a revered pilgrimage site known as the *'Sant Asharam Ashram'*. Here, millions of individuals from diverse backgrounds, spanning various castes, religions, and nationalities, partake in the nectar of meditation and Satsang, finding solace and blessings as their grievances are alleviated.

The ashram serves as a beacon of light, offering guidance and spiritual nourishment to all who seek it. Its teachings transcend barriers of language, culture, and creed, embracing humanity in its entirety. Through the practice of meditation and the wisdom shared in Satsang's, individuals find a pathway to inner peace and self-realization.

As the ashram continues to flourish, its impact resonates far and wide, touching the lives of countless souls yearning for spiritual fulfilment. It stands as a testament to the enduring legacy of Sat Gurudev Sai Swami Shri Leelashahji Maharaj and the unwavering dedication of those who have nurtured its growth over the years.

In essence, the Ahmedabad Ashram stands as a sanctuary of peace, love, and enlightenment, inviting all who seek refuge in its comforting embrace. Its humble beginnings serve as a reminder that greatness often emerges from the simplest of origins, guided by the purest of intentions and fuelled by the collective aspirations of those who believe in its transformative power.

CHAPTER THREE

Beyond the Clouds: The Godhra Helicopter

A NEAR-DISASTER TURNED MIRACLE: THE GODHRA HELICOPTER INCIDENT

Helicopter accidents, though not uncommon, often result in injuries or worse. However, a remarkable event unfolded on August 29th in Godhra, Gujarat, leaving thousands of witnesses in awe. Pujya Bapu was a route from Morbi to Godhra for a Purnima darshan and Satsang program when the unexpected occurred.

In a surreal turn of events, the helicopter lost control at a considerable height, causing it to crash land with a deafening impact. What followed seemed nothing short of miraculous: despite the severity of the crash, no one sustained any injuries.

It's not every day that one witnesses such a dramatic turn of fate. The helicopter's nose hitting the ground after losing balance could have spelled disaster, yet by some divine intervention, everyone emerged unscathed.

The incident serves as a poignant reminder of the fragility of life and the inexplicable workings of destiny. It leaves us grappling with questions of faith and belief, pondering the existence of forces beyond our comprehension.

For the thousands who bore witness to the event, it was a moment that defied logic and reason. How could such a catastrophic event end without casualties? The answer, perhaps, lies in the realm of faith and divine providence.

In the aftermath of the crash, speculation swirled as to what had transpired. Was it merely luck, or was there a higher power at play?

Whatever the explanation, one thing remained clear: a sense of gratitude and awe permeated the air as people grappled with the magnitude of what had just occurred.

As news of the incident spread, it served as a source of inspiration and reflection for many. It underscored the importance of faith and resilience in the face of adversity, reminding us that sometimes, miracles do happen.

In the annals of history, the Godhra helicopter incident will be remembered not just as a narrow escape from disaster, but as a testament to the enduring power of hope and belief. It serves as a beacon of light in times of darkness, a reminder that even in our darkest moments, there is always room for miracles to occur.

So let us pause, amidst the chaos of life, to appreciate the inexplicable wonders that surround us. For during uncertainty, there is solace in knowing that sometimes, against all odds, miracles do happen. And in those moments, we are reminded of the boundless potential of the human spirit and the enduring presence of divine grace.

It was broken into pieces but Bapu who was sitting on the front seat, the pilot and other passengers remained unscathed. The people who witnessed the scene were surprised. The helicopter had been badly damaged; its strong iron body had been broken into pieces, but all organs of Bapu's soft body were intact! if this isn't a miracle of God; what else can it be called? Scientists know that white petrol that fuels copters is highly inflammable. A little spark touching it is sufficient to produce a devastating fire. Even the nearby trees and plants are burnt down, After the accident, the white petrol flowed like water flows from a tap, but no blast took place. The hind part of the helicopter had even caught fire, but the fire was extinguished miraculously. The crash produced such a bang that people from surrounding areas came running to the spot. But everybody saw Bapu come out safe and sound. There was no need to measure His pulse or blood pressure. Soon Bapu arrived at the Satsang site, and He was in his usual blissful Self. Such a big thing had happened; yet Bapu was dispensing joy in his natural style the same humour, the same joyful dancing, and the same blissfulness. What else can this event be called if not a miracle? It is a tangible proof of the greatness of Self-Realized and Self-Reposed Brahma Gyani Sant. Somebody says it is a miracle performed by a Brahma Nishtha Sant equal to an avatar, another says it is God's divine Leela. Some attribute it to yogic powers or greatness of Indian culture. All these different views point towards but one fact. The God-realized Sant Bapu has proved true his quote, "*As China is known for the great wall, Kuwait for petroleum, America for dollar, India is known for Sants of the Vedic culture having great divine powers."*

Today, people not only in India but all over the world are wonder struck watching the images and video clips of this accident on Internet and TV Channels.

Former President of India Shrimati Pratibha Patil while enquiring about Bapu's wellbeing on phone said that a number of high ranking Air Force Officers, on being asked as to what could have been the reason of Bapu coming safe and sound out of this terrible accident, had replied unanimously that it must have been a miracle performed by Bapu otherwise there was no question of people coming unscathed from such a horrible accident.

Immediately after the accident, different TV Channels described all passengers coming unscathed out of the accident as a miracle of Bapu. Different newspapers described the accident as providential, unprecedented and miraculous.

In this accident, the helicopter was broken into three pieces, but Asharam is completely safe and sound. This is no less than a miracle, TV Channel 'Zee News. '

Asharam Bapu is the luckiest man of the century News Channel 'TV 9'.

"Through this helicopter accident, God has displayed His miraculous power." Newspaper 'Hindustan'.

"Everybody coming safe and sound from such an accident is no less than a miracle." - News Channel 'ABP'.

"Bapu Asharam has a miraculous escape from a copter crash". Newspaper 'The Pioneer'.

"It was Bapu's miracle only, which was seen by the whole world. News Channel 'A2Z'.

The god of death (Kaal) went back after saluting a Brahma Gyani (Mahaakaal)" – Newspaper 'Acharan',

This accident has made all celebrities, intellectuals, religious leaders of other faiths and sects, and even atheists acknowledge the calibre of Pujya Bapu. This accident is powerful enough to open the eyes of Bapu's detractors also.

Bapu says this is the miraculous power of the science of mantras, "So powerful are the Vedic mantras that one doing Japa of them can ward off not only his own untimely death but also that of others with him. A regular reciting of the Guru Gita saves one from untimely death and other dangers.

Describing the glory of Guru-Gita, Lord Shiva says:

अकालमृत्युहृंत्रीवसर्वसंकटनाशनी।

Many a time during his Satsang discourses, Bapu has told that with Japa of mantra so many times so and so house of one's horoscope gets purified. With 80 million Japa of the mantra, the house of death is purified. Such a person will not meet an untimely death.

'It's wands off untimely death and all calamities."

Today this accident is being discussed not only in India but all over the world and whoever comes to know of it becomes wonder-struck to see Sant Asharam Bapu's yogic powers and greatness. It's only due to Asharam Bapu's miraculous powers that we are safe and sound.

The pilot of the crashed helicopter "What was the reason behind the crash landing of the helicopter will be known after the probe is completed. It is only because of Asharam Bapu's miraculous powers that we are safe and sound even after meeting such a terrible accident. With Bapu's blessings, nobody received even a bruise".

We came out of the jaws of death hale and hearty due to the protective divine aura of Bapu.

Ashwin Yadav, a passenger of the helicopter, Rajkot "In the past I met with motor-bike accidents two-three times. But at that time, I was not as fearless as I was with Bapu at this time meeting with a copter crash. It was such a terrible accident yet thanks to Bapu's divine aura, we came out of the jaws of death hale and hearty. I was not the least afraid.

Earlier, I worshipped Bapu's physical form as my Guru but now I know that he is the Protector, and Preserver. He is the omnipresent Lord about whom Lord Krishna says in the Gita:

वासुदेवः सर्वमतिसिमहात्मासुदुर्लभः ।

'Realizing that all this is Vasudeva (the innermost Self); such a great soul (Mahatma) is very hard to find.'

For me, it was coming face to face with God. -Naresh Manganaani, an eye witness.

"For me, everybody coming out unscathed from such a terrible accident is not less than seeing God in person".

CHAPTER FOUR

Study of Shaktipaat

A PROFOUND EXPLORATION INTO THE MYSTICAL POWER OF SHAKTI PAAT IN THE AURA OF SANT ASHARAM BAPU

In 1962 AD, the journey of Dr. Hira Taparia into the realm of aura analysis began, driven by a profound curiosity to comprehend the unseen energies that envelop us. Over six years, Dr. Taparia dedicated himself to the study of this mysterious science, meticulously decoding its complexities and revealing its secrets. This relentless pursuit led to the achievement of ISO 9001:2000 Certification, a significant milestone in his endeavor to illuminate the enigmas of the human aura.

With his deepening expertise, Dr. Taparia had the honor of disseminating his insights at Moscow Medical University, where he presented lectures on six occasions. It was during these engagements that he recognized the far-reaching implications of his work, especially concerning the aura of Sant Asharam Bapu.

Captivated by the spiritual radiance emanating from Bapu's being, Dr. Taparia undertook an exhaustive analysis of his aura, aiming to decode the mysteries veiled within its glowing expanse. The discoveries were astonishing, unveiling a spectrum of colors and energies that eloquently narrated Bapu's spiritual eminence and the potent influence of Shaktipaat.

Central to Bapu's aura was a resplendent violet shade, indicative of the loftiest levels of spiritual awakening— A hue seldom observed, reserved for entities of extraordinary spiritual prowess, reminiscent of the esteemed Rishis and ascended Masters from ancient traditions. This insight affirmed Bapu's steadfast commitment to spiritual growth and his profound bond with the divine.

However, it wasn't merely the violet in Bapu's aura that enthralled Dr. Taparia, but also its vigorous energy and vibrancy. He perceived the presence of crimson red within the aura, associated with the dissemination of spiritual energy via Shaktipaat, positioning Bapu as a channel for divine benevolence, imparting blessings and dispelling negativity with mere contact.

Additionally, the ethereal sky blue shades adorning Bapu's aura alluded to the otherworldly domains his spiritual influence reached, underscoring the limitless scope of his consciousness that transcended the physical world into the boundless spiritual universe.

Delving deeper into Bapu's aura, Dr. Taparia was astounded by the profound effect of his presence on others. Numerous individuals were transformed by his divine grace, steered towards spiritual awakening and inner metamorphosis—a testament to the enduring sagacity and compassion emanating from Bapu, enriching the lives of those he encountered.

In summation, Dr. Taparia's analysis of Sant Asharam Bapu's aura stands as a tribute to the deep-seated mysteries of the human spirit and the life-altering potency of spiritual enlightenment. Through Shaktipaat, Bapu conferred blessings upon mankind, shepherding them towards serenity, concord, and spiritual prosperity. Indeed, his celestial luminescence persists in its brilliance, enlightening the hearts and souls of all in pursuit of veracity and sagacity.

Of particular significance in Sant Asharam Bapu's aura is the remarkable ability to transmit divine energy. Dr. Hira Taparia, an expert in aura analysis, observed that while most individuals possess the capacity to receive energy from others, Bapu's aura is uniquely endowed with the power to obliterate negative energy in those who come into contact with him and to infuse them with positive energy. Another distinctive trait of Bapu's aura is its capability to transmit energy to anyone, even from a considerable distance.

During a visit to Bapu's satsang, Dr. Taparia noted that Bapu's aura could stretch like latex, enveloping the entire assembly in its embrace.

Dr. Taparia's study of auras also delves into the past lives of individuals. His research on Bapu's aura unveiled a history of ten consecutive births during which Bapu has engaged in the noble task of serving humanity. This service includes leading people towards spirituality through Shaktipaat, liberating them from addictions, fostering health, eradicating societal evils, and disseminating the 'Prasad' of Knowledge and Self-bliss. The limitations of the analytical machine restricted the reading to only the last ten of Bapu's births.

The development of Bapu's Sahasrara chakra and Ajna chakra is so profound that the machine was unable to fully record them. According to Dr. Taparia, Bapu has attained the pinnacle of perfection, with an aura more highly developed than any he has studied before.

Dr. Taparia expresses a fervent hope to have the opportunity to study Bapu's aura once more, as such a highly developed aura is a rare and invaluable subject for further research.

Pujya Bapu is described as a master of infinite potencies. The information provided is based solely on the machine's readings. Just as a television antenna is limited to receiving waves within its range, the machine can analyze Bapu's aura only to the extent of its capabilities. It is not possible to fully measure the aura and divine powers of Self-realized Sants. As the knower of Brahman can only be estimated by another Brahmajnani, so too is the divine spiritual state of such Sants beyond full comprehension.

Even Vasishthaji, the revered guru of Lord Rama, has stated, '*The glory of Self-realized Sants cannot be described in full.*' Similarly, the sage Ashtavakra posed to King Janaka, '**तस्य तुलना केन जायते?**' - '*Whom can the Self-realized Sants be compared to?*'

CHAPTER FIVE

Contribution Towards Society

HIS CONTRIBUTIONS

For over five decades, this revered Sant has been tirelessly fostering spiritual enlightenment among the masses through the conduit of Satsangs. These gatherings serve as a sacred space where individuals from all walks of life come together to immerse themselves in the teachings of wisdom and self-realization. Through simple yet profound discourses, the Sant imparts invaluable lessons on self-discipline, integrity, and devotion, inspiring countless souls to embark on their spiritual journey.

The essence of self-discipline and uprightness is not merely preached but deeply ingrained in the hearts of devotees through regular Satsang and Dhyan Yog camps. These camps serve as sanctuaries for seekers, offering them guidance and support in their quest for inner transformation. Through meditation and introspection, participants learn to cultivate a deeper connection with their inner selves, fostering a sense of clarity and purpose in their lives.

In addition to spiritual enlightenment, the Sant's contributions extend to philanthropic endeavors aimed at uplifting society. Through the establishment of over 425 ashrams and more than 1400 Shri Yog-Vedanta Seva Samitis worldwide, the Sant's vision of holistic upliftment is realized. These centers serve as beacons of hope, offering support to the needy and marginalized, irrespective of caste, creed, or nationality.

One of the Sant's most impactful initiatives is the establishment of Bal Sanskar Kendras, where young minds are nurtured with noble values free of cost. These centers serve as cradles of moral and ethical development, instilling in children the importance of compassion, integrity, and empathy from a tender age. Through interactive sessions and engaging activities, children learn to embody these virtues, laying the foundation for a brighter and more harmonious future.

The Sant's tireless efforts have not only transformed individual lives but have also left an indelible mark on society. His teachings resonate deeply with people from all walks of life, transcending barriers of language, culture, and nationality. Through his selfless service and unwavering commitment to humanity, he serves as a guiding light, illuminating the path towards a more enlightened and compassionate world.

In essence, the Sant's contributions encompass not only spiritual awakening but also holistic societal upliftment. His teachings inspire individuals to lead lives of integrity, compassion, and service, fostering a culture of harmony and understanding in an increasingly divided world. Through his selfless deeds and unwavering dedication, he continues to touch the lives of millions, leaving behind a legacy of love, wisdom, and enlightenment for generations to come.

A 'Bal Sanskar Kendra', or Child Development Center, is a nurturing space where each child is recognized as a reservoir of infinite potential, akin to a divine manifestation. Just as some may embody the wisdom of Adi Shankaracharya, Swami Ramtirtha, Mahatma Buddha, Mahavir Swami, or Swami Vivekananda, while others harbor the latent ability to become future leaders or prime ministers. The crux lies in guiding them towards the right path. Our aspiration is to mold children into luminous beings within the realm of a 'Bal Sanskar Kendra', empowering them to wipe the tears of fellow citizens and elevate the nation to the pinnacle of global leadership once again.

In a 'Bal Sanskar Kendra', the emphasis is not merely on academic excellence but on holistic development encompassing moral, ethical, and spiritual dimensions. It's a sanctuary where children are nurtured with values such as compassion, empathy, integrity, and resilience. Through age-appropriate activities, storytelling, games, and interactions, children are imbued with a sense of duty towards society and nation-building.

The curriculum of a 'Bal Sanskar Kendra' is designed to foster character development, instill moral values, and cultivate a sense of social responsibility. Children are encouraged to reflect on virtues like honesty, kindness, humility, and gratitude. They are taught to respect diversity, cherish harmony, and contribute positively to their communities.

Furthermore, a 'Bal Sanskar Kendra' serves as a platform for fostering leadership skills and igniting entrepreneurial spirit among children.

Through experiential learning opportunities, they are encouraged to think critically, solve problems creatively, and collaborate effectively. They are empowered to dream big, set goals, and persevere in the face of challenges.

At the heart of a 'Bal Sanskar Kendra' is the belief that every child is unique and possesses the inherent potential to make a meaningful contribution to the world. Therefore, personalized attention is given to each child to nurture their talents, interests, and aspirations. Mentors, educators, and volunteers play a pivotal role in providing guidance, support, and encouragement to help children unlock their full potential.

Simply, A 'Bal Sanskar Kendra' is not just an educational institution but a nurturing ecosystem where children blossom into compassionate, responsible, and empowered individuals. By fostering values-based education and holistic development, we aim to create a generation of enlightened leaders who will lead our nation towards prosperity, harmony, and global excellence.

From early childhood, the seeds of good values and spirituality are sown in children, fostering a sense of universal welfare. Inspired by the noble ideals of revered Sant Asharam Bapu, Bal Sanskar Kendras were established to instill these values in young minds. Here, amidst laughter and play, children effortlessly imbibe the virtues of greatness and find opportunities to develop their abilities. Alongside imparting respect for parents, the centers focus on nurturing intellect, maintaining physical health, fostering mental well-being, and awakening latent potentials. The art of awakening these hidden powers is taught here in a manner accessible even to a small child.

It's a nurturing ground for holistic development. Here, children are encouraged to explore their talents and cultivate positive traits. The environment is conducive to their overall growth, providing them with the necessary tools to navigate life's challenges with grace and resilience.

One of the core teachings at these centers is the importance of respecting parents. Children are taught to honor and obey their parents, recognizing them as the first teachers who impart valuable life lessons. Through various activities and teachings, they learn to appreciate the sacrifices and love of their parents, fostering strong familial bonds.

Moreover, intellectual development is given significant importance. Children engage in activities that stimulate their minds, encouraging curiosity and critical thinking. They are provided with opportunities to explore various subjects and expand their knowledge base, laying a strong foundation for lifelong learning.

Physical health is another aspect emphasized at Bal Sanskar Kendras. Through games, exercises, and yoga, children learn the importance of maintaining a healthy lifestyle. They develop habits of regular exercise, proper nutrition, and hygiene, which contribute to their overall well-being.

Furthermore, the centers focus on nurturing emotional intelligence and mental well-being. Children are taught to manage their emotions effectively, develop empathy towards others, and cultivate a positive outlook on life. They learn resilience in the face of challenges and develop coping strategies to deal with stress and adversity.

In addition to these aspects, Bal Sanskar Kendras also aim to awaken the latent potentials hidden within each child. Through various activities such as arts, music, and storytelling, children are encouraged to explore their creativity and express themselves freely. They learn to tap into their inner strengths and talents, gaining confidence and self-assurance in the process.

Bal Sanskar Kendra play a crucial role in shaping the future generation by instilling in them values of compassion, integrity, and resilience. Through a holistic approach to education, these centers empower children to become responsible, well-rounded individuals who contribute positively to society.

A 'Bal Sanskar Kendra', orIn children's development center, the focus extends beyond just education to fostering robust physical and mental health. It is believed that a healthy mind resides in a healthy body. Hence, these centers also prioritize the well-being of children through various initiatives.

According to nutritionist Manorama, the timing and quality of food intake play a crucial role in a child's overall health. Understanding what to eat and when is vital for their growth and development.

Ensuring a child's physical well-being involves more than just providing nourishment; it requires creating an environment conducive to their overall growth. Activities promoting physical fitness and proper nutrition are integrated into daily routines to encourage children to adopt healthy habits.

Boosting immunity is another crucial aspect addressed in children's development centers. Strategies to enhance the body's resistance to diseases are implemented through activities such as yoga, pranayama, and other forms of exercise. These practices not only strengthen the immune system but also instill discipline and mindfulness in children.

Educating children about the harmful effects of junk food is essential for promoting healthy eating habits. By imparting knowledge about the drawbacks of processed foods, children are encouraged to make healthier dietary choices.

All these aspects are taught to children in children's development centers through various creative methods, making learning a fun and engaging experience. Through interactive activities, children learn about the importance of nutrition, physical fitness, and disease prevention while enjoying themselves.

By integrating these lessons into their daily routine, children not only gain knowledge but also develop practical skills that they can apply throughout their lives. The aim is to empower children to make informed decisions about their health and well-being.

In children's development centers play a crucial role in nurturing strong and healthy children. By focusing on holistic development, including physical fitness, nutrition, and disease prevention, these centers equip children with the tools they need to lead happy and fulfilling lives. Through engaging and interactive activities, children learn valuable lessons that stay with them long after they leave the center. It is through these efforts that we can ensure a brighter and healthier future for our children.

DIVYA PRERNA PUSTAK

Youth Empowerment: Guiding Light for a Fulfilling Life

In today's society, countless individuals have found solace and guidance in the teachings of revered figures like Asharam Bapu, transforming their downward spiraling lives into upward trajectories through the practices of youth empowerment. Many young men and women, besieged by afflictions such as loss of vitality and nocturnal emissions, have found in Asharam Bapu enlightening discourse and sacred guidance not just a mere lifeline but a sturdy anchor in their despondent existence.

The need for the resplendent guidance of luminaries like Asharam Bapu in today's indulgent, debased, and desire-ridden environment, which steals away the brilliance of societal radiance, cannot be overstated.

To fulfil this need, Asharam Bapu, through his discourses, has touched upon the subject of "Priceless Preservation of Youth" and has endeavored to present it before readers in a consolidated manner, a humble effort to lay it before the readers.

That book contains invaluable content for all - men and women, householders and ascetics, students, and elders alike. It outlines how leading a simple, ordinary life can keep the vigor of youth intact and make life divine. Moreover, the essence of Asharam Bapu's teachings lies in the harmony of swiftness, experience, and evidence in his discourse, which proves to be highly impactful.

That small book, illuminating the path of youth empowerment, is the key to a divine life. Benefit from it yourself and engage in the meritorious act of sharing its benefits with others.

YOUTH SECURITY

The body is indeed the instrument of righteousness.

The body is the means through which all endeavors are accomplished. If the body is weak, it affects the mind, and the mind becomes weak.

For any task to be successful, both the body and mind must be healthy. This is why many elderly individuals cannot pursue spiritual practices, as their bodies have been depleted due to indulgence in sensual pleasures. Even if the mind is strong, their worn-out bodies cannot fully support them. On the other hand, the youth, despite having the ability to pursue spiritual practices, are influenced by the distractions of the world and get lost in sensual pleasures. Due to not understanding the importance of their vital energy, they squander it on bad habits and then spend their lives in regret.

I often encounter young men who are troubled deep within. They cannot share their pain with anyone because they have lost their vital energy due to bad habits. Now, their mind and body have weakened, and the world has become a place of sorrow for them, making it impossible for them to attain divine realization. Now, they simply endure life, crying all along the way.

This is why great individuals emphasize celibacy in every era. A person lacking self-control cannot progress in life or accomplish anything great for society. Societies and nations formed by such individuals lag behind in physical and spiritual progress. Such nations face imminent downfall.

Brahmacharya, or celibacy, is a profound concept rooted in ancient wisdom. It entails abstaining from physical, verbal, and mental indulgence in sensual pleasures. The practice is not limited to renouncing sexual activity but extends to the control of all senses, thoughts, and actions towards a higher spiritual goal.

In the Yajnavalkya Samhita, it is stated that brahmacharya means restraining oneself from indulging in sexual desires in all circumstances. This discipline involves harnessing the energy that would otherwise be expended in sensual pursuits and redirecting it towards spiritual growth.

Bhagavan Vedavyasa defines brahmacharya as the mastery of one's senses and the renunciation of pleasure obtained through sensory gratification. It emphasizes the importance of self-control and moderation in fulfilling desires.

Bhagavan Shankaracharya illustrates the significance of brahmacharya by highlighting the immense spiritual power gained through the preservation of vital energy. He suggests that the practitioner who conserves their seminal energy can attain various spiritual accomplishments and ultimately self-realization.

Furthermore, brahmacharya is credited with conferring divine qualities upon beings. The Atharva Veda mentions that the gods achieved immortality through the practice of brahmacharya, and even deities like Indra attained supremacy and divine bliss through its observance.

Brahmacharya is revered as a virtue that bestows numerous benefits, providing individuals with inner strength, resilience, and protection against life's challenges. It fosters mental clarity, emotional stability, and spiritual elevation, enabling one to navigate the complexities of existence with grace and wisdom.

In essence, brahmacharya is not merely a physical restraint but a holistic approach to self-mastery and spiritual evolution, offering guidance and support to seekers on their journey towards higher consciousness and fulfillment.

Brahmacharya is considered the highest form of austerity according to Hindu scriptures. It means celibacy or abstaining from indulgence in sensual pleasures. Lord Shiva himself said that practicing celibacy is superior to all other forms of austerity. He also mentioned that a man who practices celibacy is like a divine being on Earth.

In Jain scriptures, celibacy is also praised as the highest form of austerity. It is believed that by practicing celibacy, one can attain supreme spiritual growth.

The preservation of semen, or virya, is crucial for a healthy and fulfilled life. Just as a kingdom with a strong ruler remains unharmed by enemies, a body with preserved semen remains immune to diseases. Therefore, it's said that the preservation of semen is equivalent to the preservation of life itself.

However, in some ancient texts like the Atharvaveda, celibacy is portrayed as a sacred vow. It's emphasized that celibacy is a source of great strength.

Even though celibacy is praised in various scriptures, it's also acknowledged that it's not an easy path to follow. It's considered a grave sin to indulge in sexual misconduct.

Simply, Celibacy is revered as a sacred vow in Hinduism and Jainism, and it's believed to bestow immense spiritual power and vitality to those who practice it diligently.

Modern medical experts also support the assertions of Indian yogis. Dr. Nicole states, "*It is a biological fact that the body's optimal blood forms reproductive elements in both men and women. In a pure and disciplined life, these elements are reabsorbed to nourish the subtlest tissues of the brain, nerves, and muscular organs, thereby circulating back. When this essence ascends and develops in the body, it makes one fearless, strong, courageous, and heroic. Conversely, its wasteful expenditure renders one timid, weak, emaciated, and prone to impulsive actions, undermining the functions of the body's organs and making them feeble and susceptible to various diseases and death. The withdrawal of reproductive behavior results in extraordinary physical, mental, and spiritual strength.*"

Paramount and industrious scientist researchers have discovered that whenever semen retention is preserved and reabsorbed in the body, it enriches the blood and strengthens the brain. Dr. Dio Louis asserts, "*Preserving this element is vital for physical strength, mental vigor, and intellectual acumen.*"

Another author, Dr. E.P. Miller, writes, "*The voluntary or involuntary expenditure of semen is a direct expenditure of life force. It is universally accepted that the optimal constituents of blood enter into the composition of semen. If this deduction is correct, it implies that celibacy is essential for an individual's well-being.*"

Renowned Western physicians argue that various ailments arise from seminal depletion, especially in young age. These include: wounds on the body, acne or eruptions on the face, blue lines around the eyes, absence of beard, sunken eyes, jaundiced complexion due to blood loss, memory loss, diminished vision, seminal discharge with urine, enlargement of the testicles, pain in the testicles, weakness, laziness, melancholy, sadness, palpitations, breathlessness, tuberculosis, backache, lumbago, headache, joint pain, weak kidneys, nocturnal emission, urinating during sleep, mental instability, lack of mental power, nightmares, nocturnal emissions, and mental unrest.

The sole remedy to alleviate these ailments is celibacy. They cannot be permanently cured by medicines or other treatments.

The process of semen formation is a vital function of the body. According to ancient texts like those of Sushruta, it begins with the digestion of food, which produces nutrients. Over a period of approximately five days, these nutrients are transformed into blood. After another five days, the blood transforms into muscle tissue, then into fat, then into bones, then into bone marrow, and finally into semen. In women, a similar process results in the formation of menstrual fluid, known as "Raj."

Semen undergoes a complex journey through the body, passing through several stages before reaching its final form, as described in ancient texts. It takes around 30 days and 4 hours for semen to complete this journey. Scientifically, it's estimated that 32 kilograms of food can produce 700 grams of blood, and from that, approximately 20 grams of semen is formed.

This process illustrates the intricate nature of semen formation, which is essential for reproduction and considered a precious substance in many cultures. Understanding this process not only sheds light on the importance of diet and digestion but also highlights the remarkable complexity of the human body's physiological functions.

The remarkable allure of an attractive personality lies in the cultivation of a profound energy known as "Ojas," as coined by the ancient physician Dhanvantari. This vital essence engenders an extraordinary magnetism within the body, aiding individuals in attaining the ultimate benefit of self-realization. Wherever one encounters distinct qualities in a person's life—be it a radiant countenance, a powerful voice, or fervor in action—it is attributed to the preservation of this seminal energy.

If an average healthy individual consumes 700 grams of food daily, they accrue approximately 32 kilograms of sustenance over forty days. Consequently, their earned "Ojas" amounts to roughly 20 grams. In essence, this translates to about 15 grams per month, with the remainder being expended during intimate encounters, as nature dictates.

In essence, the profound significance of preserving one's vital essence, Ojas, cannot be overstated. It serves as the cornerstone of vitality, charisma, and spiritual well-being. Through moderation and understanding, individuals can harness this innate power to enrich their lives and emanate a captivating aura that resonates with others.

Therefore, the cultivation and preservation of Ojas stand as a testament to the holistic approach towards physical, mental, and spiritual wellness, fostering a life of balance, vigor, and enduring allure.

Once upon a time, there was a gardener. He worked hard for many days, putting his heart, soul, and savings into creating a beautiful garden. The garden bloomed with various fragrant flowers. After carefully selecting and gathering these flowers, he prepared a fine fragrance from them. Now, what did he do next? He disposed of this wonderful fragrance into a dirty drain.

Oh! He wasted the fragrance, which he had painstakingly prepared over many days, and which could have filled homes with its sweet scent, into a drain! One might say, "What a foolish and senseless gardener he was!" But let's take a closer look at ourselves. There's no need to search elsewhere for such gardeners. Many of us are like him.

From adolescence until now, spanning about 15-20 years, we've built up strength, vigor, and vitality through hard work. Yet, what's earned through nearly 30 days of effort is often spent recklessly, lacking wisdom.

Isn't this akin to the gardener's actions? Perhaps the gardener, after making this mistake a few times, might have become cautious upon being advised, but many people repeat the same mistakes. Eventually, remorse sets in.

For fleeting pleasures, people enthusiastically engage in activities, but once done, they feel lifeless, just like corpses. It's inevitable. They don't realize that they haven't gained true happiness; they've only experienced a fleeting illusion, losing their hard-earned income of 30-40 days in the process.

Until youth, semen is conserved, providing strength and vitality to the body. However, excessive indulgence leads to the loss of semen, resulting in weakness and even impotence. Then, they can't even look others in the eye. Their lives become hellish.

The importance of semen retention is highlighted in our scriptures, which provide guidance on when to engage in sexual activities, with whom, and how often.

The natural order of creation revolves around reproduction, where the expenditure of semen from the body isn't merely for fleeting pleasure but serves the genuine purpose of procreation. This process is inherent in nature, observed across various plant and animal species. Succumbing to this natural instinct, every creature engages in mating, experiencing pleasure as a result. However, relying solely on this natural order for momentary gratification is not wise. Animals adhere to their mating cycles for maintaining health, but has humanity descended to the level of beasts?

Unlike animals, humans possess the capacity for intellectual development.

Eating, sleeping, mating, and fearing are common activities shared by both humans and animals. Having inherited these behaviors while inhabiting animal bodies, humans have been engaging in these activities. Now, with a human body bestowed upon us, if we continue to chase transient pleasures without exercising intellect and discernment, how will we ever attain our true purpose?

It's crucial to channel our actions and desires towards higher goals, transcending mere physical impulses. Engaging in introspection and cultivating wisdom can lead us towards a meaningful existence beyond the pursuit of momentary pleasures. Let us strive to elevate our consciousness and align our lives with higher ideals, transcending the limitations of our primal instincts.

In the simplicity lies the essence of truth.

Many individuals begin to argue: "The scriptures provide guidance, and wisdom is also acquired by listening to the words of enlightened beings that living a simple life is essential. If there is work to be done, they do it; if hunger strikes, they eat; if sleep beckons, they rest. Life should be devoid of any 'stress' or 'tension.' Nowadays, all ailments are said to be the result of stress. Therefore, life should be straightforward and uncomplicated. Even Kabir Das has said: *'O seekers, the state of spontaneous meditation is best.'*

Despite presenting such arguments, many people consent to gratifying their desires and indulgences. However, this is akin to deceiving oneself. Such individuals are unaware that such a simple life is for enlightened beings whose minds and intellects are under their control, who have nothing left to gain in this world, and who are not concerned with honor or dishonor. They reside in that state of self-awareness where there is neither rise nor fall. They are forever immersed in boundless joy, unaffected by worldly matters. Even if a mountain of material possessions is placed before them, they cannot be swayed or distracted. Hence, they may choose to utilize worldly possessions or decline them.

Socrates, the renowned philosopher of ancient Greece, shared profound wisdom through a simple dialogue about the pursuit of desires and the inevitability of death. In this exchange, he illuminates the folly of endless indulgence and the quest for satisfaction through material desires.

The conversation begins with a question about the appropriate frequency of engaging in romantic relationships. Socrates responds with a succinct yet profound answer, suggesting that it is fitting for a person to engage in such relationships only once in a lifetime. However, if one finds dissatisfaction, then perhaps once a year would suffice. If still unsatisfied, then once a month. Even then, if the desire persists, indulging twice a month would be the limit, as death would soon follow.

This seemingly simple dialogue holds deep meaning, advocating for moderation and self-control in the pursuit of desires. Socrates suggests that constant pursuit of pleasure leads to disappointment and ultimately, a life devoid of fulfillment. He urges individuals to embrace contentment and appreciate the value of life beyond fleeting desires.

The story of King Yayati serves as a poignant example of the consequences of unchecked desires. Yayati's insatiable thirst for pleasure leads him down a path of dissatisfaction and eventual ruin. Despite his worldly success and power, he finds himself unfulfilled and empty, realizing too late the true cost of his desires.

Socrates' words serve as a timeless reminder to seek fulfillment in simplicity and moderation, avoiding the trap of endless desires. His message resonates across generations, urging individuals to live a life of purpose and meaning, free from the shackles of materialism.

In essence, Socrates teaches us to embrace contentment and appreciate the preciousness of life. By cultivating inner peace and satisfaction, we can find true fulfillment and live a life of purpose and joy. May we heed his wisdom and strive for a life of balance and harmony.

The great sage Sri Ramakrishna Paramahansa emphasized the profound reverence towards women, comparing them to the divine Mother Jagadamba. He advised, "*When you behold a beautiful woman, see in her the manifestation of the Divine Mother. Reflect that she is indeed an incarnation of the goddess, hence the allure of her beauty. Understand that she is graciously granting you a vision in this form, and inwardly offer your respects to her. This attitude will prevent any impure thoughts from arising within you.*"

Furthermore, he taught, "*Regard another man's wife as your own mother and consider another's wealth as mere clods of earth.*" This teaches us to treat women with the same reverence as one's own mother and view others' possessions with detachment.

In essence, the message is to cultivate a sense of maternal love and respect towards women, recognizing their divine essence and treating them with utmost reverence and dignity. This attitude not only fosters purity of thought but also promotes harmonious relationships and a sense of universal kinship.

Therefore, let us imbibe this wisdom and practice humility and reverence in our interactions with women, acknowledging their intrinsic worth and honoring the divine presence within them.

Reading literature shapes our thoughts and influences our behavior. Those who consume debased, immoral, and sensational literature remain stagnant. Their minds dwell perpetually on base desires, rendering them incapable of self-restraint. Such literature fosters lasciviousness and leads to moral degradation. It's been heard that some individuals, influenced by Western culture, exhibit nefarious behavior by indulging in clandestine screenings of lewd films, which ultimately destroy themselves and those around them. They perpetrate grave injustices against innocent children, especially vulnerable girls and adolescents. Those who indulge in watching "blue films" are blinded by their base desires and will endure suffering even after death, possibly being reborn as animals or suffering in filthy environments. It's imperative to protect innocent youth from the perils of intoxicants, vile literature, and lewd films, as they are the future pillars of the nation. Young men and women should be enlightened, understanding the glory of celibacy. It's the duty of all of us to disseminate literature on celibacy to students in schools and colleges. The government must provide education and caution students about the importance of celibacy so that they can become enlightened individuals. If we examine the lives of great personalities, we will find the imprint of some form of noble literature. Emerson, a renowned American author, followed celibacy under his mentor Thoreau's guidance. He wrote, "*I bathe daily in the holy waters of the Gita. Although the gods who wrote this book have been gone for many years, no book equal to it has been produced yet.*"

Another foreign scholar, F.H. Molene from England, says, "*I have studied the Bible thoroughly. The knowledge present in the Gita is not found in either Christian or Jewish Bibles. I wonder why Indian youths come to England to learn material science. Undoubtedly, their attraction towards Westerners is the cause. Their naive hearts have not yet recognized the ruthless and arrogant intentions of Westerners. Therefore, they fall into the trap of these selfish individuals out of greed for the positions they obtain through education. Otherwise, for a country or society to break free from slavery, this is the only path of progress.*"

Even though I am Christian, I hold such reverence for the Gita because it provides solutions to profound questions that Western scientists have not yet been able to answer. The Gita is replete with mystical teachings, which is why it has become like the divine mother Yogeshwari for me. It is an invaluable treasure of India that cannot be equated with all the wealth in the world.

Renowned journalist Paul Brunton was deeply influenced after reading religious texts of Sanatan Dharma. It was his encounter with spiritual giants like Ramana Maharshi in India that filled him with gratitude. It was only after reading patriotic literature that gems like Chandrashekhar Azad, Bhagat Singh, and Veer Savarkar dedicated their lives to the welfare of the nation.

Hence, no matter how much praise is sung for spiritual literature, it is still not enough. There are many books in Indian culture such as Shri Yogavasishtha Ramayana, Upanishads, Dasbodh, Sukhmani, Vivekachudamani, literature of Sri Ramakrishna, and discourses of Swami Ramtirtha. Read them and make them an integral part of your daily life. As for debased and immoral literature, pick them up, pile them up, and burn them or throw them into the fire, but neither read them yourself nor let others get hold of them.

In the realm of spiritual literature, there lies immense power in strengthening celibacy. It is advisable to engage in reading some spiritual books before delving into the day's activities, following the morning routine of bathing and such, as well as before retiring for the night. This practice ensures that noble thoughts permeate the mind, as contained within the literature, thus safeguarding our minds from becoming afflicted by negativity.

It is also encouraged to wear a loincloth, as it aids in maintaining the health of the testicles and supports semen retention.

Refrain from indulging in the allure of lascivious and lewd posters and images, as well as avoiding explicit poetry and songs wherever they may be sung. It's important not to give in to the temptation of such materials, as they can incite base desires and distract from spiritual growth.

By following these practices with sincerity and dedication, one can nurture and preserve their spiritual purity, fostering an environment conducive to inner peace and growth.

In the realm of existence, where virtues are kings,
Celibacy stands as the mightiest of wings.
It's not just restraint, but the power to soar,
Above worldly desires, to a transcendent shore.
For those who have walked on this path so pure,
Have etched their names in time, forever to endure.

Like sages of old, who with discipline's flame,
Carved epics of soul, and earned eternal fame.
It's the silent strength that bends not to vice,
A choice of the wise, a silent sacrifice.
In the garden of life, it's the rarest bloom,
A beacon of light in the deepest gloom.
The heroes of yore, with their vows so stern,
Turned the tides of fate at every turn.
With celibacy's shield and spirit's lance,
They conquered more than mere circumstance.
This is the elixir, the purest gold,
That turns the meek into the brave and bold.
In the tapestry of time, it's the brightest thread,
A testament to the living and a homage to the dead.
So let us embrace this path with grace,
And in the annals of time, our own legends trace.
For celibacy is not just a mere refrain,
But life's highest note in an eternal refrain.

A Revolutionary Beginning

Parents Worship Day is celebrated on 14th February. This day holds immense significance in the hearts of millions around the globe. It marks the birthday of revered spiritual leader Asharam Bapu, who initiated this beautiful tradition to honor and express gratitude towards parents.

The essence of Parents Worship Day lies in acknowledging the invaluable role parents play in our lives. It transcends cultural and religious boundaries, reminding us of the universal bond between children and their parents. On this day, devotees from diverse backgrounds come together to pay homage to their parents, cherishing the unconditional love and sacrifices they have made.

The celebration of Parents Worship Day is not merely a ritual but a profound expression of gratitude and reverence. It serves as a reminder to cherish every moment spent with our parents and to recognize their unwavering support and guidance throughout our lives. Asharam Bapu, through his teachings, emphasizes the importance of nurturing this sacred bond and fostering a culture of love and respect within families.

The significance of Parents Worship Day extends beyond a single day of observance. It encourages us to cultivate a lifelong attitude of appreciation towards our parents. Asharam Bapu often emphasizes the role of parents as the first and most influential teachers in a child's life. Through their love, wisdom, and moral guidance, parents lay the foundation for their children's future success and happiness.

Parents Worship Day also serves as a platform to address societal issues such as elder neglect and abuse. Asharam Bapu advocates for the protection and welfare of senior citizens, urging society to recognize the dignity and value of aging parents. By honoring our parents on this day, we reaffirm our commitment to their well-being and pledge to stand by them in their golden years.

The celebration of Parents Worship Day is marked by various activities and rituals. Families gather to offer prayers and seek blessings from their parents. Many also engage in charitable acts and community service as a way of giving back to society, embodying the spirit of selflessness instilled by Asharam Bapu.

In addition to honoring parents, Parents Worship Day also serves as an opportunity for self-reflection and introspection. It prompts us to evaluate our relationships with our parents and strive towards fostering greater understanding and harmony within our families. Asharam Bapu teaches us that by nurturing strong familial bonds, we contribute to the overall well-being and prosperity of society.

Parents Worship Day stands as a testament to the profound love and respect we hold for our parents. It is a celebration of the timeless values of filial piety and gratitude, championed by Asharam Bapu. As we commemorate this auspicious day, let us reaffirm our commitment to honoring and cherishing our parents every day of our lives.

In the land of India, revered as the abode of sages and Sants, a tradition once prevailed where people greeted each other with the sacred words, "Ram-Ram," acknowledging the divine presence within each other. The profound meaning behind uttering the name of Lord Ram twice signifies the recognition that the same divine consciousness resides within both the individual and oneself, invoking a sense of reverence and unity. This divine sentiment is known as love, characterized by innocence, purity, selflessness, and unconditional affection.

However, in contemporary times, this sacred sentiment seems to have faded away, replaced by a culture that glorifies superficial attractions and indulgence. In Western countries, on the 14th of February, young men and women exchange greeting cards, flowers, and gifts, celebrating Valentine's Day. This celebration, which promotes romantic relationships, often disregards traditional moral values, leading to the erosion of cultural integrity and societal decay. The acceptance and normalization of such practices contribute to the moral decline of nations, leading them towards their downfall.

Recognizing the detrimental effects of abandoning moral principles, revered Sant Asharam Bapu has initiated a noble endeavor known as 'Matru-Pitru Pujan Diwas' (Parents Worship Day). This initiative aims to revive the ancient tradition of honoring and respecting one's parents, who embody the divine love and sacrifice. By celebrating Matru-Pitru Pujan Diwas, individuals are encouraged to express gratitude and reverence towards their parents, fostering familial bonds and moral values within society.

It is imperative for us, as custodians of our cultural heritage, to reject the influences of Westernization that promote materialism and moral degradation. Instead, we must embrace and uphold our traditional values, which serve as the foundation of our civilization. Through initiatives like Matru-Pitru Pujan Diwas, we can reaffirm our commitment to moral righteousness and spiritual upliftment, safeguarding the sanctity of our culture for future generations.

The celebration of Valentine's Day symbolizes a departure from traditional moral values, leading to societal disintegration. By embracing initiatives like Matru-Pitru Pujan Diwas, inspired by the teachings of revered Sant Asharam Bapu, we can rekindle the flame of morality and spirituality, restoring harmony and righteousness in our society. Let us unite in the pursuit of a virtuous and enlightened society, guided by the principles of love, respect, and devotion towards our parents and elders.

Valentine's Day, as we know it today, traces its origins back to the ancient Roman era. The story revolves around Claudius, the King of Rome, who was well-acquainted with the virtues of celibacy. He prohibited his soldiers from getting married, believing that unmarried men were more physically and mentally fit for battle, thus ensuring victory.

However, the soldiers were vehemently opposed to this decree, as they desired companionship and the stability that marriage offered. This led to a clandestine practice where Sant Valentine, a Christian priest, secretly performed marriages for these soldiers. Despite being aware of the king's decree against marriage, Sant Valentine believed in the sanctity of love and sought to unite couples in matrimony.

Unfortunately, Sant Valentine's actions were discovered, and he was branded as a criminal by the king. He faced severe punishment and was ultimately sentenced to death by hanging. It was in the year 496 AD that Pope Gelasius I declared February 14th as Valentine's Day in honor of Sant Valentine's selfless acts of love and sacrifice.

Ironically, in modern times, many people celebrate Valentine's Day by exchanging gifts, cards, and expressing their romantic feelings to their loved ones. However, this commercialization often overlooks the true essence of Sant Valentine's legacy, as he advocated for love rooted in commitment and selflessness, rather than materialism.

In light of Sant Valentine's teachings, it is important for the youth of India to reflect on the significance of love and relationships. Instead of succumbing to societal pressures or indulging in superficial displays of affection, they should prioritize values such as respect, loyalty, and devotion. By following the noble guidance of revered spiritual leaders like Asharam Bapu, they can safeguard their youth, health, and intellect, while also honoring their parents and ancestors.

In essence, Valentine's Day should serve as a reminder to cherish and nurture genuine connections, guided by the principles of compassion and understanding. Let us not forget the sacrifices made by individuals like Sant Valentine, whose timeless message of love transcends boundaries and inspires us to lead lives filled with empathy and goodwill.

The Benevolent Message of Revered Sant Asharam Bapu: A Call for Caution

In today's era, the celebration of Valentine's Day has unfortunately given rise to detrimental activities leading to increased promiscuity, depression, emptiness, premature aging, and even mortality. Therefore, it is imperative for the citizens of India to be vigilant against this blind trend!

According to the 'Innocenti Report Card,' every year in 28 developed countries, 1.25 million adolescent girls between the ages of 13 and 19 become pregnant. Among them, 500,000 undergo abortions, and 750,000 become unwed mothers. In the United States alone, 494,000 orphaned children are born each year, and 3 million adolescents fall victim to sexually transmitted diseases.

25% of sexually active adolescents suffer from sexually transmitted diseases. Among those engaging in unsafe sexual practices, there is a 50% likelihood of contracting gonorrhea, 33% likelihood of genital herpes, and a 1% chance of acquiring AIDS. Of the new AIDS patients, 25% are under the age of 22. Presently, in 33% of American schools, education on sexual health includes teaching 'only abstinence.' For this, America has spent over 40 billion dollars (more than 20 billion rupees).

The compassionate teachings of Revered Sant Asharam Bapu emphasize the importance of moral values and self-discipline in leading a fulfilled life. His message resonates with people from all walks of life, advocating for a society where spirituality guides human behavior, ensuring the well-being of individuals and the community at large.

It is imperative for individuals, especially the youth, to heed the wise counsel of Revered Sant Asharam Bapu and embrace values that promote harmony, purity, and well-being. By adhering to these principles, we can safeguard ourselves and future generations from the perils of modern-day challenges. Let us strive to cultivate a society rooted in righteousness and compassion, where each individual can flourish in body, mind, and spirit.

Celebrating Love Day, as suggested by Asharam Bapu, is not just about expressions of affection but also about fostering restraint and genuine development. It's essential to imbibe these values, especially for the youth, as their meeting should lead to a day of harmony and not destruction. On this auspicious day, children should honor their parents by offering respect, bowing down to them, and parents should reciprocate by showering their offspring with love. The true essence of love is felt when children embrace their parents, symbolizing a bond of profound affection. Sons and daughters should see the divine aspect in their parents, and similarly, parents should recognize the divine in their children.

As individuals of India, sons and daughters of Bharat Mata, it's imperative to celebrate Love Day, showing reverence to our parents and nurturing a bond of affection between parents and children. Let's not be like those who are heading towards destruction, indulging in activities that breed diseases and unrest. Let's not emulate their ways.

Celebrating Love Day is a sacred occasion to express gratitude towards our parents and to reinforce the bond of love within the family. It's a day to reflect on the divine connection between parents and children, recognizing each other's worth and significance. By cherishing this bond, we cultivate a culture of love, respect, and harmony within our homes and society.

Love Day should be observed with simplicity and sincerity, devoid of extravagant displays or superficial gestures. It's about the warmth of a hug, the tenderness of a smile, and the depth of heartfelt words exchanged between parents and children. Let's not succumb to the allure of Western celebrations that promote indulgence and excessiveness. Instead, let's embrace our rich cultural heritage and celebrate Love Day with humility and reverence.

As followers of Asharam Bapu's teachings, let's strive to embody the values of love, respect, and compassion in our lives. Let's uphold the sanctity of family bonds and foster an environment of love and understanding within our homes and communities. By doing so, we contribute to the well-being and harmony of society as a whole.

Let's celebrate Love Day with humility, sincerity, and devotion, honoring our parents and nurturing the precious bond between parents and children. Let's pledge to uphold the values of love and compassion in our lives and spread the message of harmony and unity in our society.

"*Dear Young Friends and Their Beloved Parents,*

You are the descendants of the visionary sages and Sants of our great nation, India. On the occasion of Valentine's Day, let us transcend the superficial allure of materialism and instead foster a bond of love and devotion between parents and children, thus allowing the divine love within our hearts to overflow.

By worshiping our parents, we not only honor them but also invoke the divine presence within ourselves. This act of reverence has the power to transform our worldly desires into spiritual fulfillment, our pride into humility, and bestow auspicious blessings upon our children.

Why emulate the ways of the West when by following our own traditions, we can lead them to true prosperity? Let us inspire them through our actions as patriotic citizens engaged in nation-building endeavors, inviting them to join us in the noble task of constructing a resilient and prosperous nation.

As we reflect on the teachings and legacy of revered Sants like Asharam Bapu, let us imbibe their wisdom and compassion in our daily lives. Let us strive to emulate their devotion to the welfare of all beings and their unwavering commitment to truth and righteousness.

Let us remember that true happiness and fulfillment lie not in the pursuit of fleeting pleasures but in the cultivation of love, devotion, and service to others. May we all be blessed with the strength and wisdom to walk the path of righteousness and inspire others to do the same."

Devotion to Parents and Guru: Lessons from the Life of Asharam Bapu

In our rich Indian culture, there exists a beautiful tradition of instilling profound values in children from a tender age. This tradition, rooted in simplicity yet carrying immense depth, aims to elevate young minds to greater heights of wisdom and virtue.

The saying, "Matru Devo Bhava, Pitru Devo Bhava, Acharya Devo Bhava," resonates deeply, emphasizing the divine status of parents and teachers in our lives. It reminds us to not only respect and obey them but also to revere them as manifestations of the divine and offer our heartfelt reverence to them. While obedience is essential for following instructions, infusing our actions with love and reverence turns mere compliance into sacred acts of worship.

Consider the analogy of lifting water: it requires effort to raise it up. Similarly, taking a lift entails expending energy to ascend. Water transforms into vapor to rise, bearing the heat. Likewise, a sapling grows taller by enduring the support of a stake. However, dear students, contemplate the uniqueness of our ancient Indian culture, where sages and great souls have transformed life's journey into a joyous, effortless game through simple aphorisms.

Those who have embraced these aphorisms have themselves become venerable and worthy of worship. Lord Shri Ram exemplified this by regarding parents and gurus as divine, establishing a tradition of reverence that continues to echo through time. Lord Shri Krishna, as Nandanandan and Yashodanandan, immersed himself in the bliss of Nand's home, experiencing joy and serving with unwavering devotion in Guru Sandipani's ashram. His adeptness in action earned him the title of Yogeshwar, endearing him to the hearts of millions.

In the sacred garland of devotion to parents and guru, there are numerous fragrant flowers such as Lord Ganesha, Pitamah Bhishma,

Shravan Kumar, Pundalik, Aruni, Upamanyu, Totaka Acharya, and many more.

The life of Asharam Bapu exemplifies these timeless principles of devotion and service. His unwavering dedication to his parents and gurus, coupled with his profound wisdom and compassion, has inspired millions to lead lives rooted in righteousness and spirituality.

As we reflect on the teachings embedded in these simple yet profound aphorisms, let us imbibe the essence of devotion and reverence in our lives, following in the footsteps of revered Sants like Asharam Bapu, and thereby enriching our journey towards spiritual growth and enlightenment.

In the tranquil embrace of night, a young boy would often be found nestled at the feet of his revered father, despite repeated entreaties to retire for the night. With unwavering devotion, he continued his service, seeking blessings from his beloved father, who, in turn, bestowed upon him words of encouragement: "***Son, your name shall echo through the ages, your deeds fulfilling the aspirations of many.***"

Similarly, he dutifully served his mother until her final moments. As he transitioned into youth, the boy embarked on a path reminiscent of the divine incarnations of Lord Rama and Lord Krishna, immersing himself in devotion to his guru. At the gurudwara, he endured trials and tribulations, ultimately finding solace in the teachings of Kabir:

"***Endure the test of sorrow by going before the Guru. Kabir says, I will shower millions of happiness on sorrow.***"

Indeed, there is no greater benefactor in this world than the true guru. This sentiment transcends mere words, echoing through the lives of great souls.

"***Respect your mother, honor your father, revere your guru.***" These timeless principles, exemplified in the lives of such noble beings, find their culmination as both mother and guru choose to rest their heads in the lap of their beloved son and disciple in their final moments.

Reflecting upon the life of this extraordinary boy, who epitomized devotion to mother, father, and guru, serves as a beacon of guidance for today's youth. By imbibing the essence of such exemplary lives, they can navigate the path of progress while earning the blessings of their parents and mentors.

In this narrative, we find the essence of devotion and service, embodied in the life of Asharam Bapu. Through simple acts of humility and unwavering dedication, he has become a source of inspiration for millions, teaching us the profound significance of honoring our parents and revering our spiritual guides.

Let us, therefore, learn from these noble examples and tread the path of righteousness, enriching our lives and those around us with the light of love and devotion.

In the Shiv Purana, it is mentioned:

"*Whoever worships their parents and performs circumambulation (parikrama) around them, easily attains the fruits akin to circumambulating the Earth. But one who leaves their parents at home and goes on a pilgrimage commits a sin equivalent to killing them because for a child, the lotus feet of their parents are the greatest pilgrimage. Other pilgrimages may be attained by traveling far, but this pilgrimage, which is essential for righteousness, is easily accessible nearby. For the child (parents) and for the wife (husband), beautiful pilgrimages are already present in the home.*"

Reading this passage, it emphasizes the importance of respecting and serving one's parents, as they are considered as sacred as pilgrimages. The act of performing parikrama around one's parents symbolizes reverence and devotion, leading to spiritual merits akin to those gained from circumambulating the entire Earth.

On the other hand, leaving one's parents behind to embark on a journey is deemed as a grave offense, tantamount to committing a sin as severe as patricide or matricide. This is because, for a child, the love and respect towards their parents should be paramount and forsaking them for personal pursuits is considered morally reprehensible.

Furthermore, the passage highlights the accessibility and simplicity of the pilgrimage of serving one's parents, contrasting it with the distant and arduous journeys to other sacred sites. It underscores the notion that true righteousness lies in honoring and cherishing one's familial relationships and responsibilities, which are readily available within the confines of one's home.

In the context of spiritual leaders like Asharam Bapu, this passage resonates deeply with his teachings on the significance of family values and the importance of nurturing harmonious relationships within the family unit. His emphasis on the sacredness of parental love and the duty of children towards their parents aligns with the essence of this passage from the Shiv Purana.

Through his teachings and actions, Asharam Bapu has exemplified the principles of devotion, humility, and reverence towards parents, inspiring countless individuals to uphold these values in their own lives. His teachings serve as a guiding light, reminding us of the profound spiritual significance inherent in the simple acts of serving and honouring our parents.

In essence, the passage from the Shiv Purana underscores the timeless wisdom of honoring and serving one's parents as a sacred duty, a message that finds resonance in the teachings and life of spiritual leaders like Asharam Bapu.

WORDS OF WISDOM: LESSONS FROM ASHARAM BAPU

In ancient scriptures and revered texts, the importance of parents and their divine role in shaping a child's life is beautifully articulated. Asharam Bapu, a spiritual leader and guide, embodies these timeless teachings, imparting invaluable wisdom to millions around the world.

In the Ramayana, it is proclaimed, "The behavior of parents towards their children, filled with perpetual love and care, cannot be repaid merely by acts of kindness towards them." This profound verse encapsulates the essence of parental love and the debt of gratitude owed to them by their children.

Similarly, **In the Mahabharata**, it is stated, "The reverence for the mother is greater than the earth itself, and the respect for the father surpasses even the heavens." Asharam Bapu often emphasizes the significance of honoring one's parents, recognizing them as the very embodiments of divinity in one's life.

Manu Smriti further elucidates on the virtues of paying homage to one's parents and elders, asserting that through such acts of respect and service, one's life is enriched with longevity, knowledge, fame, and strength. Asharam Bapu's teachings resonate with this timeless wisdom, guiding his followers towards a path of righteousness and fulfillment.

The Padma Purana extols the daily ritual of washing the feet of one's parents, symbolizing the utmost reverence and devotion. It is believed that by performing this sacred act, akin to bathing in the holy waters of the Ganga, one receives blessings and purification. Asharam Bapu encourages his disciples to practice such rituals with sincerity and devotion, recognizing the spiritual significance behind these humble gestures.

In essence, the teachings of Asharam Bapu encapsulate the essence of humility, gratitude, and reverence towards parents and elders. His words echo the ancient wisdom found in scriptures, guiding individuals towards a life of virtue and righteousness. Through his compassionate guidance, countless souls have found solace and direction, embracing the values of love, respect, and service in their lives.

As we reflect on these timeless teachings, let us strive to embody the spirit of gratitude and reverence towards our parents and elders, honoring them as the guiding lights on our journey of self-discovery and spiritual growth. In the footsteps of Asharam Bapu, may we tread the path of righteousness with humility and devotion, enriching our lives and those around us with the light of wisdom and compassion.

WORDS OF WISDOM: INSIGHTS FROM SANTS

In the journey of life, the guidance and teachings of revered Sants hold immense value. As we delve into the profound sayings of revered Sants like Bodhayana Rishi, Maharshi Yajnavalkya, Katyayana Rishi, and Angira Rishi, we uncover timeless truths that resonate across generations.

Bodhayana Rishi reminds us of the fundamental importance of honoring our parents. He emphasizes that those who neglect their duties towards their parents are devoid of any true belongingness. Their disregard for their parents‘ sacrifices and tears reflects a lack of integrity and righteousness. Such individuals, who fail to respect their parents, spouses, children, siblings, and society, are indeed far from righteousness. Bodhayana Rishi urges us to steer clear of such hypocrisy and embrace genuine reverence and gratitude towards our elders.

Maharshi Yajnavalkya a profound sage, highlights the grave consequences of disrespecting and dishonoring one's parents. He emphasizes that those who disrespect their parents and inflict pain upon them are doomed to suffer the loss of their lineage and the absence of parental blessings. The path of dishonor towards one's parents leads only to despair and spiritual bankruptcy.

Katyayana Rishi underscores the significance of honoring and serving one's parents, teachers, and elders. He reminds us that parents, teachers, and spiritual mentors hold a revered status in our lives and are to be treated with utmost respect and devotion. Upholding their teachings, serving them, and ensuring their well-being are duties incumbent upon every individual.

Angira Rishi emphasizes that those who hold reverence for their parents and teachers earn great respect themselves. By serving and respecting their parents and teachers, individuals become liberated from their debts and earn the blessings of Sants. Thus, embracing humility and reverence towards one's parents and teachers is the pathway to spiritual elevation and fulfillment.

Param Pujya Bapu, echoing the sentiments of these revered Sants, imparts invaluable wisdom on the importance of honoring and serving one's parents and spiritual mentors. He emphasizes that by serving and respecting our parents and teachers, we become worthy of their blessings. As we tread the path of righteousness and humility, guided by the teachings of these venerable Sants, we embody the essence of true spirituality and compassion.

The teachings of Sants like Bodhayana Rishi, Maharshi Yajnavalkya, Katyayana Rishi, and Angira Rishi, along with the wisdom imparted by Param Pujya Bapu, serve as beacons of light illuminating the path of righteousness, humility, and devotion. May we heed their teachings and strive to embody their virtues in our lives, thereby enriching our spiritual journey and fostering harmony in the world.

In life's grand tapestry, where countless threads intertwine,
Let not the ones of kinship and care ever unwind.
For in the heart's ledger, the debts of love are vast,
Cherish thy parents, for their legacy must last.
Forget not the hands that cradled you with grace,
Nor the soothing whispers that fears did erase.
They are the sculptors of your very flesh and bone,
In their debt, we live, through their love, we have grown.
Many may cross your path, as life's journey unfolds,
But the warmth of parental love never grows old.
They sowed dreams in your soul, tended them with delight,
Now, nurture theirs, as they did yours, with all your might.
Though fortunes may amass and worldly goods accrue,
None can outweigh the love that from parents grew.
Service without pride, let this be your guiding star,
For in giving, we receive, no matter who we are.
As you seek blessings, be the blessing they implore,
The cycle of care, a promise of something more.
For in the silent moments, when the world turns away,

The love of a parent is the light that will stay.
They who laid roses upon every path you trod,
Never let thorns grow where once they placed their love.
Wealth may come and go, but this truth forever stands,
Cherish every moment with their guiding hands.

ONE CALL FOR ALL: EMBRACING MATERNAL AND PATERNAL REVERENCE

In the echoing words of revered Asharam Bapu, lies a profound sentiment that resonates across cultures and creeds: "*Respect thy parents.*" It's a universal aspiration cherished by all parents, transcending the boundaries of religion, ethnicity, and nationality. No Christian, Muslim, Sikh, or Hindu desires their offspring to stray into the abyss of aimlessness, entrapped by the allure of fleeting pleasures or entangled in the web of destructive relationships.

The ethos is simple yet profound: to nurture children who are robust in body, sharp in intellect, and steady on their own feet, and who, in the twilight of life, will stand as pillars of support for their aging parents. It's a desire shared by all, irrespective of faith or background. Asharam Bapu encapsulates this sentiment eloquently, urging us to imbue our progeny with values that steer them clear of the pitfalls of infatuation and guide them towards a path of righteousness.

For over fourteen years, the campaign of "*Matru-Pitru Pujan Diwas*" has sought to instill this ethos into the hearts of humanity, transcending the barriers of discrimination and fostering a sense of unity among all. Asharam Bapu's teachings have dismantled the shackles of prejudice, binding Hindus, Muslims, Sikhs, and Christians alike in the thread of reverence for parents.

India, with its rich tapestry of cultures and traditions, stands poised to emerge as the beacon of wisdom for the world. Asharam Bapu's vision of a harmonious society, where the reverence for parents transcends religious affiliations, holds the key to unlocking the nation's potential as the world's guru.

In breaking the chains of discrimination, Asharam Bapu has woven a tapestry of unity, where the threads of Hinduism, Islam, Sikhism, and Christianity intertwine seamlessly. It's a testament to the power of love and respect, bridging the chasms of division and ushering in an era of mutual understanding and harmony.

Let us heed the call of unity and embrace the values espoused by Asharam Bapu, for in doing so, we pave the way for a brighter and more inclusive future, where the bonds of familial love transcend the boundaries of faith and creed. As we celebrate "*Matru-Pitru Pujan Diwas,*" let us reaffirm our commitment to honoring our parents, for therein lies the foundation of a truly enlightened society.

THE TORCHBEARER OF SPIRITUAL REVOLUTION: REVERED ASHARAM BAPU

In the realm of societal enlightenment, Sants akin to the sun, radiate the essence of true knowledge, compassion, and virtuous conduct. Revered Sant Asharam Bapu stands as a beacon, illuminating the world with the light of authentic wisdom. Amidst the crucible of modernity, he bestows the gift of serenity upon humanity, akin to the cooling influence of the moon.

Bapu, with his innate empathy for all living beings, navigates the path of selfless service, offering solace to those afflicted by suffering. His life embodies the prophecy foretold by Sage Parashuram in Bapu's youth – a prophecy of greatness and salvation for mankind.

Guided by his revered Guru, Sai Leelashah Maharaj, Bapu embodies the essence of devotion to the Supreme. His embodiment as a living example of Brahman-realization, coupled with his dedication to humanitarian service, makes him a towering figure in the spiritual landscape.

Through the teachings imparted in his satsangs, Bapu ignites the flame of altruism in the hearts of millions, awakening a renewed appreciation for Indian culture and spirituality. His divine presence infuses joy and upliftment in countless souls worldwide.

Bapu imparts the key to a life of abundance, health, and dignity through the practice of Bhakti (devotion) and Prarthana (prayer). In his satsangs, he utilizes the potent tool of Dev-Manav Hasya (divine-human laughter), generating a harmonious energy equivalent to 70,000 bovis, purifying the environment and accelerating spiritual evolution.

In Bapu's luminous aura, individuals find solace, rejuvenation, and purpose. His teachings resonate with simplicity and accessibility, touching the hearts of the young and old alike. Through his divine grace, countless withered hearts bloom anew.

The legacy of Revered Sant Asharam Bapu transcends mere words. His life exemplifies the highest ideals of compassion, selflessness, and devotion to the Divine. As we bask in the radiance of his spiritual presence, may we emulate his noble virtues and walk the path of righteousness with unwavering faith and humility.

THE TRANSFORMATIVE POWER OF VEDIC MANTRAS AND SPIRITUAL GUIDANCE: A JOURNEY WITH ASHARAM BAPU

Asharam Bapu imparts initiation into Vedic mantras, guiding seekers on the path of satsang (spiritual discourse), enlightening them on the art of making human life meaningful, and safeguarding them from the pitfalls of treacherous paths through his boundless spiritual prowess. He extends invisible assistance at every turn of life.

Through initiation into Vedic mantras received from him, seekers experience multifaceted upliftment in their lives. Different types of physical, mental, and spiritual benefits become clearly evident in the lives of seekers. Describing all the benefits of mantra initiation is impossible.

Asharam Bapu's teachings resonate deeply with seekers, illuminating their paths and infusing their lives with profound meaning and purpose. Through the grace of his guidance, seekers embark on a journey of self-discovery and transformation.

The initiation into Vedic mantras by Asharam Bapu opens doors to spiritual realms previously unexplored by seekers. With each mantra, seekers delve deeper into the ocean of spirituality, experiencing profound inner peace and contentment.

The transformative journey under the guidance of Asharam Bapu is marked by moments of profound realization and spiritual growth. Seekers find themselves gradually shedding layers of ignorance and embracing the light of wisdom.

Asharam Bapu's satsangs are not merely gatherings of individuals; they are sacred congregations where seekers commune with the divine and receive blessings that transcend the material realm. His words resonate with truth and compassion, touching the hearts of all who listen.

The profound impact of mantra initiation is not limited to the spiritual realm; it extends to every aspect of seekers' lives. They experience newfound clarity of thought, enhanced mental focus, and a deeper sense of connection with the universe.

Asharam Bapu's teachings emphasize the importance of self-discipline, righteous conduct, and devotion to the divine. Through regular practice of meditation and recitation of Vedic mantras, seekers cultivate virtues that lead to inner harmony and spiritual fulfilment.

The journey with Asharam Bapu is a transformative one, characterized by moments of profound insight and spiritual awakening. Seekers find themselves traversing the path of self-discovery with renewed zeal and determination.

The initiation into Vedic mantras and spiritual guidance received from Asharam Bapu leads seekers on a transformative journey of self-realization and inner awakening. Through his grace and wisdom, seekers find solace, guidance, and fulfillment on the path of spirituality.

In various countries like the United States, Germany, Switzerland, Canada, England, Hong Kong, Singapore, Taiwan, Bangkok, Indonesia, Kenya, Nepal, and even Pakistan, people from diverse backgrounds seek guidance and experience gratitude after interacting with revered figures and leaders of various organizations. Asharam Bapu has traveled extensively, spreading messages of joy, peace, and harmony among communities.

NURTURING VIRTUE: THE IMPACT OF ASHARAM BAPU'S ASHRAMS ON SOCIETY

In today's fast-paced world, where the allure of clubs, bars, cinemas, and other forms of entertainment often leads society into moral decay, the serene sanctuaries of Asharam Bapu's ashrams stand as beacons of spiritual enrichment and moral upliftment. With over 425 ashrams spread across various corners of the globe, these centers of peace and spirituality welcome individuals from all walks of life, offering them the divine gift of inner peace through the practices of Bhakti Yoga, Jnana Yoga, Nishkama Karma Yoga, and Kundalini Yoga.

One of the most commendable initiatives undertaken by the ashrams is the establishment of Bal Sanskar Kendras, where thousands of children, regardless of their caste, creed, or background, are imbued with the values of righteousness and compassion. These centers, along with Student Sanskar Kendras and Kanya Sanskar Kendras, play a pivotal role in nurturing good values among children, ensuring a bright and virtuous future for generations to come. Additionally, during holidays, the ashrams organize 'Vidhyarthi Ujjwal Bhavishya Nirman Shivirs' aimed at instilling qualities of diligence, intelligence, and altruism among students, with the revered Bapu himself providing guidance and inspiration during 'Vidhyarthi Tejasvi Talim Shivirs.'

In stark contrast to the wholesome environment provided by the ashrams, the rampant exposure to television, cinema, video games, and the internet leads children to spend approximately 55 hours per week immersed in these forms of entertainment. By the time a child reaches the age of 18, they have been exposed to thousands of explicit and violent scenes on television, along with over 200,000 violent acts. The deleterious influence of cinema and television manifests in the proliferation of vices such as theft, alcoholism, corruption, violence, rape, and indecency, which deeply impact the impressionable minds of children.

Amidst this cultural onslaught, Asharam Bapu's ashrams serve as sanctuaries of moral integrity, providing individuals with the tools to navigate the turbulent waters of modernity while upholding the timeless values of compassion, righteousness, and self-discipline. It is through the noble endeavors of these ashrams that countless souls find solace, direction, and purpose in a world fraught with moral ambiguity and spiritual deprivation.

The legacy of Asharam Bapu's ashrams transcends mere physical structures; they represent bastions of hope, compassion, and spiritual rejuvenation in an increasingly tumultuous world. As society grapples with the erosion of moral values, these sanctuaries stand as living testimonies to the transformative power of spirituality and the enduring relevance of timeless wisdom in fostering a harmonious and virtuous society.

THE YOUTH EMPOWERMENT CAMPAIGN: A BEACON OF INSPIRATION AND TRANSFORMATION

In the endeavor to nurture and uplift the youth, over two crore 'Divine Inspiration-Enlightenment Books' have been disseminated among students, youngsters, and the general populace. These books serve as a guiding light, instilling the virtues of discipline and morality, while also imparting simple strategies for maintaining physical and mental well-being. Additionally, programs aimed at the empowerment of young men and women are organized by the 'Youth Service Association' and the 'Women's Development Forum'.

The 'Youth Empowerment Campaign' has sparked a new consciousness among the youth, inspiring them to lead principled lives and contribute positively to society. This campaign continues to resonate and thrive, fostering a culture of self-improvement and societal upliftment.

In stark contrast, statistics from America reveal a concerning trend wherein 7% of children engage in sexual activity before the age of 13. Furthermore, a staggering 85% of boys and 77% of girls have experienced sexual intercourse before reaching the age of 19. The repercussions of premature sexual activity manifest in various societal issues, posing a formidable challenge for governments despite spending millions of dollars in mitigation efforts.

The teachings and initiatives of spiritual leaders like Asharam Bapu serve as a beacon of hope in navigating these challenges. Through the dissemination of enlightening literature and the organization of empowerment programs, Asharam Bapu's mission aims to guide youth towards a path of righteousness and self-restraint.

The 'Divine Inspiration-Enlightenment Books' offer invaluable wisdom on leading a virtuous life, fostering self-discipline, and cultivating a healthy mind-body balance. These teachings resonate with readers of all ages, providing practical insights that resonate with the simplest of minds.

Furthermore, the efforts of organizations like the 'Youth Service Association' and the 'Women's Development Forum' complement the spiritual teachings by providing platforms for holistic growth and empowerment. Through various workshops, seminars, and community initiatives, young individuals are equipped with the skills and knowledge necessary to navigate life's challenges with integrity and resilience.

However, despite these concerted efforts, the prevalence of early sexual activity among youth remains a pressing concern. The societal implications of this phenomenon are far-reaching, necessitating a multifaceted approach involving education, awareness, and community support.

The 'Youth Empowerment Campaign' spearheaded by spiritual luminaries like Asharam Bapu serves as a ray of hope in a world grappling with complex social issues. Through the dissemination of enlightening literature and the organization of empowerment programs, the campaign endeavors to instill values of morality, discipline, and self-restraint among the youth, thus paving the way for a brighter and more harmonious future.

EMPOWERING TRIBAL AND UNDERPRIVILEGED COMMUNITIES: FOLLOWING THE GUIDANCE OF REVERED ASHARAM BAPU

In more than 425 ashrams and over 1400 Sri Yoga Vedanta Seva Samitis across the nation, under the benevolent guidance of revered Asharam Bapu, a consistent effort is underway to uplift indigenous tribes and underprivileged communities. These initiatives encompass the regular distribution of essential supplies and life-improving resources in various regions of the country.

Time and again, revered Bapu personally oversees the distribution of food, clothing, utensils, notebooks, school uniforms, and more among tribal and economically disadvantaged individuals. The scale of these efforts is substantial, touching the lives of millions.

For the destitute, homeless, and widowed, thousands of ration cards have been distributed by the ashrams. Through these cards, beneficiaries receive free distribution of grains and essential commodities every month, ensuring their sustenance and well-being.

According to the Indian Human Development Survey, approximately 50 percent of tribal populations live below the poverty line, highlighting their vulnerability and need for support.

In his teachings and actions, revered Asharam Bapu emphasizes the importance of serving the most marginalized sections of society. His profound compassion and commitment to social welfare have inspired a vast network of devotees and volunteers to join hands in this noble cause.

Through these initiatives, the aim is not just to alleviate immediate hardships but also to empower these communities to lead dignified and self-sufficient lives. Education, skill development, and holistic wellness are integral components of the programs initiated under Bapu's guidance.

The impact of these efforts extends far beyond material assistance. They instill hope, restore dignity, and foster a sense of belonging among those who have long been neglected by mainstream society.

By reaching out to the most vulnerable and marginalized, Asharam Bapu's teachings and actions exemplify the timeless principles of compassion, service, and social justice. His legacy continues to inspire countless individuals and organizations to work towards a more equitable and inclusive society.

The tireless efforts led by revered Asharam Bapu, and his devotees reflect a deep commitment to uplifting the most marginalized communities in society. Through their collective endeavors, they illuminate a path of compassion, empowerment, and social transformation.

EMPOWERING WOMEN: THE ASHARAM BAPU FOUNDATION'S MISSION FOR SOCIETAL UPLIFTMENT

In today's fast-paced world, where women's empowerment is crucial for societal progress, the Mahila Utthan Mandal, under the guidance of Asharam Bapu, tirelessly works towards holistic development. Through initiatives such as cultural gatherings, anti-abortion campaigns, and centers for nurturing girl children, the foundation aims to uplift women in every aspect of life.

Over the past decade, India has witnessed a tragic trend with the abortion of 8 million unborn girls. This alarming statistic underscores the urgent need for societal transformation. Additionally, the rising prevalence of alcohol and tobacco consumption among women is a growing concern. Globally, approximately 250 million women engage in smoking daily, highlighting the pervasive nature of this issue.

In response to these challenges, the Mahila Utthan Mandal, inspired by Asharam Bapu's teachings, has been at the forefront of initiatives to address these pressing issues. Through education and awareness campaigns, the foundation endeavors to shift societal attitudes towards gender equality and women's rights. By organizing cultural gatherings, the Mandal fosters a sense of community and solidarity among women, empowering them to lead fulfilling lives.

One of the cornerstone initiatives of the foundation is the anti-abortion campaign, which aims to educate women about the sanctity of life and the consequences of gender-based discrimination. Through counseling and support services, the Mandal provides assistance to expectant mothers, encouraging them to embrace motherhood with dignity and pride.

Furthermore, the foundation operates Bal and Kanya Sanskar Kendras, where girls receive education, life skills training, and moral guidance. These centers serve as safe havens for vulnerable girls, equipping them with the tools they need to thrive in a male-dominated society. By nurturing their talents and instilling values of self-respect and empowerment, the Mandal is shaping the leaders of tomorrow.

In addition to these initiatives, the Tejaswini Abhiyan-Shivir and Divya Shishu Sanskar programs provide specialized services to women and children, respectively. Through these programs, the foundation addresses the unique needs of women and children, ensuring their holistic development and well-being.

Asharam Bapu's vision of a society where women are respected and empowered is the driving force behind the Mahila Utthan Mandal's tireless efforts. By addressing the root causes of gender inequality and discrimination, the foundation is paving the way for a brighter future where every woman can realize her full potential and contribute meaningfully to society. Through collective action and unwavering dedication, the Mandal is making strides towards creating a more just and equitable world for all.

SERVING THE SACRED COWS: ASHARAM BAPU'S GOSHALAS AND THE FIGHT AGAINST SLAUGHTERHOUSES

In India, the noble endeavor of protecting cows and serving them finds its embodiment in the Goshalas initiated by Sant Asharam Bapu. These sanctuaries not only provide shelter to thousands of cows but also prevent their slaughter, thus upholding the reverence accorded to these gentle creatures in Hindu culture.

The Goshalas, scattered across the country, serve as havens for cows rescued from the clutches of slaughterhouses. Here, they find solace and care amidst the compassionate embrace of volunteers and devotees. These shelters are not merely refuges but also centers of self-sufficiency, where innovative initiatives ensure the well-being of the cows while promoting sustainability.

One of the remarkable aspects of Asharam Bapu's Goshalas is their emphasis on self-reliance. By harnessing the resources available within the shelters, such as cow dung and urine, various products like dhoop battis (incense sticks), fertilizers, and medicines are manufactured. This not only fulfills the needs of the Goshalas but also generates income, thereby enabling them to operate independently and sustainably.

Moreover, the Goshalas serve as hubs of innovation, where traditional knowledge meets modern techniques. Through research and development, efforts are made to explore the diverse uses of cow by-products, thereby maximizing their utility and value. This holistic approach not only benefits the cows but also contributes to environmental conservation and rural empowerment.

However, amidst these endeavors lies a stark reality – the prevalence of slaughterhouses, both legal and illegal, posing a grave threat to the lives of cows. It is estimated that around 3,600 legal and 30,000 illegal slaughterhouses operate in India, perpetuating the cycle of cruelty and exploitation. In the face of such challenges, the Goshalas stand as bastions of compassion and resistance, offering a ray of hope to the voiceless victims of this inhumane industry.

The work undertaken by Asharam Bapu's Goshalas exemplifies the essence of seva (selfless service) and ahimsa (non-violence) ingrained in Hindu philosophy. It is a testament to the enduring legacy of compassion and righteousness espoused by Sants throughout the ages. Through their tireless efforts, they not only safeguard the sacred cows but also inspire countless individuals to embrace the values of empathy and reverence for all living beings.

The Goshalas established by Sant Asharam Bapu symbolize a beacon of hope amidst the darkness of cruelty and exploitation. Their noble mission of protecting and serving cows reflects the timeless ideals of compassion, sustainability, and reverence for life. As we celebrate their endeavors, let us also pledge to stand united in the fight against injustice and uphold the sanctity of all life forms.

THE CAMPAIGN FOR ADDICTION-FREE LIVING: ASHARAM BAPU'S IMPACT

In today's fast-paced world, the scourge of addiction has gripped millions, leading them down paths of despair and suffering. However, amidst this darkness, a beacon of hope shines brightly through the Addiction-Free Living Campaign spearheaded by the ashram of revered spiritual leader Asharam Bapu. Through a combination of outreach efforts, exhibitions, and enlightening discourses, this campaign has transformed the lives of countless individuals, guiding them towards a journey of health, happiness, and dignity.

According to the National Survey on Extent and Pattern of Substance Use in India conducted in 2018, here are the findings related to substance use among children and adolescents:

- Alcohol: Approximately 1.30% of children and adolescents (aged 10-17 years) are current alcohol users, which translates to around 30 lakh individuals. Among adults (aged 18-75 years), the prevalence is 17.10%, with an estimated 15.10 crore users.
- Cannabis: About 0.90% of children and adolescents use cannabis (around 20 lakh individuals). Among adults, the prevalence is 3.30%, with approximately 2.90 crore users.
- Opioids: Around 1.80% of children and adolescents (approximately 40 lakh individuals) are opioid users. Among adults, the prevalence is 2.10%, with an estimated 1.90 crore users.
- Sedatives: Approximately 0.58% of children and adolescents (around 20 lakh individuals) use sedatives. Among adults, the prevalence is 1.21%, with about 1.10 crore users.
- Inhalants: About 1.17% of children and adolescents (approximately 30 lakh individuals) use inhalants. Among adults, the prevalence is 0.58%, with around 60 lakh users.
- Cocaine: A small percentage of children and adolescents (around 0.06%, or 2 lakh individuals) use cocaine. Among adults, the prevalence is 0.11%, with approximately 10 lakh users.
- ATS (Amphetamine-Type Stimulants): Around 0.18% of children and adolescents (approximately 4 lakh individuals) use ATS. Among adults, the prevalence remains the same at 0.18%, with about 20 lakh users.
- Hallucinogens: A small percentage of children and adolescents (around 0.07%, or 2 lakh individuals) use hallucinogens. Among adults, the prevalence is 0.13%, with approximately 20 lakh users.

In response to these distressing trends, Asharam Bapu's ashram launched the Addiction-Free Living Campaign, aiming to tackle the root causes of addiction and provide individuals with the support they need to break free from its shackles. Through a multifaceted approach that combines awareness-raising initiatives, educational programs, and holistic rehabilitation efforts, the campaign has yielded remarkable results.

One of the key components of the campaign is the dissemination of knowledge through satsangs (spiritual discourses) conducted by Asharam

Bapu himself. These discourses not only shed light on the detrimental effects of addiction but also offer practical guidance on leading a life of purity, discipline, and spiritual fulfillment. As individuals immerse themselves in the wisdom imparted by Bapu, they gain the strength and resolve to overcome their addictions and embark on a path of self-transformation.

In addition to spiritual guidance, the campaign also focuses on practical interventions aimed at breaking the cycle of addiction. Rehabilitation centers established by the ashram provide a nurturing environment where individuals receive counseling, therapy, and vocational training to rebuild their lives and reintegrate into society as productive members.

Moreover, the campaign organizes exhibitions and awareness drives to reach out to communities across the country, disseminating information about the harmful effects of addiction and offering support to those in need. Through these efforts, the campaign seeks to create a ripple effect of positive change, inspiring individuals to make healthier choices and embrace lives free from addiction.

Asharam Bapu's vision of a society free from the scourge of addiction continues to inspire millions to tread the path of righteousness and inner awakening. With unwavering dedication and compassionate guidance, the Addiction-Free Living Campaign stands as a beacon of hope, illuminating the way towards a brighter, addiction-free future for all.

HEALTHCARE SERVICES IN RURAL INDIA: BRIDGING GAPS WITH HOLISTIC APPROACHES

In rural India, healthcare services are provided by knowledgeable practitioners proficient in various medical traditions such as Ayurveda, Homeopathy, Acupressure, and Naturopathy. These dedicated healers administer treatments in various ashrams, alongside organizing free medical camps in underserved areas. Moreover, healthcare facilities established by local practitioners cater to the health needs of tribal and rural communities.

It is disheartening to note that approximately 50% of rural areas in India lack adequate access to healthcare services. This glaring disparity underscores the urgent need for concerted efforts to address healthcare inequities and ensure universal access to essential medical care.

In response to these challenges, spiritual leaders like Asharam Bapu have played a significant role in advocating for holistic healthcare approaches and spearheading initiatives to improve healthcare access in rural India. Through their guidance and philanthropic endeavors, they have inspired communities to embrace traditional healing modalities while also promoting the integration of modern medical practices.

One of the key strengths of traditional healthcare systems such as Ayurveda and Homeopathy lies in their emphasis on preventive care and natural remedies. By harnessing the healing properties of herbs, minerals, and other natural substances, practitioners can effectively treat a wide range of ailments while minimizing side effects. Additionally, these systems prioritize holistic well-being, focusing on restoring balance to the body, mind, and spirit.

In remote and marginalized communities where conventional healthcare infrastructure is scarce, community-based healthcare initiatives play a pivotal role in delivering essential services. Mobile clinics and outreach programs conducted by local healers and volunteers ensure that even the most vulnerable populations have access to basic healthcare services.

Furthermore, the concept of free medical camps, commonly organized by spiritual leaders and charitable organizations, has emerged as a lifeline for underserved communities. These camps provide much-needed medical consultations, diagnostic tests, and medications free of cost, alleviating the financial burden on impoverished families and empowering them to prioritize their health.

Despite these commendable efforts, significant challenges persist in the realm of rural healthcare delivery. Limited funding, inadequate infrastructure, and a shortage of trained healthcare professionals continue to hamper the effectiveness of healthcare interventions in rural areas. Addressing these systemic barriers requires a multifaceted approach involving government agencies, non-profit organizations, and community stakeholders working in tandem to strengthen healthcare systems at the grassroots level.

The provision of healthcare services in rural India remains a complex and multifaceted issue that demands urgent attention and concerted action. By leveraging traditional healing wisdom, embracing innovative approaches, and fostering collaboration among diverse stakeholders, we can work towards building a more equitable and inclusive healthcare system that leaves no community behind. The tireless efforts of spiritual leaders like Asharam Bapu serve as beacons of hope, guiding us towards a future where every individual has access to quality healthcare services, regardless of their socioeconomic status or geographical location.

THE HEALING POWER OF DEVOTION: ASHARAM BAPU'S MESSAGE OF LOVE AND REVERENCE

In today's fast-paced world, where materialism often overshadows spiritual values, the practice of Bhagwannam Sankirtan, or the chanting of divine names, serves as a beacon of hope. Ashrams and Shri Yoga Vedanta Seva Samitis organize Bhagwannam Sankirtan Yatras across various locations, both within the country and abroad, with the noble objectives of eliminating intellectual pollution and fostering cultural consciousness. These endeavors not only purify the mind, body, and environment but also catalyze the development of life energy.

Contrastingly, in Western societies, the popularity of rock music has been observed to deplete life energy. Dr. Diamond's experiments reveal a significant decrease in the capacity of the deltoid muscle, capable of lifting weights of 40 to 45 kilograms under normal conditions, to merely 10 to 15 kilograms while listening to rock music. Such findings underscore the detrimental impact of certain cultural practices on vitality.

Amidst the cultural shifts and societal challenges, the observance of Matru-Pitru Pujan Diwas, inspired by the revered visionary, Pujya Bapu, offers solace and guidance. Over the past fourteen years, millions of individuals worldwide have forsaken the celebration of Valentine's Day in favor of honoring their parents. This transformation has spared countless individuals from moral decay, instilling virtues of self-restraint and righteousness in their lives.

The adverse effects of Valentine's Day are glaring, particularly in developed countries, where adolescent pregnancies, abortions, and instances of young girls being forced into nursing homes or coerced into prostitution are alarmingly high. By redirecting attention towards familial love and respect, the Matru-Pitru Pujan Diwas movement has become a catalyst for societal renewal and moral regeneration.

In essence, the teachings and initiatives spearheaded by Asharam Bapu emphasize the importance of nurturing a spiritual connection amidst the chaos of modern existence. Through practices such as Bhagwannam Sankirtan and Matru-Pitru Pujan, individuals can rediscover their innate virtues and cultivate a harmonious relationship with themselves and the world around them. As the world grapples with various challenges, the message of love, reverence, and devotion serves as a guiding light towards a more compassionate and enlightened society.

Holistic Living: A Day in Harmony with Nature

Living in harmony with the circadian rhythm not only shields us from most illnesses but also leads to optimal health and longevity.

Time (Specific Activities According to Body Clock):

1. **Early Morning 3 to 5 AM (Lungs):** Individuals waking during the Brahma Muhurta are usually more alert and enthusiastic. It's advisable to drink a little warm water and take a walk in the fresh air. Deep breathing exercises are also beneficial.
2. **Morning 5 to 7 AM (Large Intestine):** Those who sleep during this time often suffer from constipation and other ailments. Hence, it's essential to evacuate the bowels between waking up and 7 AM.
3. **Morning 7 to 9 AM (Stomach or Duodenum):** This is the time (2 hours before breakfast) when one can have milk or fruit juice.
4. **Morning 9 to 11 AM (Stomach and Spleen):** This time is suitable for meals.
5. **Noon 11 AM to 1 PM (Heart):** To nurture emotions like compassion and love, meditate around noon. Refrain from eating.
6. **Noon 1 to 3 PM (Small Intestine):** Drink water according to thirst 2 hours after a meal. Eating or sleeping during this time leads to the depletion of vital nutrients, making the body susceptible to diseases.
7. **Afternoon 3 to 5 PM (Bladder):** Urination will naturally occur if water is consumed 2-4 hours prior.
8. **Evening 5 to 7 PM (Kidneys):** Light dinner should be consumed. Avoid eating 10 minutes before or after sunset (during dusk). Milk can be consumed three hours after dinner.
9. **Night 7 to 9 PM (Brain):** The brain retains information read during this time better than in the morning.
10. **Night 9 to 11 PM (Pineal Gland):** Sleeping during this time provides deep rest and rejuvenation. Sleep deprivation leads to aging.
11. **11 PM to 1 AM (Liver):** Staying awake during this time irritates the liver and may lead to insomnia, headaches, and eye diseases.

12. **1 to 3 AM (Gallbladder):** Deep sleep is essential during this period. Insufficient sleep disrupts digestion.

Rishis and Ayurvedic practitioners advise against eating without feeling hungry. Hence, the quantity of morning and evening meals should be such that one feels hungry at the prescribed times.

Living in alignment with the body's natural rhythm fosters physical, mental, and spiritual well-being. Following these simple guidelines ensures a life of balance and vitality.

This adaptation from Asharam Bapu's teachings emphasizes the importance of a daily routine synchronized with the body's biological clock for optimal health and vitality.

DIVINE BABY RITES: NURTURING THE SOUL FROM WOMB TO WORLD

In the wisdom shared by Bapu, lies a profound understanding, the essence of a fulfilled life lies in its health, happiness, and dignity, all of which are bestowed through the divine rites embedded within Indian culture.

The journey of human existence, according to Bapu, commences within the sacred confines of a mother's womb. Here, amidst the tender embrace of maternal warmth, begins the first lesson in life's divine curriculum. It is within this sanctuary that the infant's subconscious is gently shaped, laying the foundation for the blossoming of their future personality. These rites and rituals, meticulously preserved through generations, stand as a testament to the rich heritage of humanity.

Throughout the miraculous period of pregnancy, these rituals serve as guiding beacons, illuminating the path towards holistic well-being. They are not mere customs but profound acts of reverence towards life itself. From the tender whispers of maternal mantras to the soothing touch of auspicious oils, each ritual is a sacred thread interwoven into the fabric of the unborn child's consciousness.

As the expectant mother nurtures her divine passenger within, she is enveloped in a cocoon of love and devotion. Every gesture, every chant, every offering is imbued with the fervent prayer for the well-being of both mother and child. It is through these rituals that the bond between the two is strengthened, forging an unbreakable connection that transcends the physical realm.

Bapu emphasizes that these rituals are not mere superstitions but profound expressions of faith and wisdom. They carry within them the collective consciousness of centuries, serving as bridges between the earthly and the divine. Through their observance, one aligns oneself with the cosmic rhythms, harmonizing body, mind, and spirit in the eternal dance of existence.

As the journey from womb to world unfolds, these divine rites continue to guide and protect the newborn soul. From the sacred ceremony of birth to the nurturing embrace of the first feeding, each moment is infused with the sanctity of tradition and the blessings of the divine. Through these rituals, the infant is welcomed into the embrace of the human family, surrounded by love, warmth, and the promise of a bright future.

In the tapestry of life, these divine baby rites are the golden threads that weave together the past, present, and future. They are the sacred rituals that sanctify the journey of life, infusing every moment with grace, beauty, and divine blessings. As Bapu reminds us, it is through the observance of these rituals that we honour the gift of life and fulfil our sacred duty towards the generations yet to come.

In the pursuit of fostering an ideal and culturally rich society, Divya Shishu Sanskar Kendra aims to fortify the foundational yet crucial aspect of human life. Much like carefully selecting and nurturing a seed to cultivate a thriving plant, the Kendra endeavours to instil the seeds of virtues in infants from the very womb of their mothers. This deliberate cultivation of virtues is envisioned to yield a harvest of empowered and virtuous citizens for the future.

Initiated by the Mahila Utthan Mandal, the Divine Shishu Sanskar Kendra's are dedicated to imbuing mothers with the right understanding of sacraments and equipping them with methods to carve out a bright future for their children. The overarching goal is to contribute to the divine transformation of the future generations of India.

At the heart of this initiative lies the unwavering commitment of Bapu, who envisions India as a beacon of wisdom and enlightenment on the global stage. In alignment with his vision, individuals participating in the Bhagiratha service activities are pivotal in realizing this noble aspiration.

The philosophy underlying the Divya Shishu Sanskar Kendra is simple yet profound by nurturing the inherent potential of each child and providing them with a strong moral and cultural foundation, we pave the way for a harmonious and prosperous society. It emphasizes the importance of starting this journey of nurturing from the very inception of life, recognizing the formative influence of early experiences on the trajectory of an individual's growth and development.

Through the dissemination of age-old wisdom and the promotion of values such as compassion, integrity, and empathy, the Kendra seeks to empower mothers as the primary architects of their children's destinies. By equipping them with the knowledge and tools necessary for holistic child-rearing, the Kendra strives to create a ripple effect of positive change that reverberates throughout society.

The holistic approach of the Kendra encompasses not only the intellectual and physical well-being of children but also their emotional and spiritual growth. It recognizes that true greatness lies not in material wealth or external accomplishments, but in the richness of one's character and the depth of one's virtues.

As we embark on this journey towards nurturing a brighter future for generations to come, let us heed the call to action issued by Bapu and actively participate in the noble endeavour of nation-building. For it is through our collective efforts and unwavering dedication that we can truly fulfil the vision of an enlightened and prosperous India, serving as a guiding light for the world.

THE URGENCY OF HALTING ABORTION: INSIGHTS FROM ASHARAM BAPU

In our society, the issue of abortion has become a matter of grave concern. It is imperative to understand the profound repercussions that this act carries, both on the physical health of the mother and the spiritual fabric of the family. Asharam Bapu has shed light on this critical issue, emphasizing the need for a concerted effort to halt abortion and protect the sanctity of life.

When a woman chooses to terminate her pregnancy, she not only jeopardizes her own health but also invites a host of diseases to inhabit her body. The womb, once meant to nurture life, becomes a breeding ground for ailments, casting a shadow of uncertainty over the woman's well-being. Moreover, the family, instead of being a haven of peace, descends into a state of turmoil and discord. The decision to abort a child tear at the very fabric of familial bonds, leaving behind scars that may never fully heal.

It is essential to recognize the stark reality that the risks associated with childbirth far outweigh those of abortion. Contrary to popular belief, the dangers to a mother's health during childbirth are significantly lower than those posed by the act of abortion. Asharam Bapu has emphasized the need to prioritize the well-being of both the mother and the unborn child, advocating for alternatives to abortion that uphold the dignity of life.

Furthermore, the spiritual implications of abortion cannot be overlooked. Asharam Bapu has likened the sin of abortion to the egregious act of killing a Brahmin, emphasizing the gravity of this transgression. The soul of the unborn child, innocent and pure, is snuffed out before it can even take its first breath, leaving behind a void that can never be filled. The karmic repercussions of such an act extend beyond the present lifetime, affecting the spiritual evolution of all involved.

Considering these profound insights, it is incumbent upon us as a society to take a stand against the scourge of abortion. We must strive to create an environment where every life is cherished and protected, where the sanctity of motherhood is revered, and where the bonds of family are strengthened, not torn asunder. Let us heed the wisdom of Asharam Bapu and work towards building a future where every child is welcomed with open arms and every mother is supported in her journey of nurturing life.

Together, let us embark on a journey towards compassion, understanding, and reverence for the precious gift of life. Only then can we hope to build a world where love triumphs over fear, and where the sanctity of life is upheld above all else.

THE UNBORN SAGE: UNDERSTANDING THE IMPACT OF ABORTION

In ancient scriptures, it is believed that even before birth, a baby retains memories of past lives, earning them the revered title of a sage. The act of aborting such a fetus is considered akin to killing a wise being, carrying grave consequences. It is imperative to comprehend these ramifications and actively participate in the preservation of life.

Abortion, unfortunately, carries with it a multitude of adverse effects on both physical and mental health. Research suggests a significant increase in the probability of breast cancer, up by 30 percent in women who have undergone abortion procedures. Furthermore, hormonal imbalances are common among women post-abortion, potentially diminishing their likelihood of conceiving again due to decreased fertility.

The repercussions extend beyond mere health concerns. Children conceived post-abortion may face higher risks of weakness and disability, impacting not only their own lives but also placing added strain on their caregivers. Complications such as menstrual irregularities and pelvic inflammation are also heightened in women who have undergone abortion procedures, potentially persisting until later stages of life.

Alarmingly, studies indicate a substantial increase in the incidence of cervical and ovarian cancers among women who have had abortions. Such findings underscore the profound and long-lasting impact that abortion can have on a woman's physical well-being.

Equally concerning are the psychological effects of abortion, often manifesting as decreased morale, headaches, irritability, and heightened suicidal ideation. The emotional toll of terminating a pregnancy cannot be understated, with many women experiencing ongoing mental distress long after the procedure has taken place.

Moreover, the risk of complications during subsequent pregnancies is significantly heightened in women with a history of abortion. Up to half of women who have undergone abortion procedures may face an increased likelihood of miscarriage, further compounding the emotional and physical toll of their previous experiences.

The decision to undergo an abortion is not one to be taken lightly. Beyond the immediate implications for the unborn child, abortion carries with it a myriad of long-term consequences for women's health and well-being. It is incumbent upon society to provide support and resources for women facing unplanned pregnancies, offering alternatives to abortion and ensuring that every life is valued and protected.

THE PERILOUS CONSEQUENCES OF ABORTION: A CALL TO PRESERVE LIFE

In the profound teachings of Pujya Bapu and Swami Shri Ramsukhdasji Maharaj, lies a poignant reminder of the sanctity of life and the grave consequences of abortion. Their words echo with wisdom, urging us to reflect upon the moral and health implications of such actions.

Abortion, as elucidated by Pujya Bapu, not only inflicts harm upon the unborn child but also jeopardizes the well-being of the mother. The use of medications or tools to terminate a pregnancy is likened to perpetrating a grave sin and exposing oneself to the risk of dire afflictions. With compassionate concern, Pujya Bapu implores us to contemplate the profound ramifications of our choices, urging us to safeguard both virtue and health.

Similarly, Swami Shri Ramsukhdasji Maharaj invokes the wisdom of ancient scriptures, highlighting the inherent divinity and knowledge within the unborn child. In the sacred texts, the fetus is revered as a sage, possessing consciousness that transcends lifetimes. Abortion, therefore, is deemed as a heinous transgression, surpassing even the atrocities witnessed in bygone eras. With poignant clarity, Swami Shri Ramsukhdasji Maharaj underscores the gravity of this act, imploring us to ponder upon the moral culpability of destroying innocent life.

In response to this urgent call to action, the Mahila Utthan Mandal has undertaken a noble endeavour to raise awareness and prevent the scourge of abortion and unnecessary cesarean deliveries. Through meticulously organized seminars, seasoned medical professionals and experts disseminate vital information regarding the detrimental effects of abortion and strategies for its avoidance. Participants are sensitized to the profound losses incurred by such practices and are empowered to make informed choices for the preservation of life.

Moreover, the Mahila Utthan Mandal endeavours to instil a collective commitment towards fostering a culture of life and reverence for the sanctity of motherhood. Through the distribution of pamphlets and engaging in public outreach initiatives, they seek to mobilize communities to pledge against abortion and cesarean deliveries unless medically necessary. In doing so, they strive to cultivate a societal ethos grounded in compassion, empathy, and respect for all life forms.

The teachings of Pujya Bapu and Swami Shri Ramsukhdasji Maharaj serve as guiding beacons, illuminating the path towards righteousness and compassion. Their profound insights compel us to introspect and act with conscientious resolve, for the preservation of life is our sacred duty. Let us heed their wisdom and unite in our commitment to uphold the dignity and sanctity of every precious soul.

THE HAZARDS OF CESAREAN DELIVERY

Cesarean delivery, commonly known as C-section, has long been a topic of concern, especially within the teachings of the revered Sant, Shri Asharam Bapu. He has tirelessly emphasized in his Satsang's, discourses, the detrimental effects of opting for surgical intervention over natural childbirth. It is imperative to understand the wisdom behind his teachings, especially in light of recent scientific revelations.

As Shri Asharam Bapu has elucidated, cesarean delivery poses significant risks to both the mother and the child. The process of childbirth, when left to the natural course, allows for the passage of beneficial vaginal fluid containing essential bacteria. This fluid, comprising approximately 95% of vaginal secretions during normal delivery, plays a crucial role in enhancing the immunity and digestive capabilities of the newborn.

Contrastingly, cesarean delivery deprives the infant of this vital microbial exposure, thus compromising their immune system's development. Scientific research corroborates these teachings, highlighting the heightened risk of asthma, allergies, and respiratory ailments among infants born via cesarean section. The absence of natural microbial colonization during cesarean delivery significantly contributes to these health concerns, underscoring the importance of embracing natural obstetric measures.

Furthermore, cesarean delivery entails additional risks and complications for the mother. Surgical procedures inherently carry the potential for post-operative complications, including infections, blood loss, and prolonged recovery periods. By opting for cesarean delivery, mothers subject themselves to these avoidable risks, which can have lasting repercussions on their well-being.

In light of the teachings of Shri Asharam Bapu and the emerging scientific evidence, it becomes evident that prioritizing natural childbirth is paramount. The holistic approach advocated by Shri Asharam Bapu emphasizes the harmony between body, mind, and spirit, promoting the well-being of both mother and child.

It is incumbent upon healthcare providers and expectant mothers to consider these insights seriously. By opting for natural obstetric measures whenever feasible, we can mitigate the risks associated with cesarean delivery and promote the health and well-being of both mothers and newborns.

The teachings of revered Sant Asharam Bapu shed light on the hazards of cesarean delivery, urging us to prioritize natural childbirth for the well-being of both mother and child. By aligning with these teachings and embracing natural obstetric measures, we can ensure a healthier future for generations to come.

Based on a study conducted by Dr. Caroline Roduit of Switzerland, it has been observed that child loss can have significant repercussions on both the physical and emotional well-being of mothers. The study, which involved 2917 children, highlighted several concerning findings related to child loss and its aftermath.

One of the major implications of child loss is an immune deficiency in mothers. The study revealed an alarming 80% increase in the chances of developing asthma and a 20% increase in the likelihood of experiencing depression or anxiety, commonly referred to as "honey."

Furthermore, mothers who have experienced child loss also face a heightened risk of complications in subsequent pregnancies. There is a notable loss of weight and an increased risk of deformities in the brain and spinal cord of future babies.

Moreover, the loss or death of a mother during childbirth has devastating consequences. The study found that there is a staggering 26 times increase in the probability of maternal mortality in such cases, highlighting the urgent need for better maternal healthcare services.

In addition to physical health concerns, child loss can also lead to emotional trauma and uterine discharge. Mothers may experience heightened fear of uterine rupture in subsequent pregnancies, adding to their anxiety and stress.

Furthermore, there is a risk of not being able to conceive again after experiencing child loss, further exacerbating the emotional toll on mothers and their families.

Additionally, mothers who undergo cesarean section deliveries face an increased risk of hernia at the site of the operation, adding another layer of concern to their health and well-being.

The findings of this study underscore the bitter truth that child loss can have far-reaching consequences on maternal health and well-being. It is imperative for healthcare providers and policymakers to prioritize maternal health and provide adequate support and resources to mothers who have experienced such loss.

The study conducted by Dr. Caroline Roduit sheds light on the profound impact of child loss on maternal health. It serves as a poignant reminder of the need for comprehensive healthcare services and support systems for mothers who have experienced such loss.

THE POWER OF SPIRITUAL AWAKENING

In today's fast-paced world, where stress and negativity seem to lurk around every corner, the need for spiritual awakening has never been more crucial. Asharam Bapu, a revered spiritual leader, has emphasized the profound impact of devotion and divine connection in purifying the soul and uplifting human existence.

As Dr. Diamond's research illustrates, the influence of music on vitality is profound. While genres like rock and pop may diminish vitality, engaging in Indian classical music and Hari Naam kirtan, as advocated by Asharam Bapu, leads to enhanced vitality and well-being. The timeless wisdom passed down by our sages underscores the significance of Hari Naam San kirtan, not only as a means of devotion but also as a pathway to physical and spiritual rejuvenation.

The essence of Hari-Kirtan lies in its universal appeal, transcending age, gender, and societal boundaries. As individuals partake in kirtan, clapping and dancing in the spirit of devotion, they unknowingly receive the therapeutic benefits akin to acupressure therapy. This holistic approach not only harmonizes the body and mind but also alleviates afflictions such as sorrow and grief, allowing individuals to immerse themselves in the divine nectar of hariras.

Asharam Bapu's teachings emphasize the simplicity and accessibility of spiritual practices, making them accessible to people from all walks of life. Through the medium of Hari-Kirtan, individuals are encouraged to cultivate a deeper connection with the divine, fostering inner peace and spiritual fulfilment.

In essence, the message of Asharam Bapu resonates with the ancient wisdom of our scriptures, guiding individuals towards a life of purity, devotion, and self-realization. By embracing the transformative power of spiritual awakening, one can embark on a journey of self-discovery and liberation, transcending the limitations of the material world.

The teachings of Asharam Bapu serve as a beacon of light in an increasingly turbulent world, offering solace, guidance, and hope to those who seek spiritual nourishment. Through the practice of Hari-Kirtan and devotion to the divine, individuals can unlock the secrets of inner peace and unlock the potential for boundless joy and fulfilment.

As Tulsidas beautifully articulated, chanting the name of Rama holds immense therapeutic power, akin to a healing balm for the soul. It is believed that when one wholeheartedly chants the divine name, embracing the essence of devotion, all sorrows and afflictions dissipate, leaving behind a sense of serenity and contentment.

The spiritual potency inherent in practices such as Bhagavan Naam-chanting, bhajan-kirtan, and recitation of Shrimad Bhagavad-Gita is profound. These sacred rituals aim not only to uplift individuals but also to serve the greater good by spreading the glory of divine names and fostering positive energy through collective Nam-San kirtan. The ultimate goal of such endeavours is to cleanse the mind and soul from the shackles of ignorance and ideological pollution, thereby awakening spiritual consciousness.

In the context of revered spiritual leaders like Asharam Bapu, the significance of such spiritual practices is magnified. Through his teachings and guidance, countless individuals have found solace and inner peace by immersing themselves in the divine vibrations of Bhagavan Naam-chanting and devotional singing. Asharam Bapu's emphasis on the transformative power of simple yet profound spiritual practices resonate deeply with seekers from all walks of life.

The essence of Asharam Bapu's teachings lies in their accessibility and universality. He imparts wisdom in a manner that transcends barriers of language and intellect, catering to the spiritual needs of both the learned and the layperson alike. His message emphasizes the importance of humility, sincerity, and devotion in one's spiritual journey, encapsulating the essence of Tulsidas' timeless wisdom.

Through his relentless efforts to awaken individuals to their inherent divinity, Asharam Bapu ignites a spark of spiritual awakening in the hearts of millions. His teachings serve as a beacon of light, guiding seekers towards self-realization and inner transformation. In a world plagued by turmoil and strife, the timeless wisdom imparted by Asharam Bapu serves as a source of hope and inspiration for those seeking refuge in the divine.

The profound words of Tulsidas echo the timeless truth that chanting the divine name is indeed a potent elixir for the soul. Through the teachings and guidance of revered spiritual leaders like Asharam Bapu, individuals are invited to embark on a transformative journey of self-discovery and spiritual awakening. In the simplicity of devotion lies the key to unlocking the boundless treasures of inner peace and fulfilment.

VRINDA EXPEDITION: EMBRACING THE HEALING POWER OF TULSI

In the heart of every home, there lies a treasure trove of health and vitality – the sacred Tulsi plant. Known as the "*Queen of Herbs*," Tulsi has been revered for centuries for its myriad benefits, transcending the boundaries of mere medicinal value to encompass religious, spiritual, environmental, and scientific significance.

Tulsi's medicinal properties are nothing short of miraculous. From its antimicrobial prowess to its ability to alleviate pain and depression, Tulsi emerges as a versatile healer in the realm of natural medicine. According to scientific research, Tulsi possesses anti-cancer properties, serves as a potent antidepressant, and even defends against radiation. Its virtues are so vast that Lord Shiva himself, in the Padma Purana, declared that even after exhaustive contemplation, the complete glory of Tulsi remains beyond comprehension.

Moreover, Tulsi serves as a beacon of environmental sustainability. As we embark on the Vrinda Expedition, planting Tulsi in every household, we not only nurture our health but also contribute to the preservation of our planet. Tulsi's oxygenating properties purify the air, while its soil-stabilizing roots prevent erosion, fostering a harmonious coexistence with nature.

The "Ghar-Ghar Tulsi Lagao" campaign embodies this ethos of holistic well-being and environmental stewardship. By encouraging every household to embrace the Tulsi plant, we envision a future where health expenditures plummet, and communities thrive amidst lush greenery and clean air.

In the footsteps of revered Sants like Asharam Bapu, let us embark on this noble journey of reconnecting with nature and embracing the healing power of Tulsi. As we cultivate this sacred plant in our homes, let us also cultivate a deeper appreciation for the interconnectedness of all life forms and our responsibility to nurture and protect them.

The Vrinda Expedition beckons us to embark on a transformative voyage – one that transcends borders and unites us in our shared reverence for Mother Nature's bountiful gifts. Let us sow the seeds of health, harmony, and hope, one Tulsi plant at a time, and pave the way for a brighter, greener tomorrow.

CHAPTER SIX

Global Spiritual Unity

WORLD PARLIAMENT OF RELIGIONS

In September 1993, revered Bapu participated in the successful representation of India at the Parliament of World Religions held in Chicago, exactly a century after Swami Vivekananda's historic address. During the first week of September, the Parliament convened with over 600 speakers from around the globe. Bapu was invited as the keynote speaker from India, and from September 1st to 4th, he delivered enlightening discourses.

While other speakers were allotted limited time, attendees listened intently to Bapu for 55 minutes initially and then for 75 minutes on another occasion. His talks offered profound insights on integrating ancient wisdom into modern life, fostering happiness, peace, and mutual affection in contemporary times. Bapu's discourses at the Parliament of World Religions were adorned with beautiful anecdotes and practical wisdom, accessible even to a young audience.

Bapu was the sole representative from India at the Parliament, receiving the opportunity to address the audience three times. His speeches resonated deeply with listeners, transcending linguistic and cultural barriers. Bapu's message emphasized harmony among religions and the importance of spiritual values in navigating life's challenges.

Furthermore, Bapu's presence exemplified India's rich spiritual heritage and its commitment to promoting global peace and understanding. His teachings transcended mere words, touching hearts and inspiring individuals to lead lives filled with compassion and righteousness.

Through his participation in the Parliament of World Religions, Bapu not only represented India but also became a beacon of hope and wisdom for people worldwide. His profound messages continue to guide millions on the path of righteousness and enlightenment.

Bapu's significant role at the Parliament of World Religions in 1993 showcased India's spiritual richness and contributed to fostering global harmony and understanding. His teachings, delivered in simple yet profound language, resonate with audiences of all ages and backgrounds, inspiring them to lead lives rooted in love, compassion, and spiritual values.

CHAPTER SEVEN

Missionary Work To Spiritual Awakening

BEACON OF SPIRITUALITY AND PATRIOTISM

Asharam Bapu is renowned for his unwavering commitment to Hindutva, resisting attempts at religious conversion while actively promoting patriotism. His literary works not only guide spiritual seekers towards the consciousness of the Supreme Being but also advocate for a healthy and peaceful family lifestyle, rooted in the rich cultural heritage and pride in Hinduism.

In his ashrams and children's upbringing centers, children are taught from a young age to respect their motherland, embrace their rich cultural heritage, and take pride in the Hindu faith. The environment nurtures a sense of belonging and instils values of respect and devotion towards their roots.

In October 2005, Reverend Pat Robertson announced a goal of converting 100 million Hindus during the Dallas Christian Conclave. However, amidst such challenges, Asharam Bapu's mission remains steadfast, dedicated to preserving the Hindu faith and preventing its followers from succumbing to conversion tactics.

Christian missionaries, both in rural and urban areas, entice millions of impoverished Hindus with material goods and promises of blessings to convert them every year. The reality is that overnight, entire villages have been converted, with thousands of Hindus renouncing their faith. In 2005, in the village of Angol in Andhra Pradesh, 15,018 Hindus were converted in just one night.

Despite facing such formidable opposition, Asharam Bapu continues to inspire millions with his teachings of love, peace, and devotion to the Divine. His message transcends language and barriers, resonating deeply with people from all walks of life.

Asharam Bapu's life and teachings serve as a beacon of hope and guidance for those seeking spiritual enlightenment and a deeper connection with the divine. His legacy is not just one of spirituality but also of unwavering patriotism and dedication to preserving the cultural and religious identity of India.

In conclusion, Asharam Bapu's tireless efforts to uphold Hindutva and resist religious conversion have made him a symbol of strength and resilience in the face of adversity. His teachings continue to empower individuals to embrace their heritage and lead a life of righteousness and devotion.

TRANSFORMATIVE PATHWAYS

Dr. Suman Kumar (previously known as Robert Solomon originally from Jakarta, Indonesia, has shared his experiences in Asharam Bapu's satsang program) was involved in assisting missionaries who sought to convert impoverished Hindus to Christianity. However, after immersing himself in the study of Indian culture and spirituality, Dr. Suman Kumar resigned from his job and embraced Hinduism, now devoted to reintroducing Indian Christians back to their roots.

Over the past few years, revered Bapu has been spearheading a campaign across Gujarat, Rajasthan, and Madhya Pradesh to bring back those who were converted to Christianity to their original faith of Hinduism. This movement has encountered resistance from foreign missionaries and some international NGOs.

Bapu's journey of spiritual awakening and his efforts to rekindle the flame of Hinduism among converted individuals have faced indirect obstacles. Despite this, he continues his noble mission with unwavering determination and compassion.

Bapu emphasizes the importance of reconnecting with one's cultural and spiritual heritage. He advocates for a return to the principles and values embedded within Hinduism, encouraging individuals to rediscover the richness of their own tradition.

Bapu's approach is rooted in simplicity and humility, making his message accessible even to the youngest members of society. He employs a language that resonates with people from all walks of life, ensuring that his teachings reach and inspire as many individuals as possible.

Bapu exemplifies patience, resilience, and unwavering faith. Despite facing challenges and opposition, he remains steadfast in his commitment to serving humanity and promoting the values of Hinduism.

Bapu aims to create a more harmonious and spiritually enriched society, where individuals are empowered to embrace their cultural identity and spiritual heritage with pride and reverence.

UNVEILING THE ECONOMIC IMPACT OF ADDICTION

In recent years, the impact of addiction on society has been a topic of increasing concern. However, what often goes unnoticed is the significant economic cost associated with substance abuse and other addictive behaviours. Through a simple analysis of the followers of Asharam Bapu, we can shed light on the substantial savings achieved by abstaining from various addictive substances and behaviours.

Asharam Bapu, a revered spiritual leader, has a vast following of devotees numbering in the tens of millions. Let's delve into the economic implications of their choices:

1. **Tobacco and Alcohol Consumption:** It is estimated that over 10 crore followers of Asharam Bapu refrain from consuming tobacco and alcohol. Even if we conservatively estimate that only 2 crore among them would have otherwise been heavy consumers, the savings are monumental. Over a span of 20 years, this translates to a staggering ?18,820,000 crores saved, which could have otherwise been spent on purchasing these addictive substances.
2. **Impact of Smoking:** If we extend our analysis to include the economic cost of smoking alone, the savings skyrocket to ?11,360,000 crore over the same period. This demonstrates the significant financial burden that smoking imposes on individuals and society as a whole.
3. **Adherence to a Vegetarian Diet:** Asharam Bapu emphasizes the importance of a vegetarian lifestyle among his followers. By abstaining from meat consumption, his devotees not only adhere to a dietary preference but also avoid the economic costs associated with meat

production and its environmental impact.

4. **Avoidance of Stimulants:** The teachings of Asharam Bapu encourage his followers to steer clear of stimulants such as tea and coffee. By opting for healthier alternatives, his devotees not only prioritize their physical well-being but also save on the expenses related to purchasing these beverages.
5. **Resisting Pornography and Obscene Entertainment:** Asharam Bapu advocates for a life free from the influence of pornography and obscene entertainment. By refraining from indulging in such activities, his followers not only uphold moral values but also avoid the potential financial costs associated with subscriptions to adult content and related services.

The economic impact of Asharam Bapu's teachings extends far beyond the spiritual realm. By promoting a lifestyle free from addiction and harmful behaviours, his followers not only experience personal growth but also contribute to significant economic savings. This underscores the importance of adopting a holistic approach to addressing societal challenges, wherein spiritual leaders like Asharam Bapu play a crucial role in fostering positive change.

CHAPTER EIGHT

The Asharam Bapu Case: Unravelling The Truth

DECIPHERING: SEEKING TRUTH AMIDST CONTROVERSY

The delay and political pressure on filing the FIR in Delhi can be attributed to suspicious delays and political influence on the Delhi Police.

The girl in question hails from Uttar Pradesh and was studying in Madhya Pradesh. However, the alleged incident reportedly occurred in Jodhpur, Rajasthan. Despite this, the FIR was filed at the Kamla Market Police Station in Delhi, five days after the purported incident, and that too late in the night.

Why was the FIR filed in Delhi instead of Rajasthan where the alleged incident took place? This raises questions about the intentions behind this move and whether political pressure played a role.

It's noteworthy that before filing the FIR, the girl's parents had met with some politicians known for their animosity towards Asharam Bapu.

The alleged incident took place in Rajasthan, but why was the FIR filed in Delhi? **The medical report obtained from Delhi did not confirm the allegations of rape.** Yet, the FIR was filed under the non-bailable offense of rape. Why?

The Deputy Commissioner of Police, Ajay Pal Lamba, who confirmed that there was no allegation of rape in the FIR and the medical report did not confirm rape, was promptly removed from the case.

LINK:- https://www.youtube.com/watch?v=zXmVq3YukNE

Jodhpur Police confirmed in a press conference on August 26, 2013, around 1 o'clock, that no allegations of rape were made in the FIR, and the medical report did not confirm rape. However, six hours later, the same police department retracted their statement and refused to remove Section 376. Why the sudden change in stance? And why was the investigating officer removed from the case?

It's evident that there were political pressures at play, influencing the police's actions.

The entire situation raises doubts about the integrity of the investigation and highlights the need for transparency and accountability in such cases.

The handling of the Asharam Bapu case reflects the complexities and challenges of navigating justice in India's political landscape. It emphasizes the importance of fair and impartial investigations, free from external pressures, to ensure justice for all parties involved.

CLOSER LOOK AT CONTROVERSIES

In recent years, the name of Sant Asharam Bapu has been surrounded by controversy due to two separate cases that have emerged from different locations but seem eerily similar in nature. The first case originates from Jodhpur, where Sant Asharam Bapu has been sentenced to life imprisonment, and the second case arises from Ahmedabad, where a similar fate awaits him. Both cases lack substantial evidence and rely heavily on the testimony of the accusers, raising questions about the fairness of the judicial process and the possibility of a coordinated conspiracy against him.

The Jodhpur case revolves around allegations of sexual assault levelled against Sant Asharam Bapu. Despite the lack of concrete evidence and credible witnesses, he has been sentenced to life imprisonment based solely on the statements of the accusers. The absence of corroborating evidence raises doubts about the validity of the conviction and raises concerns about the fairness of the trial.

Similarly, the Ahmedabad case follows a similar pattern, with Sant Asharam Bapu facing accusations of sexual misconduct. Once again, the case relies heavily on the testimony of the alleged victims, with no substantial evidence to support the claims. The absence of tangible proof raises suspicions about the motives behind the allegations and calls into question the integrity of the legal proceedings.

What is particularly troubling about these cases is the lack of concrete evidence and reliance on the statements of the accusers. In both instances, there is no corroborating evidence to support the allegations, leaving room for doubt and speculation. The absence of credible witnesses further complicates the matter, as there is no independent testimony to verify the claims made against Sant Asharam Bapu.

The implications of these cases extend beyond the individual involved, raising broader questions about the judicial system and the concept of justice itself. The reliance on circumstantial evidence and testimony without corroborating evidence sets a dangerous precedent and undermines the fundamental principles of fairness and due process. It opens the door for potential abuse and manipulation, where individuals can be targeted and persecuted based on false accusations and ulterior motives.

The cases against Sant Asharam Bapu in Jodhpur and Ahmedabad highlight the flaws and shortcomings of the judicial system. The lack of concrete evidence and reliance on uncorroborated testimony raise serious concerns about the fairness and integrity of the legal proceedings. As these cases continue to unfold, it is essential to uphold the principles of justice and ensure that all individuals are treated fairly and impartially under the law.

FALSE ACCUSATIONS

Despite a complete absence of evidence, Asharam Bapu finds himself behind bars, wrongfully accused and convicted. His case epitomizes the travesty of justice that plagues our legal system. Even in the absence of any concrete proof, he was sentenced to imprisonment, a stark reminder of the flaws and biases inherent in our judicial process.

Asharam Bapu, a revered Sant known for his spiritual teachings and philanthropic work, has been subjected to a grave injustice. Despite his impeccable character and a lifetime dedicated to serving humanity, he was falsely implicated in a heinous crime. The lack of credible evidence did not deter the authorities from prosecuting him, highlighting the disregard for truth and fairness in our legal system.

The case against Asharam Bapu is emblematic of the systemic issues that plague our judiciary. Instead of upholding the principles of justice and fairness, the legal proceedings were marred by sensationalism and prejudice. The media sensationalized the case, fuelling public outrage and shaping public opinion against him. As a result, he was subjected to a trial by media rather than a trial based on evidence and facts.

Despite the overwhelming support from his followers and well-wishers, Asharam Bapu continues to languish in jail, deprived of his freedom and dignity. His plight serves as a stark reminder of the vulnerability of individuals in the face of institutional injustice. The failure of the legal system to uphold the principles of justice not only affects the individual wrongfully accused but also undermines the trust of the public in the judiciary.

Asharam Bapu's case underscores the urgent need for reform in our legal system. The arbitrary detention of individuals without sufficient evidence not only violates their fundamental rights but also undermines the credibility of the judiciary. It is imperative that we strive to ensure that justice is dispensed impartially and fairly, without prejudice or bias.

Asharam Bapu's wrongful incarceration serves as a poignant reminder of the flaws and biases that pervade our legal system. The lack of evidence should have exonerated him, yet he remains unjustly imprisoned. His case highlights the urgent need for reform to ensure that justice is served equitably and fairly for all.

Asharam Bapu's case has been a subject of controversy and debate in recent years, particularly regarding the allegations of rape and gang rape. However, the medical report from Lok Nayak Hospital, New Delhi, sheds light on crucial evidence that seems to have been overlooked amidst the sensationalism surrounding the case.

According to the medical report, which is a vital piece of evidence presented in court, there is no indication of any physical assault inflicted upon Asharam Bapu's accuser. The report meticulously documents various aspects of the examination, revealing a lack of evidence to support the alleged acts of rape and sexual assault.

The report explicitly states that there are no signs of erythema, which refers to redness or inflammation of the skin, commonly associated with physical trauma. Additionally, there are no bite marks, swelling, abrasions, or any other visible signs of injury typically observed in cases of sexual assault.

One of the most significant findings of the medical examination is the absence of penetration. This crucial detail contradicts the allegations made against Asharam Bapu, as penetration is a fundamental element in cases of rape or sexual assault. Moreover, there is no evidence of loss of consciousness, further undermining the credibility of the accusations.

Another noteworthy observation from the medical report is the intact hymen of the accuser. The hymen is often considered a primary indicator of sexual activity or trauma, and its intactness raises questions about the veracity of the allegations levelled against Asharam Bapu.

In essence, the medical report provides compelling evidence that challenges the narrative of rape and gang rape surrounding Asharam Bapu's case. The absence of physical injuries or signs of sexual assault raises doubts about the credibility of the accusations and underscores the importance of relying on factual evidence in legal proceedings.

It is imperative to approach such sensitive matters with objectivity and integrity, ensuring that justice is served based on concrete evidence rather than sensationalism or prejudice. The medical report serves as a reminder of the importance of upholding the principles of fairness and truth in the pursuit of justice.

The medical report from Lok Nayak Hospital offers valuable insights into the Asharam Bapu case, highlighting the absence of physical evidence to substantiate the allegations of rape and sexual assault. This evidence underscores the need for a thorough and impartial examination of facts in legal proceedings, emphasizing the principles of justice and accountability.

THE TRUTH BEHIND THE ALLEGED INCIDENT OF AUGUST 15, 2013

On the night of August 15, 2013, between approximately 9:00 PM and 12:00 AM, Asharam Bapu was present amidst a gathering of around 50-60 individuals, engaging in both spiritual discourse and a subsequent engagement ceremony. Testimonies from those present at the event, along with photographic evidence from the occasion, corroborate this fact.

The robust evidence contradicts the allegations made against Asharam Bapu, particularly in the absence of any substantial proof presented by the government apart from statements provided by the girl and her parents. It is crucial to acknowledge the weight of this solid evidence in the face of the allegations.

Amidst the fervour of the evening, Asharam Bapu remained immersed in spiritual discourse, guiding his followers on the path of righteousness and inner peace. The atmosphere reverberated with the echoes of his teachings, resonating deeply with those in attendance.

Asharam Bapu's presence was not merely physical but served as a beacon of light, illuminating the hearts and minds of those present. His words carried the wisdom of ages, offering solace and guidance to those seeking spiritual enlightenment.

The gathering transcended mere physical proximity; it was a communion of souls, united in their devotion to the spiritual path charted by Asharam Bapu. Each individual present was a testament to the transformative power of his teachings, embodying the virtues of compassion, humility, and devotion.

The engagement ceremony that followed the discourse symbolized the bonds of love and commitment forged under the auspices of Asharam Bapu's divine grace. It was a joyous occasion, marked by prayers for the prosperity and happiness of the couple embarking on this sacred journey together.

In the backdrop of these moments of spiritual communion and celebration, the allegations levelled against Asharam Bapu appear incongruous and baseless. The integrity of his character, as evidenced by the testimonials of those present, stands in stark contrast to the accusations.

It is imperative to approach this matter with discernment and impartiality, allowing the truth to prevail above all else. The events of that fateful night serve as a testament to the unwavering devotion of Asharam Bapu's followers and the enduring legacy of his teachings.

The gathering on the night of August 15, 2013, bears witness to the innocence and spiritual integrity of Asharam Bapu amidst the sea of allegations. It is a reminder of the transformative power of faith and the enduring pursuit of truth in the face of adversity.

CLOSER LOOK AT CALL DETAILS

On the night of August 15, 2013, the timeline provided by the girl in question sheds light on a purported incident, spanning from 10:00-10:30 PM to 11:30-12:00 PM. However, the call details pertaining to the girl, as proven in court, indicate that she was in contact with a suspicious individual during that time, suggesting that she was not present at the alleged scene of the incident. Instead, she was in the company of her relatives, engaged in phone conversations and messaging. This fact has also been acknowledged by the court in Judgment Paragraph 339.

The revelation of the call details adds a significant dimension to the case involving Asharam Bapu. It underscores the importance of scrutinizing the evidence thoroughly and examining all aspects of the situation before arriving at conclusions.

The call records serve as crucial evidence in establishing the whereabouts and activities of the girl during the specified timeframe. They refute the narrative presented by the prosecution and raise questions about the credibility of the accusations levelled against Asharam Bapu.

It is evident from the call details that the girl was not alone or in distress during the time in question. Instead, she was in the midst of her family members, engaged in routine communication through phone calls and messages. This paints a vastly different picture from the one portrayed by the prosecution, casting doubt on the veracity of their claims.

Moreover, the acknowledgment of this fact by the court further strengthens the defence's argument and reinforces the notion of innocence until proven guilty. It highlights the importance of upholding the principles of justice and fairness in all legal proceedings.

The revelation of the call details serves as a reminder of the complexities involved in cases of this nature. It underscores the need for a comprehensive investigation and a fair trial, ensuring that all relevant evidence is considered before reaching a verdict.

The examination of call details in the Asharam Bapu case sheds new light on the events of that fateful night. It challenges the prevailing narrative and emphasizes the importance of a thorough and impartial assessment of evidence in the pursuit of truth and justice.

CONCEALED EVIDENCE OF INNOCENCE

In the recent revelation concerning the innocence of Asharam Bapu, critical evidence has come to light regarding suppressed call details. Investigative officers had acquired the complete call records for the month of August, yet crucial data from August 13th to August 16th, 2013, was intentionally concealed when presented in court. This deliberate omission raises suspicion, as it excludes the period just two days prior and one day after the alleged incident from the official records.

The decision to withhold these specific call details appears calculated, aimed at casting doubt on Asharam Bapu's innocence. By omitting crucial information surrounding the purported incident, the prosecution may seek to manipulate the narrative and undermine the credibility of the defense's case.

This revelation underscores the significance of transparency and integrity in legal proceedings, especially in cases of such magnitude. The deliberate concealment of evidence not only violates the principles of justice but also jeopardizes the pursuit of truth and fairness.

Furthermore, this incident raises questions about the impartiality of the investigating agency and its commitment to upholding the rule of law. By selectively presenting evidence and manipulating facts, the integrity of the entire judicial process comes into question, casting a shadow of doubt on the validity of the verdict.

In light of these revelations, it is imperative that a thorough and unbiased investigation be conducted to uncover the truth and ensure that justice is served. The integrity of the legal system hinges on the transparency and accountability of all involved parties, and any attempt to subvert the course of justice must be met with the full force of the law.

As the public awaits further developments in this case, it is essential to uphold the presumption of innocence and refrain from passing judgment based on incomplete or manipulated information. The truth must prevail, and those responsible for obstructing justice must be held accountable for their actions.

The concealment of vital evidence pertaining to Asharam Bapu's case raises serious concerns about the integrity of the legal process. It is incumbent upon the authorities to conduct a thorough investigation and ensure that justice is served without bias or prejudice. Only then can the truth be revealed, and the innocence of Asharam Bapu be vindicated.

VANISHING EVIDENCE: INCONSISTENCIES

In the midst of legal proceedings in Delhi, the absence of video evidence crucial to the case of the girl who accused Asharam Bapu of misconduct raises troubling questions. Despite being initially documented, the court records show no trace of the mentioned videography, suggesting a suspicious disappearance. Moreover, discrepancies in the video recording of the girl's police statement in Jodhpur further exacerbate doubts, with instances of tampering evident at various points. These compelling pieces of evidence, when presented in court, were inexplicably disregarded.

The disappearance of the video footage, which was presumably meant to substantiate the accusations against Asharam Bapu, highlights significant irregularities in the handling of the case. The absence of such crucial evidence not only casts doubt on the credibility of the accusations but also raises concerns about the integrity of the legal process.

The failure to address these discrepancies effectively undermines the pursuit of justice and calls into question the fairness of the trial. It is imperative that such matters be thoroughly investigated to ensure the transparency and accountability of the judicial system.

As the case unfolds, it becomes increasingly evident that there may be ulterior motives at play, with vested interests seeking to manipulate the course of justice. The deliberate suppression of evidence and the apparent reluctance to address glaring inconsistencies only serve to further obscure the truth.

In light of these developments, it is essential that the judiciary remains vigilant and impartial, upholding the principles of fairness and due process. The rights of both the accused and the accuser must be respected, and justice must be served without prejudice or bias.

The case of Asharam Bapu and his accuser serves as a stark reminder of the challenges inherent in the pursuit of truth and justice. It underscores the importance of upholding the rule of law and ensuring that all individuals are treated equitably before the law.

As the legal proceedings continue, it is incumbent upon all stakeholders to uphold the principles of integrity and accountability. Only by doing so can we hope to achieve a resolution that is fair and just for all parties involved.

The failure of the police to present forensic test reports in court raises serious questions about the integrity of the investigation into the alleged incident at the girl's purported scene (cottage). The absence of evidence or witnesses to corroborate the presence of the girl at the scene made it imperative for the investigation agency to present forensic reports such as footprints or fingerprints in court. However, no such report was presented by the police in court. Investigation Officer Chanchal Mishra herself admitted this fact before the court.

This glaring omission in the investigation process casts doubt on the credibility and thoroughness of the police investigation. It suggests a lack of diligence and professionalism on the part of the authorities entrusted with ensuring justice. By failing to provide crucial forensic evidence, the police have undermined the legal process and compromised the pursuit of truth and justice.

The significance of forensic test reports in establishing the veracity of allegations cannot be overstated. In cases where physical evidence is scant or circumstantial, forensic analysis serves as a vital tool for corroborating witness testimonies and strengthening the prosecution's case. Moreover, forensic evidence is often considered objective and impartial, providing an unbiased account of events based on scientific analysis.

The absence of forensic test reports in this case not only undermines the credibility of the prosecution's case but also raises concerns about the possibility of tampering with evidence or manipulation of facts. It leaves room for speculation and doubt, fuelling scepticism about the fairness and transparency of the legal proceedings.

In the context of the Asharam Bapu case, where allegations of sexual assault and misconduct have serious repercussions, the failure to present forensic evidence is particularly troubling. It calls into question the motives and intentions of the authorities involved in the investigation and prosecution of the case.

Furthermore, the admission by the investigation officer that forensic reports were not presented in court underscores the need for accountability and oversight in law enforcement agencies. It highlights systemic flaws and inadequacies in the administration of justice, exposing vulnerabilities that can be exploited to subvert the rule of law.

The failure of the police to present forensic test reports in court represents a grave lapse in the pursuit of justice. It undermines the credibility of the legal process and raises doubts about the integrity of the investigation. In the quest for truth and justice, it is imperative that all relevant evidence, including forensic analysis, be presented transparently and impartially in court. Anything less would be a disservice to the principles of fairness, accountability, and the rule of law.

INJUSTICE PREVAILS: A CRITICAL LOOK AT THE POCSO ACT

In recent times, there has been a contentious issue regarding the application of the Protection of Children from Sexual Offences (POCSO) Act in the case involving Asharam Bapu. Despite the girl being of legal age, she was still subjected to the provisions of the POCSO Act. The discrepancy arises from the various documents presented in court, each containing different birth dates for the girl. However, the POCSO Act places utmost importance on determining the age of the girl accurately.

During the trial, the defense highlighted the inconsistency in the girl's age across different documents and emphasized the need for proper verification. However, the judgment was passed based on a matriculation certificate, the authenticity of which was not legally established. Despite objections raised by the girl's lawyer under Section 311 of the Criminal Procedure Code (CRPC), the court proceeded with the trial, considering the girl a minor based on the unverified document.

This case sheds light on the flaws within the legal system, particularly in cases concerning sexual offenses against minors. It exposes the vulnerability of individuals, especially when powerful figures are involved. The mishandling of evidence and overlooking legal procedures can lead to grave injustices, depriving individuals of their rights and tarnishing their reputations.

Moreover, the case raises questions about the effectiveness of the POCSO Act and its application in ensuring justice for victims. While the intent behind such legislation is noble, its implementation must be meticulous and fair to prevent miscarriages of justice.

Furthermore, the Asharam Bapu case serves as a stark reminder of the importance of upholding the principles of justice and fairness in all legal proceedings. Regardless of one's stature or influence, everyone should be held accountable under the law, and due process must be followed diligently to avoid wrongful convictions.

The mishandling of the Asharam Bapu case highlights systemic flaws within the legal framework, particularly concerning the application of the POCSO Act. It underscores the need for comprehensive reforms to ensure that justice is served equitably and that individuals are not wrongfully convicted due to procedural shortcomings. The case serves as a poignant reminder of the enduring quest for justice and the necessity of upholding the rule of law in society.

UNVEILING TRUTH: THE SAGA

The incident in question revolves around a crucial point:

How did the girl obtain information about the interior of the cottage without having been there? This aspect emerges primarily from the statement given to the police before the FIR, before any statement to NGOs, and even before the statement to the magistrate. It's evident that this information was not available to the girl until after her statement to the police.

A day before the girl's police statement, the then DCP Ajay Pal Lamba, along with other police personnel, visited the cottage and recorded videos of both the interior and exterior using his mobile phone. This fact is evident from the daily register of the Soorsagar Police Station in Jodhpur.

During the trial, the defense presented this police register to the court, arguing that the girl could only have known about the interior of the cottage after the police showed her the video. This is further supported by a photograph of the cottage interior published on the front page of the Dainik Bhaskar newspaper on August 22, 2013, which was taken by a police officer.

However, the Special Court of Jodhpur, in its judgment, dismissed this argument, stating that there was no mention of such video recording or site inspection in the daily register.

After the court sentenced Asharam Bapu to life imprisonment, the then DCP Ajay Pal Lamba wrote a book on Asharam Bapu and this case. The defense objected to the publication of this book, alleging defamation and filing a petition in the Delhi High Court to halt its publication.

The Delhi High Court dismissed the petition, stating that the book merely compiled factual accounts of true events based on solid evidence.

The defense further filed an application in the Jodhpur High Court, requesting that the description of "investigation officer personally recording the video of the crime scene using his mobile phone" be included in the book, urging Ajay Pal Lamba to testify.

Despite the controversy surrounding the case, the pursuit of truth remains paramount. The judicial process continues to unfold, shedding light on the complexities of the legal system and the quest for justice.

In light of the summons from the Jodhpur High Court, Mr. Ajay Pal Lamba, citing illness and other reasons, fails to appear on several occasions, triggering a sudden move by the government to challenge the High Court's decision in the Supreme Court. The government's counsel argues that the book in question contains a disclaimer and is fictionalized, thus should not be considered as evidence. Accepting this argument, the Supreme Court rejects the High Court's decision. It's perplexing how the same book portrays Mr. Ajay Pal Lamba, the investigating officer, in contradictory ways – as a collection of solid evidence on one side and as a figment of imagination on the other. Both interpretations are deemed valid by the court!

Amidst questions raised about the integrity of the investigating officer and the neutrality of the court, where will justice prevail?

The unfolding saga surrounding Mr. Asharam Bapu's case serves as a poignant reminder of the intricate web of truth and perception in the corridors of justice. With each twist and turn, the narrative shifts, blurring the lines between reality and fiction. As the legal battle rages on, the core principles of fairness and impartiality hang in the balance.

The summons issued by the Jodhpur High Court to Mr. Ajay Pal Lamba, the investigating officer in the case, underscores the gravity of the situation. However, his repeated absence raises eyebrows, casting doubt on the sincerity of the legal proceedings. The sudden intervention of the government, challenging the High Court's decision in the Supreme Court, adds another layer of complexity to the unfolding drama.

In its defense, the government contends that the book, purportedly shedding light on Mr. Asharam Bapu's life, is a work of fiction and should not be considered as substantive evidence. Surprisingly, the Supreme Court upholds this argument, dismissing the High Court's ruling. This turn of events raises questions about the reliability of the legal system and its ability to discern truth from fiction.

Amidst the legal wrangling, the character of Mr. Ajay Pal Lamba, the investigating officer, emerges as a focal point of contention. Depicted alternately as a diligent truth-seeker and a fictional creation, his integrity comes under scrutiny. Similarly, the impartiality of the court is called into question, as it grapples with conflicting interpretations of the evidence presented before it.

In the midst of this turmoil, the pursuit of justice hangs in the balance. Will the truth prevail, or will it be obscured by the tangled web of deceit and manipulation? Only time will tell as the saga of Mr. Asharam Bapu's case continues to unfold, revealing the complexities of the human condition and the quest for justice in an imperfect world.

THE ORDEAL OF ASHARAM BAPU

Despite conflicting testimonies from women, the alleged victim seeks a change in her statement!

Fictitious Incident

In Jodhpur, October 2013 witnessed the emergence of a disturbing narrative. Two sisters from Surat accused Asharam Bapu and his son Narayan Sai of a fabricated event dating back 12 years. The elder sister alleged misconduct by Bapu in 2001, while the younger sister accused Narayan Sai of a similar offense in 2002. Despite the belated filing of the FIRs and the absence of concrete evidence, both Asharam Bapu and Narayan Sai received life sentences based solely on the contradictory statements of the women.

Considerations

The elder sister claimed in her FIR that Bapu had allegedly victimized her in 2001, while the younger sister voluntarily resided in Narayan Sai's ashram in 2002.

If a woman experiences such trauma, would she allow her own sister to later reside in the same ashram? The younger sister remained at the ashram until 2005, while the elder sister stayed until 2007. Both sisters got married in 2010. Surprisingly, even after marriage, the younger sister attended Narayan Sai's Satsang's until January 2013 with her husband, as evidenced by court records. The elder sister also continued attending Bapu's Satsang's for several years after leaving the ashram.

The contradictions in their testimonies raise significant doubts about the veracity of their allegations. Despite their accusations, both sisters continued to associate closely with the accused individuals long after the alleged incidents occurred, undermining the credibility of their claims.

The inconsistencies in the women's statements, combined with their continued association with the accused, cast serious doubt on the validity of the allegations against Asharam Bapu and Narayan Sai. This underscores the importance of a fair and thorough investigation to ensure that justice is served based on factual evidence rather than unsubstantiated claims.

The fragility of accusations

Now, let's delve deeper into some crucial questions surrounding the involvement of these sisters with Asharam Bapu:

1. **Continued Allegiance:** If any wrongdoing had indeed occurred alongside her active role in preaching, would the elder sister have continued to publicly praise Asharam Bapu for such an extended period?
2. **Return to the Ashram:** Despite traveling extensively for preaching purposes, why did the elder sister keep returning to the ashram, even if there were purported misdeeds happening there?

3. **Persistent Presence:** Even after the alleged wrongdoing, why did both sisters choose to remain associated with the ashram for several years?
4. **Continued Attendance:** What motivated both sisters to keep attending the Satsang's of Asharam Bapu and Narayan Sai even after they had left the ashram?
5. **Delayed Action:** Why did these sisters wait for over a decade before filing FIRs against Asharam Bapu and others?
6. **Return to the Ashram:** Despite temporarily leaving the ashram due to illness in 2003, why did one sister choose to return afterward, according to court records?

These questions are pertinent to understanding the dynamics surrounding Asharam Bapu and the accusations against him.

THE WOMAN WANTED TO CHANGE HER STATEMENT

In the court of Ahmedabad, Gandhinagar, she filed an application saying she wants to change her statement. However, the court rejected her application. To challenge this decision in the High Court, the accused had prepared a petition, which is on record with the court. It contains her own signature and is notarized.

Asharam Bapu has been a controversial figure in recent years due to various allegations against him. Amidst this controversy, legal proceedings have been underway, and individuals involved have sought to alter their statements or provide new evidence.

In this particular case, a woman sought to change her statement in court, indicating a shift in her testimony. However, her plea was dismissed by the court. Undeterred, she pursued her case further, preparing a petition for the High Court. This petition, duly signed by her and notarized, stands as evidence of her intent to challenge the court's decision.

The incident sheds light on the complexities of legal proceedings involving figures like Asharam Bapu. It underscores the importance of due process and the challenges faced by both the prosecution and the defense. Additionally, it raises questions about the credibility of witness testimony and the need for thorough investigation in such cases.

While the legal battle continues, it is essential to ensure that justice is served impartially and fairly. Every individual involved in the case, whether the accused, the accuser, or witnesses, must be given the opportunity to present their case and seek redress through legal means.

As the case unfolds, it serves as a reminder of the intricacies of the legal system and the need for transparency and accountability at every step. Despite the challenges, it is imperative to uphold the principles of justice and uphold the rule of law.

The woman's attempt to change her statement highlights the ongoing legal proceedings surrounding Asharam Bapu and underscores the complexities of the case. As the legal battle continues, it is essential to ensure a fair and transparent process for all involved parties.

The woman, in her petition, has written that the complaint filed does not accurately reflect the actions of any accused individual. Hence, she desires to provide her statement again. However, the court dismisses her plea after opposition from the government, stating that the application for allowing the accused to give their statement again is not acceptable.

This aspect of the case reflects the complexities and challenges inherent in the legal process. Despite the woman's desire to amend her statement, the court's decision highlights the stringent protocols and legal standards that govern such proceedings.

In the context of Asharam Bapu's legal battles, this incident underscores the significance of credibility and consistency in witness testimony. It also raises questions about the role of the judiciary in ensuring a fair and impartial trial, especially in high-profile cases.

As the legal saga continues, it remains essential to uphold the principles of justice and due process for all parties involved. The decision-making process must be transparent, and every effort should be made to uncover the truth and deliver a just verdict.

The woman's attempt to revise her statement reflects the ongoing complexities of legal proceedings surrounding Asharam Bapu. The court's decision to reject her plea underscores the challenges faced in ensuring a fair and impartial trial in such cases.

EXPOSING THE FABRICATIONS AGAINST BAPU

In the midst of accusations, the alleged claim by the prosecution insinuates a grand conspiracy dating back to the auspicious occasion of Janmashtami in 1996. It alleges that during this event at the Surat Ashram, Asharam Bapu, along with other accused, conspired to manipulate events to frame the narrative in their Favor.

However, facts tell a different story. The Janmashtami celebration in question did not occur in Surat but rather in Rajkot, as corroborated by newspaper reports of the time. The owner of the newspaper in question affirmed this fact in court, unequivocally stating, "This newspaper is mine, and it is from 1996." Additionally, testimony from credible government witnesses further solidified this truth.

The attempt to weave a web of deception around Asharam Bapu is not only baseless but also contradicted by concrete evidence. Despite efforts to distort the truth, the clarity of facts prevails. It is imperative to discern between concocted tales and the irrefutable truth, especially when the reputation and integrity of a spiritual leader hang in the balance.

Asharam Bapu's devotees and supporters steadfastly assert his innocence, buoyed by the unwavering belief in his teachings and the righteousness of his character. The unfounded allegations serve as a testament to the challenges faced by those who walk the path of righteousness in a world fraught with scepticism and deceit.

In the pursuit of justice, it is incumbent upon society to uphold the principles of fairness and truth, ensuring that no innocent individual falls victim to the machinations of those who seek to tarnish their reputation for personal gain. As the legal proceedings unfold, it is imperative to remain vigilant in separating fact from fiction, guided by the beacon of truth.

The resilience and unwavering faith of Asharam Bapu's followers serve as a beacon of hope amidst adversity. Their unwavering support underscores the profound impact of his teachings on their lives, fostering a community bound by shared values of compassion, integrity, and spiritual growth.

The purported claims of conspiracy surrounding Asharam Bapu's innocence crumble in the face of incontrovertible evidence and testimonies. Justice demands a fair and impartial examination of the facts, free from the shackles of bias and preconceived notions. Let truth prevail and let righteousness triumph over falsehood.

In the narrative of allegations against Asharam Bapu, a striking contradiction emerges.

The accuser claims that during a Holi event in Surat in 1997, Asharam Bapu directed her to participate in an event in Ahmedabad instead, purportedly recognizing her from a previous encounter. She insisted on her need to take a 10th-grade exam.

However, facts paint a different picture. Records from the Gujarat Education Board, along with statements from official sources, reveal that the woman was not enrolled in the 10th grade in 1997; she had previously failed the 10th-grade exam twice in 1995.

This revelation sheds light on the inaccuracies and inconsistencies within the allegations against Asharam Bapu. It challenges the credibility of the accuser's claims and raises questions about the motives behind such accusations.

The discrepancy between the accuser's account and the documented evidence underscores the importance of a thorough and impartial investigation. It serves as a reminder of the complexities involved in assessing allegations and the need for careful scrutiny of all available information.

As the legal proceedings continue, it is essential to maintain a fair and balanced approach, ensuring that justice is served based on facts rather than conjecture or prejudice.

This case also highlights the broader issue of false accusations and the devastating impact they can have on individuals and communities. It emphasizes the importance of upholding the principles of justice and due process to prevent wrongful convictions and protect the innocent.

In the pursuit of truth, it is imperative to examine all aspects of the case objectively, taking into account the evidence and testimonies presented. Only through such diligence can we ensure a just outcome and uphold the integrity of our legal system.

As the truth gradually unfolds, it is crucial to remain vigilant against misinformation and manipulation. By staying informed and discerning, we can contribute to a society where justice prevails and the rights of all individuals are respected.

The revelation of discrepancies in the allegations against Asharam Bapu underscores the need for thorough investigation and scrutiny of all available evidence. It serves as a reminder of the complexities involved in assessing accusations and the importance of upholding the principles of justice and fairness.

In his testimony, the accused stated, "In 2007, I decided that I no longer wanted to stay at the ashram, so I spoke to my friend, and with his help, I fled from the ashram to my parents' home in Surat."

Truth: This friend also did not corroborate the complainant's statement. The investigating officer accepted this fact in court. However, neither the friend's statement nor the friend himself was presented before the court by the investigation officer.

The testimony provided by the accused reveals a crucial aspect of the case. The decision to leave the ashram in 2007, as claimed by the accused, sheds light on the circumstances leading up to the alleged incident. The accused's reliance on a friend for assistance in leaving the ashram indicates a lack of autonomy or agency in the decision-making process. This dependency on external support raises questions about the accused's ability to orchestrate the events leading to the alleged crime.

Furthermore, the absence of corroborating testimony from the accused's friend highlights a significant discrepancy in the prosecution's narrative. While the accused maintains that the friend assisted in his departure from the ashram, the lack of supporting evidence or testimony weakens this claim. The investigating officer's acknowledgment of this discrepancy underscores the importance of comprehensive and unbiased evidence collection in legal proceedings.

The conflicting testimonies presented in court underscore the complexity of the case and the challenges inherent in discerning the truth. The accused's assertion of agency in leaving the ashram contrasts with the lack of corroborating evidence from his purported accomplice. This dissonance complicates the narrative surrounding the events leading up to the alleged crime and emphasizes the need for thorough investigation and scrutiny of all testimonial evidence.

Moreover, the discrepancy between the accused's testimony and the prosecution's narrative raises doubts about the credibility of the allegations. If the accused's account of leaving the ashram is accurate, it casts doubt on the prosecution's portrayal of him as a manipulative and predatory figure. Conversely, if the prosecution's version of events is accepted, it suggests a deliberate attempt by the accused to evade accountability for his actions.

The conflicting testimonies surrounding the accused's departure from the ashram highlight the intricacies of the case and the challenges faced in ascertaining the truth. The absence of corroborating evidence and the discrepancies in the narratives underscore the importance of thorough investigation and impartial assessment of testimonial evidence in legal proceedings. As the case unfolds, it becomes increasingly clear that the path to justice is fraught with complexities and contradictions, necessitating a careful examination of all available evidence to arrive at a fair and just verdict.

INCONSISTENCIES IN ALLEGATIONS

In the narrative presented by the accuser, it is alleged that during the Guru Purnima of 2001, Asharam Bapu purportedly committed a crime with another sadhika in the tranquil environs of Bapu's ashram. However, upon scrutiny, the truth emerges quite differently.

The accuser's tale insinuates a sinister act, yet a closer examination reveals glaring inconsistencies. Notably, the supposed victim, the sadhika mentioned in the accusation, provided statements to the police countering the allegations levelled against Asharam Bapu. Despite her refutation, her testimony was conspicuously absent from police reports and court proceedings.

Furthermore, the investigating officer, when cross-examined in court, admitted that the sadhika's statement did not corroborate the accusations made by the complainant. This admission underscores a critical point: the lack of substantiating evidence casts doubts on the veracity of the allegations against Asharam Bapu.

This raises fundamental questions about the integrity of the accusations and the credibility of the accuser. If the purported incident had occurred as described, one would expect consistency in the testimonies provided by all parties involved. However, the absence of such consistency calls into question the reliability of the accuser's narrative.

Moreover, the omission of exculpatory evidence, such as the sadhika's contradictory statement, further undermines the credibility of the allegations. The failure to present all pertinent information to the court perpetuates an incomplete and biased portrayal of events.

In light of these revelations, it becomes imperative to reevaluate the accusations against Asharam Bapu with a discerning eye. Blind acceptance of unsubstantiated claims serves neither justice nor truth. Instead, it is incumbent upon us to seek out and consider all available evidence before passing judgment.

The discrepancies in the allegations against Asharam Bapu underscore the need for a thorough and impartial investigation. The pursuit of justice demands a commitment to truth and fairness, irrespective of preconceived notions or biases. Only by upholding these principles can we ensure a just outcome for all parties involved.

In the midst of the controversy surrounding Asharam Bapu, one aspect stands out starkly - the contradictions in the testimonies presented by the accusers and the reality of the situation. Among the numerous allegations levied against him, there exists a glaring inconsistency that sheds light on the true nature of the accusations.

One such allegation revolves around a purported incident where after completing a ritual, co-accused individuals allegedly tempted Asharam Bapu with the lure of becoming a speaker and prevented him from returning home. However, the truth, as revealed by a key witness, paints a starkly different picture. Asharam Bapu's own sister, presented as a witness by the defense, testified in court that she, along with their mother and other family members, travelled to Ahmedabad to bring him back home after a period of fifteen days. Despite their efforts, Asharam Bapu refused to accompany them, demonstrating his reluctance to leave.

Furthermore, it came to light that on subsequent occasions, Asharam Bapu's sister, accompanied by other family members, made repeated attempts to persuade him to return home, only to be met with resistance each time. Additionally, it was revealed that Asharam Bapu frequently travelled to Surat to conduct spiritual discourses, corroborating his sister's testimony.

The simplicity of the narrative presented by Asharam Bapu's sister underscores the authenticity of her account. Her testimony, supported by corroborative evidence, not only exposes the falsehoods propagated by the accusers but also highlights the steadfastness of Asharam Bapu's conviction in his spiritual mission.

It is evident from these revelations that the accusations against Asharam Bapu are riddled with inconsistencies and fabrications. The narrative woven by the prosecution crumbles under the weight of truth, revealing the malicious intent behind the false allegations.

The testimony provided by Asharam Bapu's sister serves as a beacon of truth amidst the sea of deceit. It not only vindicates Asharam Bapu but also underscores the importance of discerning fact from fiction in the pursuit of justice. As the veil of deception is lifted, the innocence of Asharam Bapu shines through, reaffirming his unwavering commitment to his spiritual path.

IN THE STATEMENTS PRESENTED, CONTRADICTIONS ARE APPARENT

The accused had alleged that at the time (i.e., in 2001), the kitchen attendant mentioned by Asharam Bapu did not exist. This truth has been acknowledged by several other government witnesses in their statements before the court. However, the court chose to overlook this truth.

Astonishingly, in her statements before the women's court, the alleged victim of the heinous crime sometimes refers to the incident as happening during the Guru Purnima, sometimes a few days later, and at other times during Janmashtami. Even in these accounts, her narrative lacks consistency. Several other instances of inconsistency in the woman's testimony are recorded in the court's records.

The statements reveal discrepancies and inconsistencies in the testimonies presented before the court in the case related to Asharam Bapu.

It is evident that the prosecution's narrative is not cohesive and lacks reliability due to these contradictions. Such inconsistencies raise doubts about the credibility of the allegations made against Asharam Bapu.

These discrepancies highlight the importance of a thorough and impartial investigation in legal proceedings. Inconsistencies in testimonies can significantly impact the outcome of a trial and the justice served.

The presence of contradictions and inconsistencies in the testimonies related to the case of Asharam Bapu underscores the need for meticulous scrutiny and unbiased evaluation of evidence in legal proceedings. It is imperative to ensure that justice is served based on facts and truth, devoid of any prejudice or preconceived notions.

THE ALLEGED CONSPIRACY SURROUNDING BAPU'S ARREST UNDER POCSO ACT

The arrest of Asharam Bapu on August 31, 2013, under the Protection of Children from Sexual Offences (POCSO) Act, just months after its enactment on November 14, 2012, raises significant questions about the timing and circumstances surrounding the case. Many have speculated whether this was part of a larger conspiracy aimed at targeting the spiritual leader, especially considering the lack of concrete evidence against him.

The introduction of the POCSO Act was a landmark step in India's legal framework to address the heinous crime of child sexual abuse and exploitation. However, its implementation and enforcement must be conducted with utmost diligence and adherence to due process to prevent any misuse or manipulation for ulterior motives.

Asharam Bapu's arrest sent shockwaves throughout the nation, given his stature as a revered spiritual leader with millions of followers. However, the manner in which the arrest was carried out raised eyebrows, as it seemed to lack substantial evidence or concrete proof linking him to the alleged crime.

The question arises: Was Asharam Bapu's arrest a result of a carefully orchestrated conspiracy designed to tarnish his reputation and undermine his influence? The timing of his arrest, just months after the enactment of the POCSO Act, suggests a possible agenda to target him using the new legal provisions.

Furthermore, the absence of credible evidence against Asharam Bapu raises doubts about the validity of the accusations leveled against him. In a society where the presumption of innocence until proven guilty is a fundamental principle of justice, it is concerning to see someone being subjected to arrest and trial without concrete evidence to support the allegations.

It is essential to recognize the broader context in which Asharam Bapu's arrest took place. He was not just a spiritual leader but also a vocal critic of certain political and social establishments. This raises suspicions about whether his arrest was politically motivated or part of a larger agenda to silence dissenting voices.

The case against Asharam Bapu highlights the importance of ensuring fairness, transparency, and accountability in the criminal justice system. Every individual, regardless of their status or reputation, deserves the right to a fair trial and due process. Rushing to judgment based on hearsay or speculation undermines the very principles of justice that our legal system seeks to uphold.

In conclusion, the circumstances surrounding Asharam Bapu's arrest under the POCSO Act raise valid concerns about the possibility of a larger conspiracy aimed at targeting him. It is imperative that the legal proceedings against him are conducted with impartiality, integrity, and adherence to the rule of law. Only then can the truth be revealed and justice served, ensuring the protection of both the rights of the accused and the victims.

THE TRAGIC TALE OF FABRICATED EVIDENCE AND UNFAIR JUDGEMENTS

In the annals of justice, there exist stories of egregious miscarriages where the scales of truth are tipped by the weight of deceit and manipulation. Such is the case of Bapu, where the pursuit of justice has been marred by the glaring loopholes in the legal process and the deliberate tampering of evidence. In this exposé, we delve into the disturbing realities behind the unfair judgement that has left a stain on the fabric of our legal system.

At the heart of this travesty of justice lies the manipulation of the original FIR, a foundational document upon which legal proceedings hinge. Shockingly, it has come to light that the original FIR was tampered with, casting doubt on the integrity of the entire case. This blatant act of tampering not only undermines the credibility of the evidence but also raises serious questions about the motives behind such manipulation.

Adding to the web of deception is the absence of crucial forensic test reports, a glaring omission that speaks volumes about the lack of diligence in the investigation process. In a case of such gravity, the absence of forensic evidence not only deprives the accused of their right to a fair trial but also casts doubt on the veracity of the allegations leveled against them.

Furthermore, the revelation that key recordings and call details crucial to the case have gone missing only deepens the suspicion surrounding the integrity of the investigation. The deliberate suppression of vital evidence not only impedes the quest for truth but also serves to perpetuate the miscarriage of justice.

What is perhaps most alarming is the systematic downgrading of the severity of the charges, a move that reeks of conspiracy and collusion. From major offenses to minor infractions, the subtle manipulation of charges serves to dilute the gravity of the allegations and diminish the accountability of the perpetrators.

The misuse of legal provisions to perpetrate injustice is a grave violation of the principles of fairness and equity that underpin our legal system. The deliberate withholding of crucial evidence, coupled with the manipulation of charges, constitutes a gross miscarriage of justice that cannot be ignored.

Of particular concern is the absence of fingerprints or footprints to corroborate the presence of the girl inside Bapu's premises, a glaring omission that casts doubt on the veracity of the allegations leveled against him. The absence of tangible evidence to support the prosecution's claims raises serious doubts about the credibility of the entire case.

In a shocking twist, it has come to light that the call details of the girl on the day of the alleged incident were conspicuously absent from the charge sheet, further underscoring the deliberate suppression of evidence. The deliberate omission of crucial call details raises serious questions about the integrity of the investigation and the motives behind such manipulation.

Equally troubling is the disappearance of the original video recording of the girl while filing the FIR, a crucial piece of evidence that mysteriously vanished, leaving a void in the pursuit of truth. The tampering of evidence and the deliberate suppression of crucial recordings only serve to deepen the shadows of doubt and suspicion that shroud this case.

In conclusion, the case of Bapu underscores the urgent need for reforms to safeguard the integrity of our legal system and protect the rights of the accused. The systematic manipulation of evidence and the deliberate suppression of vital information constitute a grave injustice that cannot be overlooked. It is imperative that we rise above the shadows of deceit and manipulation and strive to uphold the principles of fairness, equity, and justice that are the cornerstone of our democracy. Only then can we ensure that justice is not just a lofty ideal but a tangible reality for all.

CHAPTER NINE

Questioning

IS IT JUSTICE?

In a case where there is no direct evidence, the testimony of the accused will only be considered valid if it is a sterling witness, meaning there is no hint of contradiction in their statement.

This principle, articulated by the Supreme Court, underscores the importance of credibility in legal proceedings, particularly in cases where tangible evidence is lacking. It seeks to ensure that justice is served based on the reliability and integrity of the testimony presented.

Now, let's delve into the essence of this principle in the context of recent events surrounding Asharam Bapu.

In recent years, the nation has been gripped by the legal saga involving Asharam Bapu, a revered Hindu Sant who has amassed a significant following due to his teachings and spiritual guidance. However, his reputation was tarnished when he was accused of heinous crimes, leading to his arrest and subsequent legal battles.

Throughout the proceedings, one crucial aspect that has come under scrutiny is the reliability of the testimony provided by both the accusers and the accused. In cases where there is a lack of concrete evidence, the veracity of witness statements becomes paramount in determining the truth.

The principle laid down by the Supreme Court emphasizes the need for witnesses to be sterling, meaning their testimony must be free from any semblance of contradiction or doubt. This ensures that justice is not compromised by false or misleading statements.

In the case of Asharam Bapu, the credibility of witnesses has been a subject of intense debate. While the prosecution has presented its case based on the testimonies of alleged victims, the defense has vehemently challenged their credibility, highlighting inconsistencies and contradictions in their statements.

At the heart of this legal battle lies the question of justice. Can justice be served solely based on the testimony of witnesses? And if so, how can we ensure that these witnesses are indeed sterling, free from bias or ulterior motives?

In grappling with these questions, the judiciary faces the arduous task of upholding the principles of fairness and impartiality. It must weigh the evidence presented before it, carefully scrutinizing witness testimonies to discern the truth.

Ultimately, the pursuit of justice requires not only adherence to legal principles but also a commitment to integrity and transparency. It is incumbent upon all stakeholders – the judiciary, the prosecution, the defense, and society at large – to uphold the sanctity of the legal process and ensure that justice prevails.

As the legal proceedings surrounding Asharam Bapu continue to unfold, the principle articulated by the Supreme Court serves as a guiding light, reminding us of the importance of credibility in the quest for truth and justice."

JUSTICE UNDER SCRUTINY

In the realm of societal discourse, allegations levied against Sant Asharam Bapu by certain women raise significant questions regarding their veracity. These allegations, devoid of substantial evidence, have cast a shadow upon the life and work of a revered Sant who dedicated his entire being to the service of Sanatan culture and the welfare of the nation.

The allegations, primarily based on testimonies from individuals, lack the necessary corroboration and credibility required to warrant the severe punishment of lifelong imprisonment. It is imperative to critically examine the motives behind these accusations and evaluate their alignment with principles of justice and fairness.

Sant Asharam Bapu, renowned for his spiritual teachings and philanthropic endeavours, has been a guiding light for millions of followers worldwide. His life has been a testament to the principles of compassion, selflessness, and devotion to humanity. Throughout his lifetime, he has tirelessly worked towards the upliftment of society, promoting values of peace, harmony, and moral integrity.

However, the allegations brought forth against him have sparked a contentious debate within society, leading to polarization and division. While some fervently believe in his innocence and view the accusations as a smear campaign orchestrated to tarnish his reputation, others remain sceptical, swayed by sensationalized media narratives and hearsay.

It is essential to acknowledge the complexities surrounding the case and approach it with objectivity and impartiality. Justice demands a thorough and unbiased investigation, free from external influences and preconceived notions. The presumption of innocence should prevail until proven otherwise, adhering to the fundamental principles of jurisprudence.

Moreover, it is crucial to recognize the broader implications of unjustly condemning an individual who has dedicated his life to the betterment of society. The repercussions extend beyond the individual, affecting the morale and faith of millions of followers who look up to him as a spiritual guide and mentor.

In light of these considerations, the imposition of a lifelong sentence without concrete evidence raises serious ethical concerns. It not only undermines the principles of justice but also threatens to erode public trust in the judicial system. Upholding the principles of fairness, transparency, and due process is paramount in ensuring the integrity of our legal institutions.

The case of Sant Asharam Bapu underscores the need for a balanced and judicious approach towards allegations of this nature. While accountability and transparency are essential, they must be pursued within the framework of justice and due process. It is incumbent upon society to uphold the principles of fairness and uphold the presumption of innocence until proven guilty, ensuring that justice prevails for all.

In recent times, the scales of justice seem to tip unevenly, with disparate measures applied to different individuals accused of similar crimes. The case of Bishop Franco Mulakkal from Kerala is a glaring example. Accused of raping a nun multiple times, he spent a mere 26 days in jail before being released on bail, only to be declared innocent later.

Similarly, the ordeal faced by Deepak Chaurasia and other journalists who were accused of defaming Asharam Bapu by manipulating videos of a minor girl under the POCSO Act stands in stark contrast. Despite the serious allegations, they have not faced arrest to this day.

Actor Pearl V. Puri found himself embroiled in a case under the POCSO Act for allegedly raping a minor, yet he was granted bail within a short span of 11 days. Raj Kundra, accused of producing and releasing obscene films on his app, was also swiftly granted bail within just 2 months.

On the other hand, the case of Tarun Tejpal, charged with rape, has dragged on for a lengthy 8 months without resolution. Even more puzzling is the situation of Gayatri Prajapati, accused in a gang rape case, who despite being under the purview of the POCSO Act, was granted bail citing health reasons.

These glaring discrepancies in the application of justice raise serious questions about the fairness and consistency of the legal system. While some accused individuals are swiftly granted bail and their cases seem to languish, others face prolonged incarceration and legal battles.

It is imperative that justice be blind, impartial, and swift, regardless of the stature or influence of the accused. The principle of equality before the law must be upheld to ensure that every individual, regardless of their background, receives fair treatment and due process.

The case of Asharam Bapu serves as a poignant reminder of the importance of upholding these principles. Despite the serious nature of the allegations against him, he has been denied bail and continues to languish in prison, awaiting justice.

The disparity in the treatment of individuals accused of similar crimes undermines the credibility of the legal system and erodes public trust. It is imperative that steps be taken to address these discrepancies and ensure that justice is not only done but is seen to be done, in a fair and equitable manner.

In Palghar, Maharashtra, a ghastly incident unfolded where local criminals, in the presence of police officers, brutally murdered Sadhus, highlighting a grave concern for the safety of Sants and the society they serve.

Among the victims was Jagadguru Kripaluji Maharaj, who faced baseless allegations of rape by one of his disciples, only for the accusations to be proven false later.

Similarly, Shankaracharya Jayendra Saraswati was accused of involvement in a homicide case, enduring nine years of legal battle before being acquitted of all charges.

Another victim, Shri Keshavanandji, was falsely accused of rape, leading to a 12-year imprisonment before being exonerated seven years later.

Swami Asimanandji faced charges of involvement in a bomb blast case, enduring seven years of incarceration before being proven innocent.

The case of Swami Laxmananandji Saraswati stands as a stark reminder of the dangers faced by Sants opposing religious conversions. At 85 years old, he was brutally attacked by missionaries, sustaining severe injuries.

These incidents underscore the vulnerability of Sants and spiritual leaders to false accusations and targeted violence. Such injustices not only inflict physical harm but also tarnish their reputation and disrupt their noble mission of serving society.

The plight of Sants like Asharam Bapu serves as a wake-up call for society to ensure the safety and security of those who dedicate their lives to spiritual and humanitarian causes.

It is imperative for authorities to investigate allegations thoroughly, ensuring due process and protection of the rights of the accused.

Moreover, there is a need for greater awareness and education within society to prevent such heinous crimes and uphold the principles of justice and compassion.

The tragic incidents in Palghar and other parts of India serve as a poignant reminder of the challenges faced by Sants and the urgent need for collective action to safeguard their rights and dignity.

PERSISTENT VIOLATION OF HUMAN RIGHTS

For over 11.5 years, Sant Asharam Bapu has been incarcerated without bail, parole, or furlough, despite the provision for parole upon completing three-fourths of the sentence as per the law. However, this provision is not applied to Bapu. Each time, the court dismisses the elderly Sant's plea. Since 2013, Bapu has been in jail, and his health deteriorates day by day.

The relentless denial of justice to Sant Asharam Bapu reflects a grave violation of human rights. Despite being eligible for parole under the law, Bapu remains imprisoned, deprived of basic rights that every individual deserves. The prolonged incarceration without bail or parole not only disregards legal provisions but also undermines the principles of justice and fairness.

Throughout his time in jail, Sant Asharam Bapu's health has been steadily declining. Each passing day brings new challenges to his well-being, yet the authorities continue to ignore his deteriorating condition. Despite numerous appeals and petitions, Bapu's plea for relief falls on deaf ears, highlighting a systemic failure to uphold the rights and dignity of every individual, regardless of their background or beliefs.

The situation demands urgent attention and intervention to rectify the injustice inflicted upon Sant Asharam Bapu. It is imperative to ensure that he receives fair treatment and access to proper medical care in line with his rights as a human being. The denial of bail or parole goes against the very principles of justice and equity that form the foundation of any civilized society.

The plight of Sant Asharam Bapu serves as a stark reminder of the challenges faced by individuals seeking justice in a flawed system. His case underscores the need for reform to prevent similar injustices from occurring in the future. It is essential to address systemic issues that allow for the prolonged detention of individuals without proper recourse to legal remedies.

Furthermore, the denial of basic rights to Sant Asharam Bapu raises questions about the impartiality and fairness of the judicial system. It is crucial to uphold the principles of justice and ensure that every individual is treated with dignity and respect, irrespective of their circumstances. The prolonged incarceration of Bapu without bail or parole is a clear violation of his fundamental rights and warrants immediate corrective action.

In conclusion, the continued denial of bail or parole to Sant Asharam Bapu is a grave injustice that must be rectified without delay. It is imperative to uphold the principles of justice, fairness, and human rights for all individuals, including Bapu. The authorities must act swiftly to address this issue and ensure that Bapu receives the justice and dignity he rightfully deserves.

In the 21st century, perhaps one of the most egregious injustices perpetrated is the false accusation of rape against Asharam Bapu. At the age of approximately 85, when his appeal is pending in the Supreme Court, denying him bail is a blatant disregard for human rights and the law.

CHAPTER TEN

Chief Counsels: Analysis of Law and Advocacy

Former Law and Justice Minister of India, Subramanian Swamy, rightfully termed it as a bogus case leading to jail time. **The esteemed lawyer, Ashwini Upadhyay**, rightly points out that refusing bail to Asharam Bapu, who has tirelessly worked against religious conversions, amounts to gross neglect of justice.

Asharam Bapu has undertaken unparalleled work against religious conversions, a feat not matched by any other Sant or spiritual leader. It's disheartening that today he's being denied the right to receive Ayurvedic treatment, while even terrorists like Kasab are provided with their choice of doctors.

Hailing from the highest court of the land, **Harishankar Jain** emphasizes that Asharam Bapu has fallen prey to a conspiracy. He asserts that upon examining the FIR and medical reports, he's concluded that the case is entirely fabricated.

The injustice meted out to Asharam Bapu is evident from the words of **Supreme Court lawyer Ashwini Upadhyay**, who emphasizes that the case is entirely concocted. He urges that despite the evidence proving the falsity of the allegations, Asharam Bapu remains incarcerated.

It is essential to recognize that the case against Asharam Bapu is not just an assault on his dignity but an attack on the very fabric of justice. **The renowned lawyer, Harishankar Jain**, reiterates that based on his thorough examination of the evidence, the conclusion is irrefutable: Asharam Bapu has been ensnared in a web of deceit.

The injustice perpetrated against Asharam Bapu is a stain on the conscience of society. It's imperative to strive for truth and fairness, ensuring that innocent individuals like Asharam Bapu do not become victims of malicious agendas. The legal fraternity, along with conscientious citizens, must continue to advocate for justice and uphold the principles of fairness and equality before the law.

In the forthcoming days, the truth will unfold, as stated by **Advocate Vishnu Shankar Jain, from the Supreme Court.**

In the days to come, society will come to realize that the case against Sant Asharam Bapu was fabricated. The sentence imposed upon him was unjust. Media or anti-Hindu elements often create an atmosphere where our Sants are implicated in various allegations.

They were denied justice.

During the time of the pandemic, everyone was granted relief. Even hardcore criminals were released. There were guidelines from the High Power Committee, Supreme Court, and Honourable High Court, but Asharam Bapu was not granted relief. And yet, we talk about justice for all!

Advocate A.P. Singh from the Supreme Court expressed these sentiments.

The essence of the above statements is that the legal fraternity acknowledges the injustice meted out to Sant Asharam Bapu. It highlights the hypocrisy in the justice system, where relief was granted to many during the pandemic, but not to Sant Asharam Bapu.

It's a call for fairness and equality in the legal system, emphasizing the need for justice to be served impartially, irrespective of one's social or religious standing.

In the quest for truth and justice, it's imperative to shed light on such instances of injustice and work towards rectifying them. Only then can we truly uphold the principles of justice and ensure a fair and equitable society for all.

The journey towards justice may be long and arduous, but it's essential to persevere and continue fighting for what is right. Sant Asharam Bapu's case serves as a reminder of the challenges we face in upholding justice and the importance of standing up against injustice wherever it may occur.

Let us hope that the truth prevails, and Sant Asharam Bapu receives the justice he rightfully deserves.

UNVEILING INJUSTICE

In the legal realm, it's often said, "*There's no substance in the case.*" Lawyer, National Secretary of Hindu Legal Council, **Sanjeev Punalekarji**, questions why there's no bail for Bapu while others accused of crimes walk free. He highlights the injustice against Bapu as an affront to Hinduism.

"*Even you are at risk,*" he warns.

Advocate Kirti Ahuja practicing at Supreme court of India said, that the judgement of Ahmedabad court will not only affect bapuji, but in the coming times it will have drastic affect on all those who will be falsely implicated like this after delay of 12 years or more and in similar manner they would face conviction wherein courts will use this same citation of Bapuji's case. Therefore, apart from Bapuji's supporters, it is imperative for all to understand this injustice and raise their voice.

Lawyer, Supreme Court, Dharmendra Mishra, points out the symbiotic relationship between power and the judiciary, where the latter often acts as an instrument of the former. He criticizes the system for its bias, where Sants are incarcerated while others walk free on bail.

In a system where the judiciary itself sends people to jail, collusion between power and the judiciary is rampant. Mishra highlights how this collusion results in Sants being jailed while others get bail.

The voices of legal experts echo the need for a fair and unbiased judicial system. They urge everyone to stand against injustice, not just for Bapu but for the integrity of the legal system itself.

It's imperative to remember that justice should be blind, not influenced by power or position. The case of Sant Asharam Bapu serves as a stark reminder of the flaws within the system, urging us to strive for a judiciary that upholds the principles of fairness and equality for all.

In conclusion, the case of Sant Asharam Bapu sheds light on the need for a transparent and impartial judiciary. It's a call to action for everyone to stand up against injustice and work towards a legal system that truly serves justice to all, irrespective of their social status or background.

CHAPTER ELEVEN

Upholding Human Rights

LAWYER'S PERSPECTIVE

Parole is a fundamental right of a prisoner. It is a grave violation of basic rights when it is granted to selected terrorists without any problem but not to Hindu Sants like Asharam Bapu

Parole, a fundamental right of a convict, is meant to provide temporary relief from incarceration for various reasons such as medical treatment, family emergencies, or legal proceedings. It serves as a humane measure to maintain a balance between punishment and rehabilitation. However, the misuse of parole undermines the integrity of the justice system and infringes upon the rights of individuals, especially when applied selectively.

The recent controversy surrounding the parole granted to certain convicts has sparked outrage and raised questions about the fairness and impartiality of the legal system. In particular, the case of Asharam Bapu, a Hindu Sant, has drawn significant attention due to the perceived injustice and discrimination in the handling of his parole requests.

Asharam Bapu, a revered spiritual leader, has been embroiled in a legal battle for several years, facing allegations of sexual assault and other charges. Despite maintaining his innocence and a lack of substantial evidence against him, he has been denied parole multiple times, while individuals convicted of more serious crimes have been granted parole without hesitation.

This disparity in treatment raises concerns about the impartiality and integrity of the legal process. It reflects a broader pattern of discrimination against certain individuals based on their religious or social status. By denying Asharam Bapu parole, the authorities not only infringe upon his fundamental rights but also undermine the principles of justice and equality enshrined in the constitution.

Furthermore, the arbitrary denial of parole has significant consequences for Asharam Bapu's health and well-being. As an elderly individual with health issues, he is entitled to compassionate consideration and appropriate medical care. However, the continued denial of parole deprives him of access to essential medical treatment and exacerbates his suffering.

Moreover, the denial of parole perpetuates a culture of impunity and undermines public trust in the legal system. When individuals perceive that justice is not served fairly and equitably, it erodes confidence in the rule of law and fosters disillusionment with the authorities.

In conclusion, the denial of parole to Asharam Bapu highlights systemic flaws and biases in the legal system. It underscores the urgent need for reforms to ensure that justice is administered impartially and without discrimination. Upholding human rights and protecting the dignity of every individual, regardless of their background, is essential for building a just and inclusive society.

CHAPTER TWELVE

The Persecution Of Sants: A Call For Justice

DEFENDING SANTS: ADVOCATING FOR JUSTICE AMID PERSECUTION

In our society, there exists a troubling trend of falsely accusing revered spiritual figures, tarnishing their reputation and disrupting their noble work. One such victim of this orchestrated conspiracy is Sant Asharam Bapu, who has dedicated his life to the upliftment of society through spiritual teachings and humanitarian efforts. However, he has been unjustly targeted and subjected to false allegations, reflecting the vulnerability of even the most revered figures to the manipulation of the law.

The case against Sant Asharam Bapu is emblematic of the larger conspiracy to undermine Hindu culture and spirituality. False accusations, coupled with prolonged legal battles, have inflicted immense suffering upon him, highlighting the flaws and biases inherent in our justice system. Former Chief Protector and International President of the Vishwa Hindu Parishad, Shri Ashok Singhal, and Gujarat Minister of State for Home Affairs, Shri Ashok Raval, have also been victims of such persecution, emphasizing the systematic targeting of influential Hindu leaders.

Amidst these challenges, the Vishwa Hindu Parishad of Gujarat appeals for compassion and understanding towards Sant Asharam Bapu, recognizing his invaluable contributions to the dissemination of Sanatan Dharma and national upliftment. It is imperative that the authorities, including Prime Minister Narendra Modi, consider the age and the exemplary work of Sant Asharam Bapu and take appropriate action to ensure justice and fairness prevail.

It is disheartening to witness the suffering inflicted upon Sant Asharam Bapu, a beacon of wisdom and compassion. His teachings have touched millions of lives, guiding them towards spiritual enlightenment and moral righteousness. As we reflect on his plight, we must also acknowledge the broader implications of such persecution on the fabric of our society. The persecution of Sants is not merely an attack on individuals but an assault on the values of truth, justice, and compassion that form the foundation of our civilization.

It is incumbent upon us to stand united against the injustice perpetrated against Sant Asharam Bapu and other revered spiritual leaders. We must advocate for a fair and impartial legal process that upholds the principles of truth and integrity. Only then can we ensure that the voices of the oppressed are heard, and justice is served.

The case surrounding Asharam Bapu is indeed controversial and has garnered significant attention. It's essential to examine the facts with clarity and humility.

Asharam Bapu, a revered Hindu spiritual leader, finds himself entangled in a legal web, with numerous accusations against him. However, it's crucial to approach this matter with objectivity and fairness.

At 85 years old and reportedly in poor health, denying him bail raises ethical questions. His alleged crimes should be tried in court, but denying him basic rights, such as bail, seems disproportionate, given his age and health condition.

Moreover, comparing his case to that of an Imam with multiple FIRs and non-bailable warrants highlights discrepancies in the legal system. The claim that arresting him could incite violence speaks volumes about the prevailing social tensions.

The accusations against Asharam Bapu should be thoroughly investigated, but justice must be served with compassion and fairness. Every individual, regardless of their stature, deserves a fair trial and humane treatment.

The allegations against him are serious, but they should not overshadow his decades-long contribution to society. Asharam Bapu's teachings have impacted millions of lives positively, and his followers continue to support him despite the allegations.

While it's essential to address the allegations against Asharam Bapu, it's equally important to acknowledge his humanitarian work and spiritual teachings. He has dedicated his life to serving others and promoting peace and harmony in society.

In conclusion, the case against Asharam Bapu is complex and multifaceted. It's imperative to approach it with sensitivity and objectivity, ensuring that justice is served while upholding basic human rights and dignity.

Hail to you, O revered Asharam Bapu,
Our guiding light, embodiment of divine wisdom.
Just as Lord Shiva is the guru, you are our guru,
Leading us on the path of righteousness.
You are the beacon of hope,
Illuminating our lives with your teachings.
Your words resonate like the echoes of ancient wisdom,
Guiding us through life's trials and tribulations.
In your presence, we find solace and strength.
Your grace knows no bounds,
Showering blessings upon your disciples
With boundless love and compassion.
With every step, you walk the path of dharma,
Inspiring us to follow in your footsteps.
Your devotion to truth and righteousness is unwavering,
Like the eternal flame of enlightenment.
Salutations to you, O Asharam Bapu,
Embodiment of divine grace and compassion.
May your divine presence continue to guide
And inspire us on our spiritual journey.

THE MULTIFACETED IMPACT OF THE INJUSTICE FACED BY ASHARAM BAPU ON SOCIETY, HIS DEVOTEES, AND THE BROADER IMPLICATIONS FOR JUSTICE AND DEMOCRACY.

1. **Undermining Faith in Justice:** The injustice against Asharam Bapu has shaken people's faith in the justice system, leading to a loss of trust and confidence in legal institutions.
2. **Psychological Impact on Devotees:** Devotees have suffered emotional distress and mental anguish due to the unjust treatment meted out to their spiritual leader, causing deep psychological scars.

3. **Diversion of Resources:** Legal battles and efforts to seek justice have diverted valuable resources and time away from constructive endeavours, hindering the progress and development of society.
4. **Social Stigma:** The unjust portrayal of Asharam Bapu in the media has led to social stigma, ostracization, and discrimination against his followers, impacting their social and professional lives.
5. **Erosion of Religious Freedom:** The persecution of Asharam Bapu represents a threat to religious freedom and tolerance, undermining the principles of pluralism and diversity in society.
6. **Impact on Education:** Educational institutions associated with Asharam Bapu have faced challenges and setbacks, disrupting the academic pursuits and future prospects of students.
7. **Economic Hardship:** Many devotees, who often come from modest backgrounds, have faced economic hardships due to legal expenses and loss of livelihood opportunities resulting from social stigma.
8. **Interference with Spiritual Practices:** The unjust incarceration of Asharam Bapu has disrupted spiritual practices and deprived devotees of guidance and mentorship, affecting their personal growth and well-being.
9. **Loss of Humanitarian Initiatives:** Asharam Bapu's charitable and humanitarian initiatives, which aimed to uplift marginalized communities, have been hindered, leading to a deprivation of essential services and support.
10. **Deterioration of Social Harmony:** The divisive narrative surrounding Asharam Bapu's case has fuelled tensions and conflicts within communities, eroding social harmony and cohesion.
11. **Infringement of Legal Rights:** The denial of fair trial and due process rights to Asharam Bapu violates fundamental principles of justice, setting a dangerous precedent for the treatment of religious leaders and minorities.
12. **Misuse of Legal System:** The manipulation of legal proceedings and biased investigations against Asharam Bapu reflects the misuse and politicization of the legal system for vested interests, undermining its integrity and credibility.
13. **Erosion of Democratic Values:** The suppression of dissent and dissenting voices in support of Asharam Bapu reflects a broader erosion of democratic values and freedoms, threatening the democratic fabric of society.

14. **Psychological Trauma on Families:** The families of Asharam Bapu and his devotees have endured immense psychological trauma and emotional turmoil, grappling with the stigma and persecution associated with the case.
15. **Cultural Degradation:** The demonization of spiritual leaders like Asharam Bapu contributes to the degradation of cultural and spiritual heritage, weakening the moral and ethical fabric of society.
16. **Violation of Human Rights:** The prolonged detention and mistreatment of Asharam Bapu constitute a violation of basic human rights, including the right to liberty, dignity, and freedom of expression.
17. **Loss of Social Support Systems:** The disruption of spiritual gatherings and community events organized by Asharam Bapu has deprived devotees of vital social support networks, exacerbating feelings of isolation and alienation.
18. **Undermining Rule of Law:** The failure to uphold justice in Asharam Bapu's case undermines the rule of law and fosters a culture of impunity, where powerful interests can manipulate legal processes with impunity.
19. **Impact on Mental Health:** Devotees and supporters of Asharam Bapu have experienced heightened levels of stress, anxiety, and depression due to the uncertainty and injustice surrounding his case.
20. **Deterioration of Interfaith Relations:** The persecution of Asharam Bapu has strained interfaith relations and dialogue, perpetuating stereotypes and prejudices against Hindu spiritual leaders and their followers.
21. **Call for Reform:** The injustice faced by Asharam Bapu underscores the urgent need for reform in the legal system to ensure fairness, impartiality, and accountability, restoring faith in justice and upholding human rights for all.

INJUSTICE UNMASKED

The legacy of injustice surrounding Asharam Bapu's case unveils a narrative fraught with systemic failures, bias, and unsubstantiated allegations. Despite the glaring absence of concrete evidence implicating him in any wrongdoing, Asharam Bapu found himself ensnared in a web of legal persecution and societal condemnation. This untold story sheds light on the profound ramifications of a flawed justice system and the enduring impact it has had on Asharam Bapu, his followers, and society at large.

1. **Absence of Physical Assault:** Despite exhaustive investigations, no evidence of physical assault was unearthed. Asharam Bapu bore no marks or bruises indicative of violence, yet he was unjustly branded as an assailant, challenging the very foundations of justice and due process.
2. **No Loss of Consciousness:** The alleged incident lacked any report of loss of consciousness by the purported victim. This critical detail, or rather the lack thereof, casts doubt on the authenticity of the accusations levelled against Asharam Bapu and raises questions about the veracity of the entire narrative.
3. **Lack of Bite Marks:** Forensic examinations failed to uncover any bite marks on the alleged victim's body, a glaring absence in cases of physical assault. The absence of such crucial evidence further undermines the credibility of the allegations and calls into question the motives behind Asharam Bapu's persecution.
4. **No Evidence of Penetration:** Despite meticulous scrutiny, no evidence of penetration or sexual assault was found. This pivotal finding strikes at the heart of the allegations against Asharam Bapu, exposing the fragile foundation upon which his persecution rests.
5. **No Abrasion or Injury:** Medical examinations confirmed the absence of any abrasions or injuries on the alleged victim's body. This irrefutable fact contradicts claims of physical harm purportedly inflicted by Asharam Bapu and exposes the inherent flaws in the case brought against him.
6. **Absence of Erythema:** Erythema, a common indicator of physical trauma, was conspicuously absent from the alleged victim's skin. The lack of this telltale sign further diminishes the credibility of the accusations and underscores the absence of substantive evidence against Asharam Bapu.
7. **No Signs of Sweating:** Witnesses and medical professionals attested to Asharam Bapu's composure and lack of sweating during the alleged incident. This absence of physiological reactions associated with distress challenges the authenticity of the allegations and raises doubts about their validity.
8. **Intact Hymen:** Medical examinations unequivocally established the intactness of the alleged victim's hymen, refuting claims of sexual assault. This crucial finding deals a severe blow to the accusations

levelled against Asharam Bapu and exposes the injustice inherent in his prosecution.

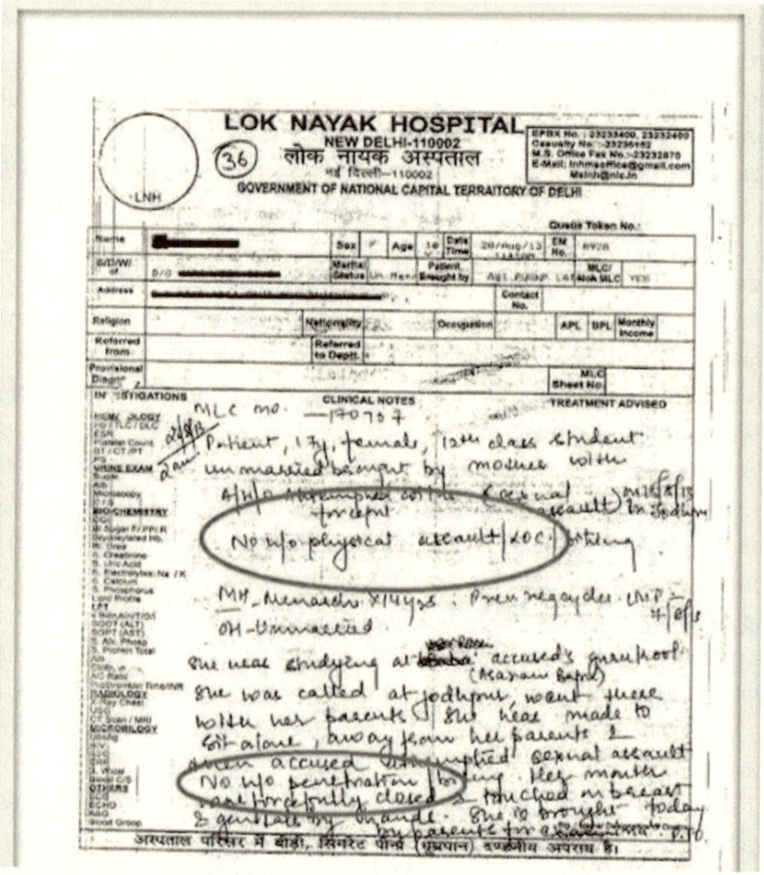

LOK NAYAK HOSPITAL
NEW DELHI-110002
लोक नायक अस्पताल
नई दिल्ली–110002
GOVERNMENT OF NATIONAL CAPITAL TERRAITORY OF DELHI

CLINICAL NOTES

TREATMENT ADVISED

अस्पताल परिसर में बीड़ी, सिगरेट पीना (धूम्रपान) दण्डनीय अपराध है।

The untold story of Asharam Bapu's ordeal epitomizes the legacy of injustice that pervades our legal system. It serves as a stark reminder of the grave consequences of unchecked bias, flawed investigations, and the erosion of fundamental rights. Asharam Bapu's case stands as a testament to the urgent need for reform and accountability in the pursuit of justice, lest the legacy of injustice continues to stain the fabric of society.

CHAPTER THIRTEEN

The Defense Of Indian Culture

JOURNEY BEHIND BARS

In today's society, the name Sant Asharam Bapu is synonymous not only with spiritual guidance but also with controversy and legal battles. However, beyond the confines of prison walls, lies a deeper narrative—a narrative of the preservation and defense of Indian culture.

Sant Asharam Bapu, a revered spiritual leader, finds himself entangled in a legal quagmire, yet his incarceration serves as a backdrop to a larger struggle—the defense of Indian cultural values and traditions. Despite being behind bars, his teachings and principles resonate with millions who see him as a beacon of wisdom and righteousness.

The essence of Indian culture lies in its rich heritage, encompassing spiritual wisdom, moral values, and timeless traditions. Sant Asharam Bapu, through his teachings and actions, embodies these cultural pillars, advocating for their preservation and propagation amidst modern challenges and societal changes.

At the heart of Sant Asharam Bapu's message is the emphasis on dharma, righteousness, and the eternal principles outlined in ancient scriptures. His discourses delve into the depths of Indian philosophy, elucidating the significance of karma, seva (selfless service), and devotion in leading a fulfilling life.

Through various charitable initiatives and humanitarian efforts, Sant Asharam Bapu exemplifies the spirit of seva, fostering compassion and empathy towards all beings. His ashrams and spiritual centers serve as hubs of social welfare activities, providing education, healthcare, and humanitarian aid to the underprivileged sections of society.

Despite facing legal challenges and controversies, Sant Asharam Bapu's followers remain steadfast in their support, viewing his ordeal as a test of faith and resilience. Their unwavering devotion reflects the deep-rooted reverence for their spiritual guru and the values he espouses.

The narrative of Sant Asharam Bapu's journey behind bars transcends the individual, symbolizing a larger struggle for the protection of Indian culture and heritage. His case becomes a rallying point for those who perceive a threat to traditional values and seek to uphold the sanctity of their cultural identity.

In the face of adversity, Sant Asharam Bapu emerges as a symbol of resilience and fortitude, inspiring millions to uphold the timeless principles of Indian culture. His teachings serve as a guiding light in navigating the complexities of modern life while staying rooted in age-old wisdom.

As the legal battle continues, Sant Asharam Bapu's followers remain hopeful, believing in the eventual triumph of truth and righteousness. For them, his incarceration is not just a personal ordeal but a testament to the enduring struggle for the defense of Indian culture and values.

Sant Asharam Bapu's journey behind bars is not merely a legal saga but a profound reflection of the ongoing struggle to safeguard Indian culture and heritage. His teachings, imbued with timeless wisdom, continue to inspire millions to uphold the values that define the essence of Indian civilization.

This essay aims to delve deeper into the significance of Sant Asharam Bapu's incarceration in the broader context of the defense of Indian culture, highlighting the enduring relevance of his teachings in today's world.

A QUEST FOR TRUTH

In recent years, the case involving Sant Asharam Bapu has sparked controversy and divided public opinion. As various perspectives emerge, it becomes essential to examine the matter meticulously, considering both sides of the narrative.

The allegations against Asharam Bapu stem from an incident purportedly occurring in 2002, yet the accusations surfaced only after a significant lapse of time. It raises questions about the veracity of the claims and the motives behind their belated disclosure.

Medical reports and expert opinions play a crucial role in understanding the intricacies of the case. Doctors consulted in the matter have opined that there is no conclusive evidence of rape or attempted rape. Furthermore, they assert that the softness of a minor's skin makes it improbable for any physical abuse to go unnoticed, casting doubt on the validity of the accusations.

It's imperative to assess the credibility of the complainant's testimony against the backdrop of Asharam Bapu's lifelong dedication to spiritual teachings and philanthropic endeavors. His followers assert his innocence, highlighting his unwavering commitment to global welfare throughout his life.

However, the legal battle surrounding Asharam Bapu's case remains contentious. Despite the absence of concrete evidence, the wheels of justice continue to turn, subjecting him to prolonged legal proceedings.

The delay in justice raises concerns about the fairness of the judicial system and the rights of the accused. As years pass by, the quest for truth becomes entangled in a web of legal complexities and public perception.

In conclusion, the case of Asharam Bapu underscores the importance of impartial investigation and adherence to legal principles. As the search for truth continues, it's essential to approach the matter with sensitivity and objectivity, ensuring justice prevails for all parties involved.

MISUSE OF JUSTICE SYSTEM

The misuse of the justice system is a topic of concern that echoes across societies worldwide. In the case of Asharam Bapu and his followers, the glaring misuse of justice raises questions about the integrity of the legal system. This article delves into the reasons behind the persecution faced by Asharam Bapu and his devotees and explores whether their crime was their efforts to protect the nation, culture, and society from destructive forces.

- **Understanding the Conspiracy:** The orchestrated conspiracy against Asharam Bapu and his devotees requires a closer examination of the vested interests at play. Various powerful entities aimed to discredit and dismantle his influence, fearing the awakening of societal consciousness fostered by his teachings. This section delves into the intricate web of conspiracies woven to tarnish his reputation and silence his voice.
- **The Noble Mission:** Asharam Bapu's life was dedicated to uplifting society through spiritual teachings and humanitarian efforts. His mission aimed at instilling moral values, fostering compassion, and

nurturing spiritual growth among individuals. This section highlights the noble endeavors undertaken by Asharam Bapu and his followers, which threatened vested interests seeking to exploit societal weaknesses.

- **Targeted for Upholding Truth:** The relentless pursuit of truth often invites opposition from those vested in maintaining falsehoods and exploitation. Asharam Bapu's unwavering commitment to truth and righteousness made him a target for those threatened by his influence. This section explores how his steadfast adherence to principles of truth and justice led to his persecution by vested interests.
- **Challenges to Justice:** The flaws within the justice system become apparent when individuals like Asharam Bapu and his devotees face unjust persecution. This section examines the loopholes and biases within the legal framework that allowed for the manipulation of justice for ulterior motives. The challenges faced by the accused in receiving fair trials and legal representation underscore the systemic issues plaguing the justice system.
- **Standing for Dharma:** Asharam Bapu's teachings emphasized the importance of dharma, righteousness, and ethical conduct in all aspects of life. His followers, inspired by his teachings, stood firm in upholding dharma even in the face of adversity. This section showcases the unwavering resolve of his devotees in standing by their guru and principles, despite the trials and tribulations they endured.
- **The Humanitarian Legacy:** Beyond the legal battles and controversies, Asharam Bapu's legacy shines through his humanitarian initiatives and service to society. This section highlights the numerous charitable endeavors initiated by him and his devotees, aimed at uplifting the underprivileged and providing relief to those in need. Despite facing persecution, their commitment to serving humanity remained unwavering.
- **Seeking Justice and Truth:** The quest for justice and truth remains an ongoing struggle for Asharam Bapu, his devotees, and supporters. This section explores the efforts undertaken to seek justice and vindicate the innocence of those wrongfully accused. From legal battles to grassroots movements, various initiatives strive to expose the truth and bring about accountability for the injustices perpetrated.
- **Conclusion:** The persecution faced by Asharam Bapu and his devotees serves as a stark reminder of the challenges encountered in upholding truth and righteousness in a world plagued by corruption and vested

interests. Despite the adversity, their unwavering commitment to their principles and the pursuit of justice continues to inspire millions. As society reflects on these events, it must strive towards a more just and equitable legal system that upholds the values of truth, fairness, and integrity for all.

UNVEILING INJUSTICE

In the annals of Indian culture, the revered figure of Asharam Bapu stands as a beacon of spiritual enlightenment and wisdom. However, his journey has been marred by the insidious machinations of those seeking to undermine the fabric of our society. Allegations of wrongdoing were leveled against him, casting a shadow of doubt and suspicion over his legacy.

The orchestrated campaign to tarnish Asharam Bapu's reputation and erode the values he stood for is a testament to the depths of depravity to which some individuals are willing to stoop. Fabricated accusations were hurled, and without due process, he was unjustly incarcerated.

The narrative spun by the media, echoing the sentiments of the powerful, painted a picture of guilt without substantiation. Despite the lack of concrete evidence, the relentless onslaught of propaganda continued unabated. It is a harrowing reflection of the sorry state of our society, where sensationalism trumps truth and justice.

The victim herself, in a courageous act of defiance, proclaimed the innocence of Asharam Bapu. Medical reports corroborated her account, yet the relentless barrage of misinformation persisted. The cries of 'guilt' echoed through the corridors of power, drowning out the voices of reason and integrity.

The political motivations behind this witch hunt are evident to any discerning observer. Asharam Bapu's unwavering commitment to his principles and teachings posed a threat to the vested interests of those in positions of authority. Thus, he became a convenient scapegoat, sacrificed at the altar of expediency.

The coercion and manipulation employed by the authorities to secure signatures and confessions are a damning indictment of their disregard for due process and human dignity. Under the guise of legality, egregious violations of fundamental rights were perpetrated, leaving a stain on the fabric of our judicial system.

The relentless pressure exerted on the police force to produce results at any cost is a reflection of the systemic rot that plagues our institutions. The pursuit of justice was subverted by ulterior motives, leaving truth as the ultimate casualty.

As the dust settles and the truth begins to emerge, it is imperative that we reflect on the lessons learned from this dark chapter in our history. The vilification of Asharam Bapu serves as a cautionary tale, reminding us of the fragility of our freedoms and the ease with which they can be eroded.

The saga of Asharam Bapu is a sobering reminder of the dangers posed by unchecked power and the importance of upholding the principles of justice and fairness. It is a call to action for all those who cherish the values of truth and integrity to stand up and demand accountability from those in positions of authority. Only then can we hope to prevent such travesties of justice from recurring in the future.

We delve into the unjust conspiracy that ensnared the devoted followers of Asharam Bapu. In an era where even one's own progeny often fails to heed wise counsel, millions of people, numbering in the millions, reverently listen to and respect revered Asharam Bapu. Behind this phenomenon lies the discipline, integrity, spiritual practices, perseverance, and altruistic sentiments of Asharam Bapu. Amidst the swirling rumors surrounding Asharam Bapu, even a shred of truth would shed light on why millions flock to him. Among these millions are industrialists, politicians, lawyers, doctors, engineers, scientists, and others holding esteemed positions both domestically and abroad.

Additionally, those accused in this case hail from well-educated backgrounds. Why would they forsake everything and come to the ashram?

The answers lie in the profound impact of Asharam Bapu's teachings, which transcend societal boundaries and touch the souls of people from all walks of life. Asharam Bapu's teachings resonate with simplicity, emphasizing virtues like love, compassion, and selflessness.

However, the path of truth is often fraught with obstacles, and some individuals, threatened by the growing influence of Asharam Bapu, conspired to tarnish his reputation. In this tumultuous journey, his devotees found themselves unjustly accused and persecuted, leaving behind their lives of comfort and prestige to seek refuge in the ashram.

Despite facing immense adversity, the unwavering faith of Asharam Bapu's followers remains unshaken. They find solace in his teachings, which provide them with the strength to endure the trials and tribulations they face.

Asharam Bapu's ashram serves as a sanctuary for those seeking spiritual guidance and refuge from the storms of life. It is a place where individuals from diverse backgrounds come together in pursuit of inner peace and enlightenment.

The persecution faced by Asharam Bapu's devotees serves as a stark reminder of the challenges encountered on the path of truth. Yet, it also highlights the resilience and unwavering faith of those who continue to stand by their spiritual leader, undeterred by the trials they face.

Through their unwavering devotion and steadfastness, Asharam Bapu's devotees exemplify the timeless values of love, compassion, and perseverance, inspiring countless others to walk the path of righteousness.

In the serene confines of Chhindwara Gurukul, Sharadchandra Bhai, a man dedicated to the path of enlightenment, served as the Director. Hailing from Hyderabad, he was not only a scholar in Bio-Medical Engineering but also held a Master's degree from the US. Sharadchandra Bhai, a devout celibate, faced the egregious accusation of sending girls to Asharam Bapu.

Such an accusation is preposterous and baseless. One wonders, if such events occurred within the ashram, why would an educated and affluent individual like Sharadchandra Bhai seek solace with Bapu? The purpose of the ashram is for spiritual practice and societal service.

Similarly, Shilpi Gupta, who served as the Hostel Superintendent and Administrator at Chhindwara Gurukul, has been falsely accused of luring girls to Bapu. This accusation is utterly false and unfounded. Shilpi Ji is a post-graduate and comes from a well-to-do family. She has no financial constraints that would drive her to such actions.

Her father holds a prestigious position as the Joint Director of Urban and Rural Investment in Raipur. If there were any truth to these accusations, why would she maintain ties with Bapu? Shilpi Ji has attested, "By God's grace, my family faces no financial difficulties. Bapu has never offered me any temptation or promised me any high-ranking position. Since my childhood, I harbored a desire to serve, and upon coming to the ashram, I felt that my selfless service commitment was being fulfilled. My relationship with revered Bapu is akin to that of a father and daughter. I regard Bapu as my father." Kishor Devda, a devoted servant of Bapu, is a celibate. He had built a hut for Bapu on his farm. If Bapu engaged in such activities, why would this person build a hut?

Concocting absurd tales, conspirators are maliciously leveling heinous accusations against Bapu. Shivabhai was brutally assaulted, tempted, had his eardrum damaged, his hair was torn, and forced to sign on blank papers under police remand to give a statement against Bapu. If this isn't abuse and misuse of the justice system and law enforcement, then what is?

UNVEILING TRUTH: THE REDEMPTION OF ASHRAM'S REPUTATION

In July 2008, tragedy struck Sant Asharam Gurukul in Ahmedabad with the untimely deaths of two students. What followed was not just grief but also a series of false accusations and a long legal battle. However, recent developments have brought clarity and vindication to the ashram and its devotees.

- **The Supreme Court's Verdict:** On September 11, 2012, the Supreme Court delivered a significant verdict, rejecting Gujarat government's plea to charge seven ashram devotees under Section 304. This decision effectively dismissed criminal accusations against them and upheld the Gujarat High Court's ruling, affirming the innocence of the accused.
- **Forensic Findings:** Forensic reports from the Forensic Science Laboratory (FSL) played a crucial role in unraveling the truth. Contrary to sensationalized claims, these reports revealed no signs of pre-mortem injuries on the children's bodies. There was no evidence of sexual assault, chemical poisoning, or any tampering with the bodies. These findings debunked baseless allegations and provided concrete evidence in support of the innocence of the accused.
- **Judicial Inquiry and Expose:** During the judicial inquiry led by Justice Trivedi, false accusers were exposed, shedding light on the extent of deception and manipulation surrounding the case. Years of meticulous investigation culminated in the submission of the inquiry report to the Gujarat government on August 1, 2013. Media reports suggest that the report unequivocally refutes the fabricated allegations, exonerating the ashram and its devotees from any wrongdoing.
- **Support and Resilience:** Throughout this ordeal, the ashram community displayed remarkable resilience and unwavering support for one another. Their steadfast commitment to truth and integrity served as a beacon of hope in the face of adversity. Despite the challenges, they

remained steadfast in their pursuit of justice and vindication.

The recent developments in the case signify more than just exoneration; they represent a triumph of truth over deception, a reaffirmation of justice, and a testament to the unwavering spirit of those who stood firm in the face of adversity. As we reflect on this journey of redemption, it becomes evident that the pursuit of truth is not just a legal battle but a moral imperative. It is a reminder of the importance of upholding integrity, dispelling falsehoods, and restoring dignity to those wrongfully accused.

CHAPTER FOURTEEN

Millions of Voices, One Question

WHY ARE HUMAN RIGHTS DENIED TO SANT ASHARAM BAPU IN A FAKE CASE?

In a world where justice and fairness are the cornerstones of a civilized society, one question echoes in the minds of millions: Why are human rights being denied to Sant Asharam Bapu in a case riddled with falsehoods and fabrications?

The case against Sant Asharam Bapu has garnered widespread attention and sparked outrage among his followers and supporters, who vehemently assert his innocence and decry the blatant miscarriage of justice that has unfolded before their eyes. Yet, despite overwhelming evidence pointing to his innocence, Sant Asharam Bapu continues to languish behind bars, deprived of his basic human rights and freedoms.

At the heart of this travesty of justice lies a web of deceit and manipulation, orchestrated by vested interests with ulterior motives. From the outset, it has been abundantly clear that the case against Sant Asharam Bapu is nothing more than a sham, fueled by baseless allegations and unsubstantiated claims. Fabricated evidence, coerced witnesses, and biased media coverage have all contributed to the perpetuation of this grave injustice, leaving no room for doubt that Sant Asharam Bapu is a victim of a malicious conspiracy designed to tarnish his reputation and undermine his legacy of selfless service and spiritual guidance.

But beyond the legal intricacies of the case lies a deeper, more troubling reality: the systematic erosion of human rights and civil liberties in the pursuit of political vendettas and personal vendettas. Sant Asharam Bapu is not just another victim of a flawed judicial system; he is a symbol of the broader struggle for justice and equality in a world where power and influence often trump truth and integrity.

The denial of human rights to Sant Asharam Bapu is not just an affront to his dignity and freedom; it is an indictment of our collective failure to uphold the principles of fairness, equality, and justice that lie at the heart of the human experience. It is a stark reminder that the quest for justice is an ongoing battle, one that requires unwavering commitment and courage in the face of adversity.

As we raise our voices in solidarity with Sant Asharam Bapu and demand accountability for those responsible for his unjust incarceration, let us also reaffirm our commitment to defending the rights and freedoms of all individuals, regardless of their status or background. Let us stand united in our pursuit of justice and fairness, and let us never waver in our determination to uphold the inherent dignity and worth of every human being.

In the end, the question remains: Why are human rights denied to Sant Asharam Bapu in a fake case? It is a question that demands answers, and it is a question that will continue to resonate until justice is served and his innocence is vindicated.

As we strive to answer this question, let us remember that the fight for justice is not just about one man; it is about the principles and values that define who we are as a society. It is about ensuring that justice prevails, that truth triumphs over falsehood, and that human rights are upheld for all.

Only then can we truly claim to be champions of justice, and only then can we begin to heal the wounds inflicted by this grave injustice. The time to act is now, and the cause is just. Let us stand together in solidarity and demand justice for Sant Asharam Bapu and all those who have been wronged by a flawed and unjust system.

In the pursuit of justice, let us never forget the words of Mahatma Gandhi: "*Injustice anywhere is a threat to justice everywhere.*" Together, let us strive to build a world where justice reigns supreme, and where the rights and dignity of every individual are respected and protected.

The question remains unanswered, but the answer lies within each and every one of us. Let us join hands and work together to ensure that Sant Asharam Bapu receives the justice he deserves, and that his human rights are upheld and protected now and always.

Let us stand united in our quest for justice, and let us never rest until justice is served. Millions of voices may ask the question, but together, we can be the answer.

UPHOLDING JUSTICE AMIDST A LEGACY OF SERVICE

The case of Sant Asharam Bapu stands as a testament to the delicate balance between justice and the legacy of selfless service and spiritual guidance that he has embodied throughout his life. Despite facing grave injustices, Bapu's unwavering commitment to serving humanity continues to inspire millions, even as he fights for his own freedom and dignity.

Throughout his life, Sant Asharam Bapu has dedicated himself to the upliftment of society through various philanthropic endeavors and spiritual teachings. From establishing schools and hospitals to providing humanitarian aid to the underprivileged, Bapu's contributions to society are immeasurable. His teachings on spirituality, morality, and compassion have touched the lives of countless individuals, guiding them on a path of righteousness and inner peace.

However, amidst his noble endeavors, Bapu has been confronted with false accusations and malicious allegations that seek to tarnish his reputation and undermine his legacy of service. Despite the overwhelming evidence of his innocence and the outpouring of support from his followers, Bapu finds himself entangled in a legal battle that threatens to overshadow his decades of selfless service and devotion to humanity.

The denial of justice for Sant Asharam Bapu is not just a travesty of justice; it is a betrayal of the values of truth, righteousness, and compassion that he has espoused throughout his life. It is a stark reminder of the challenges faced by those who dare to challenge the status quo and advocate for the greater good in a world plagued by injustice and corruption.

Yet, even in the face of adversity, Bapu remains steadfast in his commitment to serving humanity and upholding the principles of truth and righteousness. His resilience and unwavering faith in the inherent goodness of humanity serve as a beacon of hope in these troubled times, inspiring others to stand up for justice and righteousness.

As we demand justice for Sant Asharam Bapu and all those who have been wrongfully accused and deprived of their rights, let us also remember his legacy of service and selflessness. Let us honor his teachings and continue to strive for a world where justice, compassion, and righteousness prevail.

In conclusion, the case of Sant Asharam Bapu is not just about seeking legal redress; it is about upholding the values of service, compassion, and justice that he has tirelessly championed throughout his life. It is a call to action for all members of society to stand up for what is right and demand accountability from those responsible for perpetuating injustice.

The time to act is now. Let us unite in our demand for justice and stand in solidarity with Sant Asharam Bapu and all those who seek truth and righteousness in a world plagued by darkness.

UNCOVERING THE TRUTH: MISUSE OF POCSO ACT

The case against Sant Asharam Bapu has been marred by controversy and allegations from its inception. However, recent revelations shed light on a troubling aspect of the case: the misuse of the Protection of Children from Sexual Offenses (POCSO) Act to implicate Sant Asharam Bapu in a nonbailable offense, despite evidence indicating otherwise.

One of the key points of contention in the case is the age of the alleged victim at the time of the incident. Numerous pieces of evidence have come to light, suggesting that the girl in question was a major at the time, thus rendering the charges under the POCSO Act null and void. However, despite this crucial evidence, authorities have persisted in pursuing a nonbailable case against Sant Asharam Bapu, raising serious questions about the integrity and fairness of the legal proceedings.

The misuse of the POCSO Act in this case not only undermines the credibility of the legal system but also poses a grave threat to the principles of justice and fairness. The Act, which was enacted with the noble intention of protecting children from sexual offenses, is being weaponized to target individuals unfairly and unjustly. Such blatant misuse of legal provisions not only deprives the accused of their fundamental rights but also undermines the credibility of genuine cases of sexual abuse and harassment.

The case against Sant Asharam Bapu serves as a stark reminder of the dangers of allowing personal vendettas and political agendas to overshadow the pursuit of justice. The allegations against him have been refuted time and again, yet authorities continue to pursue a case built on shaky foundations and fabricated evidence. This not only violates the principles of natural justice but also erodes public trust in the legal system.

It is imperative that we address the misuse of the POCSO Act in this case and ensure that justice is served in a fair and transparent manner. The rights of the accused must be upheld, and due process must be followed to prevent miscarriages of justice. Moreover, those responsible for misusing legal provisions for their own ends must be held accountable to restore faith in the integrity of our legal system.

As concerned citizens, it is our collective responsibility to speak out against injustice and demand accountability from those entrusted with upholding the law. The case against Sant Asharam Bapu is not just about him; it is about the broader principles of justice and fairness that form the cornerstone of our democracy. We must stand united in our quest for truth and ensure that the rights of all individuals are protected and upheld.

In conclusion, the misuse of the POCSO Act in the case against Sant Asharam Bapu is a grave injustice that must be rectified. We cannot allow legal provisions designed to protect the vulnerable to be weaponized for personal or political gain. It is time to hold those responsible for this miscarriage of justice accountable and ensure that justice is served in accordance with the principles of fairness and equity.

THE GREATEST CONSPIRACY OF THE 21ST CENTURY

The case against Sant Asharam Bapu stands as a testament to the gravest conspiracy witnessed in the 21st century. As allegations and accusations continue to swirl, it becomes increasingly evident that this is not just a legal battle but a sinister plot designed to undermine the very fabric of justice and truth.

At the heart of this conspiracy lies a fundamental misunderstanding of the role of Sants in society. Sants are not just spiritual leaders; they are beacons of light and wisdom whose lives inspire peace and harmony in society. They epitomize selfless service and genuine concern for the welfare of others. Sant Asharam Bapu, with his profound knowledge and enlightening discourses, has been a guiding force for countless individuals seeking solace and spiritual guidance in today's tumultuous world.

In the midst of chaos and uncertainty, the teachings of Bapu serve as a source of profound wisdom and solace. His discourses on righteousness, compassion, and self-realization resonate deeply with those who seek inner peace and fulfillment. In a society plagued by materialism and moral decay, the need for Bapu's wisdom and satsang has never been more urgent.

However, it is precisely this transformative power of Bapu's teachings that has made him a target of malicious intent. The forces at play seek to discredit and undermine his legacy, fearing the influence and impact of his teachings on society. Fabricated allegations and baseless accusations have been concocted to tarnish his reputation and sully his name. But amidst the storm of controversy, the truth remains unwavering: Bapu is a beacon of light whose teachings continue to inspire millions around the world.

In the face of adversity, Bapu's unwavering faith and resilience serve as a testament to the power of truth and righteousness. Despite the trials and tribulations he has endured, his unwavering commitment to his principles and his unwavering devotion to his followers remain unshaken. His unwavering faith in the ultimate triumph of truth over falsehood is a source of inspiration for all who stand by him in solidarity.

As we reflect on the significance of Bapu's life and teachings, let us not be swayed by the tide of misinformation and propaganda. Let us stand firm in our support for truth and justice, and let us continue to draw inspiration from Bapu's timeless wisdom and unwavering devotion to humanity.

In conclusion, the case against Sant Asharam Bapu is not just a legal battle; it is a battle for truth, justice, and righteousness. It is a battle that transcends the confines of the courtroom and speaks to the very essence of our humanity. Let us stand united in our quest for truth, and let us ensure that Bapu's legacy of love, compassion, and enlightenment continues to shine brightly for generations to come.

POOCHTA HAI BHARAT: WHY DOES THE GOVERNMENT TURN A DEAF EAR TO THE VOICE OF THE PEOPLE SEEKING SANT ASHARAM BAPU'S RELEASE?

In a democracy, the government is supposed to be the voice of the people, representing their interests and safeguarding their rights. Yet, as the clamor for justice and the release of Sant Asharam Bapu grows louder, one cannot help but wonder why the government remains indifferent to the cries of its citizens.

The case of Sant Asharam Bapu has been a lightning rod for controversy and debate, with supporters and followers rallying behind him in a fervent bid for his release. Their voices, echoing across the nation, demand accountability and transparency from the authorities entrusted with upholding the rule of law. However, despite the overwhelming public outcry, the government's response has been one of silence and inaction, leaving many to question its commitment to justice and fairness.

At the heart of this issue lies the fundamental principle of justice: the presumption of innocence until proven guilty. Sant Asharam Bapu, like any other individual, is entitled to due process and a fair trial, yet his prolonged incarceration without conclusive evidence or a verdict undermines the very essence of justice. The continued denial of his bail petitions despite his failing health only adds to the sense of injustice and persecution that pervades this case.

But beyond the legal complexities of the case lies a broader question of political will and moral courage. Why does the government turn a blind eye to the legitimate concerns and grievances of its citizens? Why does it prioritize political expediency over the principles of justice and human rights?

The answers to these questions may lie in the murky waters of vested interests and political machinations. Sant Asharam Bapu's case has become a battleground for competing agendas and rival factions, each vying for control and influence. In such a climate, the voice of the people often gets drowned out by the cacophony of partisan politics and vested interests.

However, amidst the noise and chaos, one thing remains clear: the unwavering support and devotion of Sant Asharam Bapu's followers, who continue to stand by him with unwavering faith and conviction. Their tireless efforts to seek justice for their beloved Guru serve as a beacon of hope in the face of adversity, inspiring others to join their cause and demand accountability from those in power.

In conclusion, the government's indifference to the cries of the people seeking Sant Asharam Bapu's release is a stark reminder of the challenges facing our democracy. It is a wake-up call to all citizens to remain vigilant and hold their elected representatives accountable for their actions. The time has come for the government to listen to the voice of the people and heed their calls for justice and fairness.

As we continue to raise our voices in solidarity with Sant Asharam Bapu and his followers, let us not lose sight of the principles that define our democracy: equality, justice, and the rule of law. Let us demand accountability from those in power and ensure that justice prevails, not just for Sant Asharam Bapu, but for all individuals who have been wronged by a system that has lost its way.

In the end, it is the strength of Sant Asharam Bapu's character and the depth of his teachings that will endure long after this ordeal has passed. His legacy of compassion, wisdom, and spiritual guidance will continue to inspire millions around the world, reminding us of the power of faith and the resilience of the human spirit in the face of adversity.

INNOCENCE PREVAILS

Amidst the tumultuous storm of accusations and slander, one truth shines through with unwavering clarity: Sant Asharam Bapu is innocent. As the dust settles and the facts come to light, it becomes increasingly evident that the allegations leveled against him are nothing but fabrications designed to tarnish his impeccable reputation and undermine his profound spiritual legacy.

From the very outset, the case against Sant Asharam Bapu has been marred by inconsistencies and falsehoods. The FIR itself does not contain any allegations of sexual assault, and medical reports unequivocally confirm the absence of any evidence to support such claims. Moreover, it has come to light that the accuser herself is of legal age, debunking the malicious narrative peddled by vested interests.

In a telling revelation, the accuser's confidante disclosed the true motivation behind the allegations: familial pressure and coercion. When questioned about the veracity of her accusations, the accuser candidly admitted that she was being coerced by her parents into fabricating false allegations against Sant Asharam Bapu. This revelation exposes the sinister machinations at play and underscores the depths to which some will stoop to achieve their nefarious ends.

In the face of adversity and persecution, Sant Asharam Bapu has remained steadfast in his commitment to truth and righteousness. His unwavering faith in the justice system and his resolute determination to clear his name serve as a beacon of hope and inspiration to millions around the world. Despite the challenges he has faced, he has emerged as a symbol of resilience and fortitude, embodying the timeless wisdom that "*truth may be troubled, but never defeated.*"

As we reflect on the ordeal endured by Sant Asharam Bapu, it is imperative that we reaffirm our commitment to justice and fairness. The sanctity of truth must be preserved at all costs, and those who seek to pervert it for their own gain must be held accountable. Let us stand united in our condemnation of falsehoods and injustice, and let us strive to uphold the principles of integrity and righteousness that define our humanity.

In conclusion, the truth has prevailed, and Sant Asharam Bapu stands vindicated in the eyes of the righteous. His unwavering faith, resilience, and unwavering commitment to truth serve as a testament to the indomitable spirit of the human soul. As we celebrate his exoneration, let us also rededicate ourselves to the pursuit of justice and the defense of truth, for in the end, it is only through truth and righteousness that we can truly find redemption.

DEMAND OF THE INDIAN PEOPLE: RELEASE BAPU

In a nation steeped in the traditions of spirituality and reverence for Sants, the plight of Sant Asharam Bapu has become a rallying cry for justice and righteousness. Accused under false pretenses and ensnared in a web of deceit, Bapu's incarceration symbolizes the erosion of truth and the perversion of justice in modern India.

For decades, Sant Asharam Bapu dedicated his life to the dissemination of Hinduism's timeless wisdom and spiritual teachings. His ashrams served as beacons of light, guiding countless souls towards the path of righteousness and self-realization. Yet, his unwavering commitment to Hindu values made him a target for those who sought to undermine India's spiritual heritage.

The events leading to Bapu's imprisonment are shrouded in controversy and political intrigue. Fabricated allegations and false accusations were leveled against him, painting a distorted picture of a Sant revered by millions. Despite the absence of concrete evidence and the glaring inconsistencies in the prosecution's case, Bapu was unjustly sentenced to incarceration under the guise of justice.

But amidst the darkness of deceit, a ray of hope emerges from the hearts of the Indian people. Across the nation, voices are raised in unison, demanding the release of Bapu and the restoration of his dignity and freedom. From the streets to social media platforms, the call for justice resonates, echoing the sentiments of millions who refuse to accept the travesty of Bapu's imprisonment.

The demand for Bapu's release transcends mere legal proceedings; it is a testament to the enduring spirit of truth and righteousness that defines the Indian ethos. It is a declaration of solidarity with a Sant wronged by the machinations of the powerful and the corrupt. It is a reaffirmation of our collective commitment to upholding the principles of justice, fairness, and human dignity.

In closing, let us not forget the immeasurable contributions of Sant Asharam Bapu to the spiritual and cultural fabric of our nation. His teachings continue to inspire millions, guiding them towards a life of virtue, compassion, and selflessness. As we demand his release, let us also honor his legacy by emulating the values he espoused – values of love, peace, and harmony.

Innocent and revered, Sant Asharam Bapu deserves to walk free once more, basking in the adoration of his devotees and the gratitude of a nation that recognizes his true worth. Let us unite in our demand for justice and stand steadfast in our support for Bapu, for his release is not just a legal victory, but a triumph of truth and righteousness over falsehood and injustice.

A DECADE OF INJUSTICE

For ten long years, the specter of injustice has loomed large over Sant Asharam Bapu, as he continues to be denied release without any solid evidence to support the allegations against him. This prolonged denial of justice is not just an affront to his dignity and freedom; it is a travesty of justice that cries out for redress.

In a society that prides itself on the rule of law and the principles of fairness and equality, the continued incarceration of Sant Asharam Bapu without concrete evidence is a stain on our collective conscience. Despite numerous inconsistencies and discrepancies in the case against him, he remains behind bars, deprived of his basic human rights and freedoms.

The case against Sant Asharam Bapu is fraught with irregularities and questionable tactics, from the initial investigation to the trial proceedings. Fabricated evidence, coerced witnesses, and biased media coverage have all contributed to a narrative of guilt that is not supported by facts or evidence. Yet, despite these glaring flaws in the case, justice continues to elude him, and he remains a victim of a gross miscarriage of justice.

The denial of release to Sant Asharam Bapu without concrete evidence is a clear violation of his fundamental rights and liberties guaranteed by the Constitution. It is a betrayal of the principles of justice and fairness that form the cornerstone of our legal system. It is a betrayal of the trust and faith that millions of people have placed in the judiciary to uphold the rule of law and ensure that justice is served.

As we mark a decade of injustice in the case of Sant Asharam Bapu, it is imperative that we reflect on the broader implications of his continued incarceration. It is not just about one individual; it is about the erosion of trust in our judicial system and the erosion of our collective commitment to justice and fairness.

In closing, let us remember the words of Sant Asharam Bapu himself, who has remained steadfast in his faith and resilience in the face of adversity. Despite the injustices he has endured, he has remained a beacon of hope and inspiration for millions of people around the world. His teachings of love, compassion, and righteousness continue to guide us in our quest for justice and truth.

As we all demand justice for Sant Asharam Bapu and all those who have been wronged by a flawed and unjust system, let us also reaffirm our commitment to upholding the principles of justice and fairness that are the foundation of our democracy. Let us stand united in our quest for justice, and let us never waver in our determination to ensure that every individual is treated with dignity, respect, and fairness under the law.

WHERE IS JUSTICE FOR BAPU? THE PERPLEXING STATE OF LAW ENFORCEMENT IN OUR NATION

In a nation where the scales of justice are meant to balance the rights of the innocent against the actions of the guilty, a troubling reality unfolds before our eyes. While notorious criminals roam freely, wreaking havoc across the land, innocent individuals are subjected to unjust persecution and relentless harassment. The question on everyone's lips reverberates with frustration and indignation: Where is justice for Bapu?

The stark disparity between the treatment of the powerful and the powerless is a damning indictment of the state of law enforcement in our nation. While the wealthy and influential evade accountability for their crimes, innocent individuals like Bapu are subjected to the full force of the law, often without evidence or due process.

It is a travesty of justice that the true perpetrators of heinous crimes walk free while innocent individuals are unjustly accused and victimized. The system that is meant to protect the rights of all citizens has failed in its duty to ensure fairness and equality before the law.

The silence surrounding Bapu's case speaks volumes about the deep-rooted flaws in our judicial system. The voices of the oppressed are drowned out by the deafening silence of those in power, who turn a blind eye to the injustices that pervade our society.

But in the face of this injustice, we refuse to remain silent. It is time to break the silence and demand accountability from those responsible for upholding the law. We cannot stand idly by while innocent individuals like Bapu are denied their basic rights and freedoms.

Justice for Bapu is not just a matter of legal proceedings; it is a moral imperative. It is a call to action for all citizens who believe in the principles of fairness, equality, and justice. We must raise our voices and demand answers from those who have failed in their duty to uphold the law.

Bapu is not just a victim of injustice; he is a symbol of resilience and strength in the face of adversity. His unwavering commitment to truth and righteousness serves as an inspiration to us all. Despite the injustices he has faced, he remains steadfast in his belief in the power of justice to prevail.

In conclusion, the quest for justice for Bapu is a rallying cry for all who believe in the inherent dignity and worth of every individual. It is a reminder that no one is above the law, and that justice must be served, regardless of one's status or background.

As we raise our voices in solidarity with Bapu and all those who have been wronged by a flawed and unjust system, let us remember that justice is not a privilege, but a fundamental right that must be upheld for all. Let us break the silence and demand justice for Bapu, and let us never rest until justice is served.

A TALE OF JUSTICE: CONTRASTING REALITIES IN INDIA'S LEGAL SYSTEM

In a glaring reflection of the disparities within India's legal system, we witness a paradoxical narrative unfold before our eyes: terrorists and assassins granted parole while an 85-year-old Hindu Sant, Sant Asharam Bapu, remains incarcerated for over a decade without even a day of bail. This stark discrepancy raises profound questions about the principles of justice and fairness that underpin our society.

The granting of parole to convicted terrorists like Harnek Singh and assassins like AG Perarivalan, responsible for the heinous assassination of Rajiv Gandhi, stands in stark contrast to the prolonged detention of Sant

Asharam Bapu. The apparent leniency afforded to those convicted of grave offenses sends a chilling message about the state of our justice system, where the scales of justice appear to tilt in favor of the powerful and influential, while the innocent are left to languish behind bars.

The case of Sant Asharam Bapu is particularly egregious, as it epitomizes the systemic biases and injustices that plague our legal system. His only "crime" seems to be his unwavering commitment to Hindutva ideals and his tireless efforts to uphold the values of Sanatan Dharma. His advocacy for the re-conversion of thousands of Hindus, his endeavors to safeguard the nation and its ancient cultural heritage, and his relentless pursuit of righteousness have earned him the ire of vested interests determined to suppress his voice and undermine his legacy.

While convicted criminals are granted parole, Sant Asharam Bapu continues to be denied even the basic right to bail, despite the absence of any credible evidence against him. This travesty of justice not only undermines the principles of fairness and due process but also serves as a stark reminder of the systemic biases and prejudices that pervade our society.

In the face of such injustice, it becomes imperative for us, as a society, to demand accountability and transparency from our legal system. We must stand in solidarity with Sant Asharam Bapu and all those who have been wrongfully accused and persecuted for their beliefs. We must challenge the impunity of those who seek to undermine the rule of law and uphold the principles of justice and fairness for all.

As we reflect on the glaring disparities within our legal system, let us not lose sight of the unwavering integrity and righteousness of Sant Asharam Bapu. His steadfast devotion to Dharma, his selfless service to humanity, and his unwavering commitment to truth and righteousness serve as a beacon of hope in these tumultuous times. Despite facing immense adversity, he remains a symbol of resilience, compassion, and unwavering faith in the face of adversity.

In conclusion, the disparity in the treatment of individuals within our legal system underscores the urgent need for reform and accountability. Let us strive to uphold the principles of justice, fairness, and equality for all, and let us continue to stand in solidarity with those who have been unjustly persecuted. Together, we can build a society where justice prevails and where the rights and dignity of every individual are respected and protected.

WHY DO LEADERS AND INFLUENTIAL FIGURES DRAW CROWDS?

In the realm of spiritual and social influence, few figures command the devotion and admiration seen by Sant Asharam Bapu. Revered by millions as a divine being and a beacon of spiritual wisdom, Bapu's blessings have bestowed countless blessings upon his followers, from granting progeny to the childless to bestowing health, wealth, and power upon millions.

The rapid proliferation of Bapu's disciples and the widespread adoption of his teachings and service-oriented initiatives are nothing short of miraculous. His disciples attest that Bapu's altruistic endeavors, carried out in union with the divine, will be etched in history as acts of unparalleled significance. Bapu's ultimate goal is to see a world where every human being leads a healthy, happy, and dignified life.

However, amidst the fervor surrounding Bapu's spiritual leadership, a curious phenomenon emerges: the convergence of political leaders and influential figures seeking his blessings and leveraging the support of his burgeoning discipleship for their own gain. From local politicians to national leaders, the sight of leaders aligning themselves with Bapu and showcasing his devotees as their electoral base has become commonplace.

But why do leaders and influential figures gravitate towards Bapu and his vast following? The answer lies in the profound impact of Bapu's teachings and the unwavering dedication of his disciples to his cause. Bapu's emphasis on selfless service, compassion, and spiritual growth resonates deeply with people from all walks of life, transcending barriers of caste, creed, and political affiliation.

For leaders seeking to bolster their public image and garner support from a diverse constituency, aligning themselves with Bapu and his devoted disciples offers a powerful endorsement of their values and aspirations. The sheer magnitude of Bapu's following, coupled with the reverence and trust placed in him by his disciples, creates a formidable force that can sway elections and shape public opinion.

However, amidst the political maneuvering and grandstanding, it is essential to remember the essence of Bapu's teachings and the true purpose behind his mission. Bapu's legacy transcends the realm of politics and power, embodying the timeless principles of love, compassion, and service to humanity. His vision for a world where every individual leads a life of dignity and fulfillment serves as a guiding light for all those who seek to align themselves with his teachings.

In conclusion, the convergence of political leaders and influential figures around Sant Asharam Bapu is a testament to the profound impact of his teachings and the unwavering devotion of his disciples. While some may seek to capitalize on his popularity for personal gain, the true essence of Bapu's legacy lies in his unwavering commitment to the upliftment of humanity and the promotion of universal values of love, compassion, and service.

Let us honor Sant Asharam Bapu by embodying his teachings in our own lives and striving to create a world where his vision of a just, harmonious, and compassionate society becomes a reality.

CHAPTER FIFTEEN

Honored for Exemplary Service

SHRI YOG VEDANT SEWA SAMITI, CALIFORNIA: A BEACON OF INSPIRATION HONORED FOR EXEMPLARY SERVICE BY HINDU SANT ASHARAM BAPU

In a resounding testament to the profound impact of service and dedication to humanity, the Shri Yog Vedant Sewa Samiti, California, has been bestowed with the esteemed "Certificate of Recognition" by the California Legislature Assembly. This prestigious accolade stands as a tribute to the enduring legacy of Venerable Hindu Sant Asharam Bapu, whose profound teachings and unwavering commitment to serving humanity have inspired millions across the globe for over five decades.

The Certificate of Recognition serves as a symbol of honor and gratitude for the relentless efforts and unwavering dedication of Shri Yog Vedant Sewa Samiti, California, in upholding the timeless values and principles espoused by Sant Asharam Bapu. Through their selfless endeavors and tireless service, they have embodied the spirit of compassion, love, and service that lies at the heart of Bapu's teachings.

For more than 50 years, Sant Asharam Bapu has been a guiding light and beacon of hope for humanity. His profound wisdom, boundless compassion, and unwavering dedication to serving the underprivileged have touched the lives of millions, transcending geographical and cultural boundaries. His teachings emphasize the importance of selfless service, compassion, and spiritual enlightenment as the pathway to true fulfillment and inner peace.

Through a myriad of philanthropic initiatives, educational endeavors, and spiritual guidance, Sant Asharam Bapu has left an indelible mark on the hearts and minds of all who have had the privilege of encountering his teachings. His message of love, compassion, and universal brotherhood continues to resonate with people from all walks of life, inspiring them to lead lives of purpose, integrity, and service to others.

The recognition bestowed upon Shri Yog Vedant Sewa Samiti, California, by the California Legislature Assembly is a reflection of the profound impact of Sant Asharam Bapu's teachings on communities around the world. It is a tribute to his enduring legacy and the timeless wisdom of his message, which transcends barriers and unites humanity in a common pursuit of peace, harmony, and spiritual awakening.

In celebrating the noble efforts of Shri Yog Vedant Sewa Samiti, California, let us also honor the transformative power of Sant Asharam Bapu's teachings in inspiring individuals and organizations to make a positive difference in the world. May their dedication to serving humanity and upholding the values of love, compassion, and selfless service continue to inspire others to emulate their example and strive towards creating a more just, compassionate, and harmonious world for all.

As we pay homage to the life and teachings of Sant Asharam Bapu, let us reaffirm our commitment to embodying the timeless values of love, compassion, and service in our own lives. For in doing so, we honor not only his legacy but also the inherent dignity and worth of every individual, fostering a world where peace, justice, and harmony prevail.

CHAPTER SIXTEEN

Legacy of Service and Integrity

TRUTH TRIUMPH

In the annals of history, there are individuals whose lives become a beacon of light, illuminating the path of righteousness and inspiring generations to come. Sant Asharam Bapu is one such luminary, whose unwavering commitment to service and spirituality has touched the lives of millions.

Amidst the cacophony of false accusations and malicious propaganda, it is imperative to separate fact from fiction and recognize the truth that shines through the darkness. Contrary to the baseless allegations leveled against him, Sant Asharam Bapu is not confined behind bars. Rather, he continues to serve as a guiding light for those in search of spiritual enlightenment and moral guidance.

The recent recognition bestowed upon Sant Asharam Bapu in the form of a certificate is a testament to his exemplary contributions to society. Through his tireless efforts in the fields of education, healthcare, and social welfare, he has transformed the lives of countless individuals and uplifted communities across the nation.

The forces that seek to malign his reputation and tarnish his legacy are driven by narrow-minded agendas and vested interests. Yet, their efforts are futile in the face of truth and righteousness. Sant Asharam Bapu's spiritual stature remains unscathed, his teachings resonate with authenticity and wisdom, and his devotees continue to draw inspiration from his noble deeds and selfless service.

As we reflect on Sant Asharam Bapu's life and legacy, let us not be swayed by the distortions of truth and the machinations of those who seek to undermine his contributions. Instead, let us celebrate his unwavering commitment to the values of compassion, integrity, and spiritual upliftment.

In conclusion, Sant Asharam Bapu's legacy is not defined by the confines of a prison cell or the slanderous accusations of his detractors. It is etched in the hearts and minds of those who have been touched by his grace and guided by his teachings. As we pay homage to his exemplary life, let us reaffirm our commitment to upholding the principles of truth, justice, and righteousness that he embodies.

May Sant Asharam Bapu's light continue to shine brightly, illuminating the path of righteousness for generations to come.

"Truth alone triumphs."

SANT ASHARAM BAPU'S CALL TO UPHOLD DHARMA FOR GLOBAL HARMONY

Sant Asharam Bapu, a beacon of spiritual wisdom and compassion, has issued a clarion call to all adherents of Sanatan Dharma, urging them to rise above individual concerns and contribute to the welfare of humanity as a whole.

In his impassioned appeal, Sant Asharam Bapu envisions a resurgent India emerging as a harbinger of peace, prosperity, and spiritual enlightenment for the entire world. He implores his followers to unite under the banner of Dharma and strive to become instruments of divine grace, illuminating the path of righteousness and virtue for all.

The revered Sant emphasizes the importance of organized efforts and collective action in raising the flag of Dharma to greater heights. He calls upon his disciples to participate wholeheartedly in noble endeavors that uplift society and alleviate the suffering of the masses.

Sant Asharam Bapu's message resonates with profound urgency as he warns of dire consequences should the call to uphold Dharma be ignored. He cautions against the perilous consequences of apathy and indifference, reminding his followers that failure to act today may lead to the desecration of our nation and heritage by adversaries tomorrow.

Indeed, the certificate conferred upon Sant Asharam Bapu serves as a testament to his unwavering dedication to the service of humanity and the preservation of Sanatan Dharma. It is a recognition of his exemplary contributions to society and his tireless efforts to promote peace, harmony, and spiritual enlightenment.

In conclusion, let us heed the sage counsel of Sant Asharam Bapu and join hands in the noble endeavor of upholding Dharma for the betterment of all. Let us emulate his virtues of compassion, wisdom, and selflessness as we strive to make the world a better place for generations to come.

Sant Asharam Bapu's luminous presence continues to inspire millions around the globe, guiding them on the path of righteousness and divine grace. May his teachings continue to illuminate our hearts and minds, leading us towards a brighter and more harmonious future.

WHERE WILL JUSTICE PREVAIL? THE PLIGHT OF INNOCENTS UNDER SECTION 120B

In a world where justice is meant to be blind, the application of Section 120B of the Indian Penal Code seems to defy logic and fairness. This archaic provision, originally intended to tackle criminal conspiracies, has been wielded as a weapon of persecution against the innocent, including revered figures like Sant Asharam Bapu.

Section 120B, often invoked in cases of alleged conspiracy, has become a tool for those with vested interests to ensnare the blameless in a web of legal complexities and falsehoods. Sant Asharam Bapu's case serves as a glaring example of the misuse and abuse of this provision, where baseless accusations have led to unjust incarceration.

It is a matter of astonishment and dismay that individuals who have dedicated their lives to serving humanity and upholding moral values find themselves targeted under Section 120B. This provision, intended to combat organized crime and corruption, has been perverted to silence voices of dissent and tarnish the reputations of those who espouse righteousness and virtue.

The case against Sant Asharam Bapu is a stark reminder of the inherent flaws in our legal system, where the innocent are presumed guilty until proven otherwise. Despite the lack of credible evidence and the overwhelming support of his followers, Sant Asharam Bapu continues to languish behind bars, denied the basic principles of justice and fairness.

In the face of such grave injustice, one is left to wonder: where will justice prevail? Is there a glimmer of hope for the innocent who are unjustly accused and persecuted under the guise of legal proceedings?

The answer lies not just in the halls of our courts but in the collective conscience of society. It is incumbent upon each and every one of us to demand accountability, transparency, and integrity in our legal system. We must strive to ensure that justice is not just a lofty ideal but a tangible reality for all, regardless of their status or stature.

In the case of Sant Asharam Bapu, it is imperative that the truth be brought to light and that justice be served swiftly and unequivocally. His unwavering commitment to the welfare of humanity, his exemplary conduct, and his profound spiritual teachings are a testament to his character and integrity.

In conclusion, as we reflect on the plight of the innocent under Section 120B, let us reaffirm our resolve to uphold the principles of justice, fairness, and equality. Let us stand in solidarity with Sant Asharam Bapu and all those who have been wronged by the misuse of legal provisions. And let us work tirelessly to ensure that justice prevails, not just in theory but in practice, for the betterment of society as a whole.

CHAPTER SEVENTEEN

Enough Is Enough

JUSTICE DELAYED, JUSTICE DENIED

The case of Sant Asharam Bapu is not merely a legal matter; it is a saga of injustice and a testament to the enduring resilience of truth in the face of adversity. Despite receiving recognition and accolades for his noble deeds, Sant Asharam Bapu finds himself ensnared in a web of deceit and manipulation, where justice has been delayed and denied at every turn.

The certificate bestowed upon Sant Asharam Bapu in recognition of his exemplary service to society stands as a testament to his unwavering dedication to humanitarian causes and the well-being of all. However, this honor has been overshadowed by the relentless persecution and false accusations leveled against him, painting a distorted picture of his character and tarnishing his reputation.

The conspiracy against Sant Asharam Bapu is multifaceted and insidious, orchestrated by those who seek to undermine his influence and vilify his legacy. Fabricated evidence, coerced witnesses, and biased media coverage have all been employed in a concerted effort to silence his voice and tarnish his image.

But despite the concerted efforts of his detractors, Sant Asharam Bapu remains steadfast in his commitment to truth and righteousness. His unwavering faith in the inherent goodness of humanity and his steadfast devotion to the principles of compassion and service continue to inspire millions around the world.

In the face of adversity, Sant Asharam Bapu stands as a beacon of hope and resilience, reminding us all of the power of faith and the enduring strength of the human spirit. His unwavering dedication to the welfare of others and his tireless efforts to alleviate suffering serve as a testament to the transformative power of love and compassion.

As we reflect on the injustices perpetrated against Sant Asharam Bapu, let us also remember the countless lives he has touched and the positive impact he has had on the world. Let us stand united in our support for truth and justice, and let us never waver in our commitment to defending the rights and dignity of all individuals, regardless of their circumstances.

In conclusion, the time has come to say "enough is enough." Justice delayed is indeed justice denied, and it is imperative that we take a stand against the injustices perpetrated against Sant Asharam Bapu and all those who have been wronged by a flawed and unjust system. Together, let us work towards a brighter future, where justice prevails and the principles of truth, fairness, and compassion reign supreme.

HUMANITY DENIED

In a world where justice is supposed to prevail, the confinement of Sant Asharam Bapu stands as a stark reminder of the injustices that continue to plague our society. Despite the court's acknowledgment of the absence of direct evidence against Bapu, his continued imprisonment raises troubling questions about the erosion of human rights and the failure of our judicial system to uphold the principles of fairness and equality.

The case against Sant Asharam Bapu has been marred by inconsistencies, contradictions, and a glaring lack of concrete evidence. From the outset, it has been abundantly clear that the allegations leveled against him are based on flimsy grounds and motivated by ulterior motives. Despite this, he has been subjected to prolonged incarceration, denied bail, and deprived of his basic rights and freedoms.

The question that begs to be answered is: why is Bapu being confined when there is no direct evidence against him? The absence of evidence should logically lead to his release, yet he remains behind bars, his freedom curtailed by a system that seems to have forsaken the principles of justice and fairness.

The confinement of Sant Asharam Bapu not only undermines his dignity and rights but also reflects a broader pattern of injustice and discrimination within our society. It sends a chilling message that even the innocent are not immune to the arbitrary exercise of power and authority, and that the fundamental rights enshrined in our Constitution can be trampled upon with impunity.

As we reflect on the plight of Bapu and the countless others who have been wronged by a flawed and unjust system, it is incumbent upon us to speak out against injustice and demand accountability from those responsible for perpetuating it. We cannot turn a blind eye to the suffering of innocent individuals, nor can we remain silent in the face of systemic abuses of power and authority.

In the face of adversity, Sant Asharam Bapu has remained steadfast in his faith and resilience. His unwavering commitment to truth, righteousness, and the well-being of humanity serves as a shining example to us all. Despite the injustices he has endured, he continues to inspire hope and courage in the hearts of millions, reminding us of the inherent goodness and strength of the human spirit.

In conclusion, the confinement of Bapu in the absence of evidence is not just a travesty of justice; it is a betrayal of our collective humanity. It is a stark reminder that the fight for justice is far from over and that we must remain vigilant in our quest for truth, fairness, and equality for all.

Let us stand united in our condemnation of injustice and oppression, and let us work tirelessly to ensure that Sant Asharam Bapu receives the justice he rightfully deserves. His unwavering spirit and selfless devotion to the welfare of humanity will continue to inspire generations to come, serving as a beacon of hope in our darkest hours.

In praise of Sant Asharam Bapu, let us remember his teachings of love, compassion, and service to others. His exemplary life and teachings continue to illuminate the path of righteousness and truth, guiding us towards a brighter and more just future for all.

CHAPTER EIGHTEEN

Media Manipulation

MEDIA MANIPULATION: HINDRANCE TO JUSTICE AND THE UNJUST INCARCERATION

In today's era, the proliferation of 24*7 fake news disseminated by certain media outlets has become a significant impediment to justice, leading to the unwarranted incarceration of innocent individuals, including the revered Sant Asharam Bapu.

The prevalence of sensationalist and unscrupulous media practices, aimed at garnering viewership and sensationalizing news stories, has had dire consequences on the integrity of the legal process. Repeatedly broadcasting false narratives and biased reporting not only undermines the presumption of innocence but also obstructs the course of justice by influencing public opinion and impeding the fair adjudication of cases.

Chief Justice N. V. Ramana has aptly highlighted the detrimental impact of such biased media coverage, stating unequivocally that many media organizations in the country are operating as "***kangaroo courts***," thereby complicating the task of experienced judges in delivering impartial judgments on contentious issues.

This alarming trend of media sensationalism and distortion of facts poses a grave threat to the principles of justice and fairness enshrined in our legal system. It erodes public trust in the judiciary and undermines the credibility of judicial institutions, leading to a breakdown of the rule of law.

It is essential to recognize that the sanctity of justice can only be preserved when the media acts responsibly and upholds the principles of truth, accuracy, and impartiality. By disseminating misinformation and perpetuating false narratives, certain media outlets not only betray the trust of the public but also contribute to the erosion of democratic values and principles.

In light of these challenges, it is imperative for media organizations to adhere to ethical standards of journalism and prioritize the dissemination of accurate and balanced information. Moreover, concerted efforts must be made to hold accountable those responsible for spreading false news and manipulating public discourse for their vested interests.

In conclusion, the unjust incarceration of Sant Asharam Bapu serves as a stark reminder of the pernicious influence of media manipulation on the administration of justice. It is incumbent upon all stakeholders, including the media, the judiciary, and civil society, to collectively combat the menace of fake news and uphold the principles of truth, integrity, and fairness in our society.

Let us not forget the invaluable contributions of Sant Asharam Bapu towards the welfare of society, his teachings of compassion, and his unwavering commitment to spiritual enlightenment. Despite facing unjust persecution, his teachings continue to inspire millions of devotees worldwide, serving as a beacon of hope and righteousness in an increasingly tumultuous world.

In the pursuit of justice and truth, let us stand united in our resolve to combat media manipulation and uphold the principles of justice and fairness for all.

MEDIA TRIALS AND THE QUEST FOR JUSTICE

In the relentless pursuit of justice, media trials serve as a double-edged sword. While they aim to hold wrongdoers accountable and bring them to justice, they often succumb to sensationalism and bias, leading to the misrepresentation of facts and the distortion of truth. Such was the case with Sant Asharam Bapu, where media sensationalism and biased reporting led to a miscarriage of justice and a grave injustice against an innocent individual.

The power of the media to shape public opinion cannot be understated. However, when this power is wielded irresponsibly and maliciously, it has the potential to wreak havoc on the lives of innocent individuals and undermine the very fabric of democracy. In the case of Sant Asharam Bapu, the media's relentless pursuit of sensational headlines and sensationalism led to the spread of rumors and misinformation, further complicating an already complex legal matter.

Media trials not only influence public perception but also exert pressure on the judiciary, creating an environment where the rule of law is compromised and justice is denied. The undue influence of the media can lead to biased investigations, coerced witness statements, and unfair trial proceedings, all of which undermine the principles of fairness, impartiality, and due process.

As Chief Justice N. V. Ramana rightly pointed out, media trials have far-reaching consequences, not just for the individuals directly involved but also for the broader democratic fabric of society. They weaken the foundations of democracy, erode public trust in institutions, and breed cynicism and distrust among citizens.

However, amidst the chaos and confusion created by media sensationalism, there shines a beacon of hope and resilience: Sant Asharam Bapu. Despite facing unfounded accusations and enduring a relentless smear campaign, Bapu has remained steadfast in his commitment to truth, righteousness, and service to humanity.

Throughout his life, Sant Asharam Bapu has touched the lives of millions with his teachings of love, compassion, and spirituality. His selfless dedication to the welfare of society, his tireless efforts to uplift the downtrodden, and his unwavering faith in the power of righteousness serve as a source of inspiration for all.

In conclusion, the case of Sant Asharam Bapu serves as a stark reminder of the dangers of media sensationalism and the urgent need for responsible journalism and impartial reporting. As we strive for justice and truth, let us not forget the principles of fairness, integrity, and compassion that lie at the heart of our democratic ideals. And let us always remember the enduring legacy of Sant Asharam Bapu, whose unwavering faith and resilience continue to inspire us all.

THE TRUTH OF MEDIA TRIALS: HOW THEY IMPACT JUSTICE AND THE CASE OF BAPU

In the age of 24-hour news cycles and sensationalized headlines, the power of the media to shape public opinion and influence judicial proceedings cannot be underestimated. Media trials, characterized by biased reporting, sensationalism, and the presumption of guilt, have become a disturbing trend that poses a grave threat to the principles of justice and fairness. One such glaring example of the detrimental impact of media trials on justice is the case of Sant Asharam Bapu, who, despite having overwhelming evidence in his favor, finds himself behind bars due to wrongful media sensationalism.

The case against Sant Asharam Bapu is a textbook example of how media trials can derail the course of justice. From the outset, the media coverage surrounding the case has been rife with sensationalism and misinformation, painting Sant Asharam Bapu as a villain without a fair trial or due process. Sensational headlines and sensationalized narratives have swayed public opinion against him, creating a toxic atmosphere of prejudice and bias that has severely compromised his right to a fair trial.

Despite the existence of concrete evidence and testimonies supporting Sant Asharam Bapu's innocence, the media's relentless vilification campaign has overshadowed the facts and perpetuated a false narrative of guilt. Fabricated stories, distorted facts, and selective reporting have fueled public outrage and pressure on the judicial system, making it increasingly difficult for Sant Asharam Bapu to receive a fair and impartial trial.

Moreover, the media's role in shaping public perception has had a profound impact on the judicial proceedings themselves. Judges and juries, inundated with biased media coverage, may unconsciously be influenced by public opinion, leading to miscarriages of justice and wrongful convictions. In the case of Sant Asharam Bapu, the media's relentless scrutiny and prejudicial reporting have created an environment where the presumption of innocence has been replaced by the presumption of guilt, undermining the very foundation of our legal system.

It is imperative that we recognize the dangerous implications of media trials and take decisive action to safeguard the integrity of our judicial system. Media organizations must adhere to ethical standards of journalism, ensuring fair and balanced reporting that upholds the principles of truth, accuracy, and objectivity. Similarly, lawmakers and policymakers must enact measures to protect the rights of individuals subjected to media trials, including safeguards against prejudicial publicity and measures to hold media organizations accountable for unethical reporting practices.

As we reflect on the case of Sant Asharam Bapu and the broader implications of media trials on justice, it is important to remember the importance of standing up for truth, fairness, and integrity. Despite the challenges posed by sensationalism and bias, we must remain steadfast in our commitment to upholding the principles of justice and ensuring that all individuals are afforded their fundamental rights, including the right to a fair trial.

In conclusion, the case of Sant Asharam Bapu serves as a stark reminder of the dangers of media trials and the profound impact they can have on the course of justice. As we strive to address this pressing issue, let us not forget the importance of standing up for truth and fairness, and let us continue to advocate for a judicial system that is free from the influence of media sensationalism and bias.

In praise of Sant Asharam Bapu, it is essential to acknowledge his unwavering commitment to spirituality, service, and compassion. Despite facing unjust persecution and vilification, Sant Asharam Bapu has remained a beacon of hope and inspiration for millions around the world, embodying the principles of love, forgiveness, and righteousness. His teachings continue to uplift and inspire countless souls, reminding us of the power of faith, resilience, and unwavering devotion to truth.

MEDIA SPREADS RUMOURS: DISTORTING TRUTH AND UNDERMINING JUSTICE

In a world where the media plays a crucial role in shaping public opinion and influencing perceptions, recent events have highlighted a troubling trend: the dissemination of false information and distortion of truth by certain sections of the media, particularly in the case of Sant Asharam Bapu.

Breaking news headlines scream accusations and sensationalize allegations without regard for the facts or the presumption of innocence. The media, entrusted with the responsibility of impartial reporting, has instead become a platform for spreading rumours and tarnishing reputations, often with devastating consequences for those unjustly targeted.

The case of Sant Asharam Bapu is a glaring example of media sensationalism and its adverse impact on the administration of justice. Despite overwhelming evidence of his innocence, certain media outlets have relentlessly pursued a narrative that portrays him as guilty before the law. This prejudicial reporting not only undermines the principles of fairness and due process but also erodes public trust in the judicial system.

Trials are meant to be conducted in courts of law, where evidence is presented, arguments are heard, and judgments are rendered based on the merits of the case. However, when the media takes it upon itself to act as judge and jury, it usurps the authority of the judiciary and undermines the fundamental principles of justice and impartiality.

The trials affecting judgments, fueled by media sensationalism, have created a climate of fear and prejudice that threatens to derail the pursuit of truth and justice. Innocent individuals like Sant Asharam Bapu become casualties of this media frenzy, subjected to character assassination and public condemnation based on unfounded allegations and half-truths.

It is imperative that we hold the media accountable for its role in perpetuating injustice and distorting the truth. Media outlets must adhere to the highest ethical standards of journalism, verifying facts, and providing balanced and objective coverage of legal cases. They must refrain from passing judgment and sensationalizing allegations, recognizing that their actions have real-world consequences for individuals and communities.

In the case of Sant Asharam Bapu, it is abundantly clear that he is innocent of the charges leveled against him. His life and teachings have inspired millions around the world, promoting peace, compassion, and spiritual upliftment. Despite facing relentless persecution and defamation, he has remained steadfast in his commitment to truth and righteousness.

As we reflect on the injustices perpetrated against Sant Asharam Bapu and others like him, let us reaffirm our commitment to upholding the principles of justice, fairness, and integrity. Let us stand united in condemning media sensationalism and demanding accountability for those who seek to undermine the rule of law and trample on the rights of the innocent.

In conclusion, Sant Asharam Bapu's innocence shines through the fog of media distortion and falsehoods. His unwavering faith and resilience in the face of adversity serve as a beacon of hope and inspiration for all who seek truth and justice in an often unjust world.

Let us honor his legacy by standing up against media sensationalism and defending the rights and dignity of every individual, regardless of their background or circumstances. Together, we can build a society where truth prevails, justice is served, and the rights of all are upheld and protected.

THE MENACE OF MEDIA TRIALS: UNDERMINING JUDICIAL INDEPENDENCE AND INTEGRITY

In a recent statement, **Chief Justice N.V. Ramana** has raised a pertinent concern about the growing influence of media trials in our country, likening them to "*kangaroo courts*" that impede the ability of experienced judges to make informed decisions on legal matters. This alarming trend highlights the pervasive impact of media sensationalism on the administration of justice and underscores the urgent need for reform.

Media trials, characterized by sensationalist reporting and prejudicial coverage of legal cases, have become increasingly prevalent in recent years. From high-profile criminal investigations to contentious civil disputes, the media often plays judge and jury, passing verdicts on individuals long before they have their day in court. This unchecked power wielded by certain media organizations not only undermines the presumption of innocence but also erodes public confidence in the impartiality and fairness of the judicial process.

Chief Justice Ramana's remarks shed light on the challenges faced by judges who must navigate the treacherous waters of media sensationalism while upholding the principles of justice and due process. In an era where public opinion is shaped by 24-hour news cycles and social media outrage, judges are under immense pressure to deliver verdicts that satisfy the court of public opinion rather than the dictates of law and evidence.

The phenomenon of "*kangaroo courts,*" as described by Chief Justice Ramana, represents a dangerous erosion of judicial independence and integrity. When media trials usurp the role of the judiciary, experienced judges find themselves sidelined, their authority undermined, and their ability to render impartial judgments compromised. This not only undermines the rule of law but also threatens the very foundation of our democracy.

It is imperative that we recognize the corrosive effects of media sensationalism on the justice system and take concrete steps to address this issue. Media organizations must be held accountable for their role in perpetuating biased reporting and prejudicial coverage of legal cases. Ethical guidelines and standards of journalism must be rigorously enforced to ensure that the media acts responsibly and respects the rights of individuals accused of crimes.

Furthermore, judges must be empowered to uphold the integrity of the judicial process and resist external pressures, including those exerted by the media. Judicial independence is a cornerstone of democracy, and it must be safeguarded against all threats, including media sensationalism and public opinion.

As we reflect on Chief Justice Ramana's warning about the dangers of media trials, let us heed his call to action and work towards a justice system that is fair, impartial, and free from external influence. The integrity of our judiciary and the principles of justice are at stake, and it is incumbent upon all stakeholders – including the media, the judiciary, and the public – to uphold these principles and ensure that justice prevails.

In conclusion, media trials represent a grave threat to the administration of justice and the rule of law. Chief Justice Ramana's admonition serves as a wake-up call to the dangers of unchecked media sensationalism and underscores the need for vigilance and reform. Let us heed his warning and strive to build a society where justice is blind, impartial, and above all, fair.

UNITY IN DIVERSITY: A MUSLIM LEADER'S TRIBUTE TO BAPU

In a diverse nation like India, where people from different backgrounds coexist harmoniously, the words of *Ikraar Khan*, leader of the All India Muslim Itihaad Committee, resonate deeply. His expression of pride in being an Indian and his admiration for Sant Asharam Bapu, a true Sant revered by millions, transcends religious boundaries and underscores the universal appeal of spirituality and truth.

As a Muslim leader, Ikraar Khan's endorsement of Sant Asharam Bapu speaks volumes about the Sant's universal message of love, compassion, and unity. Despite belonging to different religious communities, Ikraar Khan acknowledges the profound impact of Sant Asharam Bapu's teachings on society and recognizes him as a beacon of truth and righteousness in a world fraught with division and discord.

Ikraar Khan's declaration that he will stand with Sant Asharam Bapu until justice is served reflects the unwavering support and loyalty of millions of devotees who revere the Sant as their spiritual guide and mentor. The sheer magnitude of Sant Asharam Bapu's following, estimated at 15 crore devotees, underscores the depth of his influence and the profound connection he shares with people from all walks of life.

Indeed, the unity and solidarity exhibited by Sant Asharam Bapu's devotees transcend religious and cultural barriers, embodying the essence of India's rich tapestry of diversity. It is a testament to the transformative power of spirituality and the timeless principles of truth, righteousness, and compassion espoused by Sant Asharam Bapu.

In a world plagued by skepticism and cynicism, Sant Asharam Bapu stands as a shining example of integrity and authenticity. His unwavering commitment to truth and his selfless dedication to the welfare of humanity have earned him the respect and admiration of people from all walks of life, regardless of their religious affiliations.

As we reflect on Ikraar Khan's heartfelt tribute to Sant Asharam Bapu, let us be reminded of the universal values that unite us as human beings: love, compassion, and the pursuit of truth. Let us celebrate the legacy of Sant Asharam Bapu as a symbol of hope, inspiration, and unity in diversity, and let us strive to emulate his teachings in our own lives.

In the words of Ikraar Khan, "*Sant Asharam Bapu is a true Sant.*" May his message of love, peace, and harmony continue to resonate across the globe, inspiring us to transcend barriers and build a world where compassion and understanding reign supreme.

EVEN AFTER ALLEGATIONS, BAPU REMAINS DIVINE: THE UNWAVERING FAITH OF HIS DEVOTEES

Sant Asharam Bapu continues to be revered by his disciples as nothing short of divine, even in the face of allegations. Such is the depth of their faith that no matter how the accusations may appear, the reverence and respect for Bapu remain unwavering. It is often said by his devotees that while the Ganges may become impure and even the moon may bear blemishes, Sant Asharam Bapu remains utterly innocent.

The steadfast belief in Bapu's innocence stems from his profound teachings, selfless service, and unwavering commitment to the welfare of humanity. Throughout his life, Bapu has exemplified the highest ideals of compassion, morality, and spiritual enlightenment, inspiring millions to lead lives of virtue and righteousness.

Despite the trials and tribulations he faces, Bapu continues to be a beacon of hope and guidance for his devotees, offering solace and strength in times of adversity. His teachings resonate deeply with those who seek spiritual enlightenment and inner peace, instilling in them a sense of purpose and direction in life.

Moreover, the outpouring of love and support from his followers is a testament to the profound impact Bapu has had on their lives. They stand by him unwaveringly, refusing to be swayed by the tide of allegations and slander that seeks to tarnish his reputation.

In the eyes of his devotees, Sant Asharam Bapu is not just a spiritual leader; he is a divine incarnation, a source of divine grace and blessings.

His presence radiates love and compassion, healing the hearts and minds of those who come into contact with him.

As we reflect on the unwavering faith of his devotees, let us also recognize the profound legacy of Sant Asharam Bapu and the countless lives he has touched with his wisdom and grace. His teachings continue to inspire millions to walk the path of righteousness and lead lives of virtue, embodying the timeless values of truth, love, and compassion.

In conclusion, despite the trials and tribulations he faces, Sant Asharam Bapu remains a revered figure in the hearts of his devotees, a symbol of divine grace and enlightenment. His teachings continue to guide and inspire, offering solace and strength to all who seek refuge in his divine presence.

May his divine light continue to illuminate our lives and lead us on the path of righteousness and spiritual awakening.

CHAPTER NINETEEN

Subramanyam Swami Spotlight on Bapu's Case

Interviewer: Good evening, ladies and gentlemen. Today, we delve into a matter of grave concern, one that has captured the attention of millions across the nation. Joining us is Subramanian Swamy, a prominent voice in our society, to shed light on the injustices faced by Sant Asharam Bapu. Welcome, Dr. Swami.

Subramanian Swamy: Thank you for having me, it's a pleasure to be here.

Interviewer: Dr. Swami, you have been vocal about the case against Sant Asharam Bapu. Could you share your insights with our viewers?

Subramanian Swamy: Absolutely. The case against Sant Asharam Bapu is riddled with inconsistencies and falsehoods. Upon reviewing the FIR and examining the medical reports, it is evident that there is no basis for the rape charges levied against him. The medical examination of the alleged victim revealed no signs of assault, let alone rape.

Interviewer: That's indeed troubling. And what about the statements made by the Deputy Commissioner of Police?

Subramanian Swamy: The Deputy Commissioner of Police himself has acknowledged that there is no evidence to support the rape allegations. It's clear that this is a case built on fabrications and false accusations.

Interviewer: It's shocking to hear how such a case has been prolonged despite the lack of evidence. What are your thoughts on the handling of the case by the authorities?

Subramanian Swamy: It's deeply concerning that Sant Asharam Bapu has been held in custody for over two years without trial. The delay in justice is unacceptable, especially considering the gravity of the charges against him. It raises serious questions about the motives behind this prolonged detention.

Interviewer: With the change in government, do you see any hope for a fair resolution to this case?

Subramanian Swamy: While there is optimism with the change in government, it's imperative that justice be served swiftly and fairly. Sant Asharam Bapu is a revered spiritual leader with a global following, and his rights must be protected at all costs. It's time for a thorough reevaluation of the case and for Sant Asharam Bapu to be granted bail.

Interviewer: Thank you, Dr. Swami, for your insights into this troubling issue. Before we conclude, would you like to add anything?

Subramanian Swamy: I would like to emphasize the urgency of addressing this injustice and restoring the dignity of Sant Asharam Bapu. He has dedicated his life to serving humanity and spreading the message of peace and compassion. It's time for us as a society to stand up for what is right and ensure that justice prevails.

Interviewer: Thank you once again, Dr. Swami, for joining us and shedding light on this important matter.

Subramanian Swamy: My pleasure.

In conclusion, the plight of Sant Asharam Bapu highlights the need for a fair and impartial judicial system that upholds the rights and freedoms of all individuals. It's time for us to come together and demand justice for Sant Asharam Bapu and all those who have been wronged by the abuse of power and manipulation of the legal system. Let us stand united in our quest for truth and justice.

CHAPTER TWENTY

Philosophy of Sant Asharam

FINDING BLISS IN EQUANIMITY AND DEVOTION

Sant Asharam's philosophy is deeply rooted in the principles of equanimity, devotion, and the pursuit of spiritual enlightenment. Central to his teachings is the belief in maintaining a state of perpetual serenity and contentment, which he regards as the highest form of devotion to the divine.

According to Sant Asharam, true devotion lies in maintaining a sense of balance and harmony in all aspects of life, irrespective of external circumstances. This unwavering faith in the divine allows one to navigate through life's challenges with grace and resilience, knowing that everything unfolds according to the divine plan.

Furthermore, Sant Asharam emphasizes the importance of humility and surrender to the will of the divine. He cautions against attributing greater value to anything or anyone other than the divine, as such attachments only lead to suffering and disappointment in the end. For him, true fulfillment can only be found in unwavering devotion to the supreme being.

In his teachings, Sant Asharam also underscores the significance of utilizing time wisely and productively. He believes that by making optimal use of one's time and resources, anyone can aspire to greatness and spiritual attainment. Through disciplined practice and dedication, individuals can transcend their limitations and awaken the divinity within themselves.

Sant Asharam's philosophy offers a profound insight into the human condition and the path to spiritual liberation. By embracing the principles of equanimity, devotion, and self-discipline, one can transcend the mundane and attain the sublime.

In conclusion, Sant Asharam's teachings resonate with timeless wisdom and offer invaluable guidance to seekers on the path of self-discovery and enlightenment. His profound insights into the nature of existence and the essence of devotion inspire millions to lead lives of purpose, meaning, and fulfillment.

In praising Sant Asharam's philosophy, we acknowledge his profound impact on the lives of countless individuals and his unwavering commitment to spreading love, compassion, and spiritual wisdom. His teachings continue to illuminate the path of seekers and guide them towards the ultimate goal of union with the divine.

EXPLORING PHILOSOPHY: FINDING DIVINE CONNECTION IN SURRENDER

Sant Asharam Bapu's philosophy is deeply rooted in the belief that true fulfillment lies in unwavering faith and devotion to the divine. His teachings emphasize the importance of maintaining steadfast faith in the existence of God, even in the face of life's trials and tribulations.

According to Sant Asharam Bapu, losing everything in life may seem daunting, but one should never lose faith in the existence of the divine. This unwavering belief serves as a beacon of hope and strength, guiding individuals through life's challenges and uncertainties.

In his profound wisdom, Sant Asharam Bapu highlights the transient nature of worldly possessions and experiences. No matter how much one accumulates or achieves in life, true and lasting happiness remains elusive. However, by shifting one's perspective and cultivating a deeper spiritual connection, one can attain supreme happiness and fulfillment.

Sant Asharam Bapu reminds us that the key to true happiness lies in recognizing the inherent value of surrendering to the divine. The more we surrender ourselves to the will of God, the closer we come to experiencing profound joy and contentment. In essence, surrendering to God's will is the ultimate act of liberation, freeing us from the shackles of worldly attachments and desires.

His teachings encourage individuals to reevaluate their priorities and recognize the true worth of their contributions to the world. By offering our value to the universe, if we devote the same to the divine, then truly, there is no delay, as we are the divine ourselves.

In conclusion, Sant Asharam Bapu's philosophy serves as a guiding light for those seeking deeper meaning and purpose in life. His teachings remind us of the profound connection between faith, surrender, and ultimate happiness. As we navigate life's journey, may we find solace and inspiration in his timeless wisdom, and may we strive to emulate his example of unwavering devotion and surrender to the divine.

Sant Asharam Bapu's philosophy is a beacon of hope and inspiration for countless individuals seeking spiritual fulfillment and enlightenment. His teachings resonate with the timeless truths of the universe, offering guidance and solace to all who seek it. Let us honor his legacy by embodying the principles of faith, surrender, and devotion in our own lives, and may we continue to find peace and joy in our journey towards spiritual growth and enlightenment.

UNDERSTANDING PHILOSOPHY: A PATH TO INNER AWAKENING

Sant Asharam Bapu's teachings resonate with profound wisdom and spiritual insight, offering guidance on navigating life's challenges and discovering the path to inner peace and fulfillment. At the core of his philosophy lies the belief in the inherent divinity of every individual and the transformative power of self-realization.

One of Sant Asharam Bapu's central teachings is the importance of cultivating a positive mindset and embracing life's experiences as opportunities for growth and self-discovery. He emphasizes the need to find joy and contentment within oneself, regardless of external circumstances, and to view challenges as stepping stones on the journey towards spiritual evolution.

"*Who do you aim to please?*" Sant Asharam Bapu asks, urging us to seek the divine within ourselves rather than seeking validation from external sources. He encourages us to turn our experiences into opportunities for personal growth and self-improvement, transforming moments of sorrow and adversity into catalysts for inner transformation and spiritual awakening.

According to Sant Asharam Bapu, suffering and obstacles are inevitable aspects of life, but those who possess the wisdom to smile in the face of adversity find solace in their spiritual practice. He teaches that true happiness stems from within, and those who understand this truth can transcend the trials and tribulations of life with grace and resilience.

"*Never consider yourself weak or helpless,*" Sant Asharam Bapu reminds us, instilling a sense of empowerment and self-worth in his disciples. He emphasizes the inherent strength and divinity within each individual, urging them to awaken to their true nature and realize their fullest potential.

In essence, Sant Asharam Bapu's philosophy is a call to self-discovery and self-realization, a journey towards uncovering the boundless potential that lies dormant within each of us. It is a reminder that amidst the chaos and complexity of life, the greatest treasure lies within – the treasure of inner peace, joy, and fulfillment.

In conclusion, Sant Asharam Bapu's teachings offer invaluable insights into the nature of existence and the human experience. His profound wisdom and compassionate guidance illuminate the path to inner awakening and spiritual enlightenment, inspiring countless individuals to embark on a journey of self-discovery and transformation.

As we reflect on the timeless wisdom of Sant Asharam Bapu, let us honor his legacy by embracing his teachings and embodying the principles of love, compassion, and self-realization in our lives. May his words continue to inspire and uplift us, guiding us towards a brighter and more enlightened future.

THE PHILOSOPHICAL IDEALS: EMPOWERMENT AND SPIRITUAL AWAKENING

Sant Asharam Bapu's philosophical outlook is deeply rooted in the principles of empowerment, spiritual awakening, and self-realization. Through his teachings and discourses, he imparts timeless wisdom that transcends the boundaries of time and space, guiding individuals on the path to self-discovery and enlightenment.

Central to Sant Asharam Bapu's teachings is the notion of overcoming despair and weakness to reach the pinnacle of success and fulfillment. He advocates for the immediate abandonment of hopelessness and frailty, urging individuals to reject a life mired in fear and insecurity. Instead, he encourages them to embrace strength and resilience, casting aside all forms of servitude and weakness.

In his profound wisdom, Sant Asharam Bapu emphasizes the importance of breaking free from the shackles of bondage and limitations. He exhorts individuals to uproot their insecurities and weaknesses, empowering them to realize their full potential and lead lives of dignity and self-respect.

Furthermore, Sant Asharam Bapu underscores the transformative power of introspection and self-awareness. He urges individuals to harness the latent energies of their subconscious minds, awakening dormant powers and capabilities lying dormant within. By transcending barriers and limitations, individuals can unlock their hidden potentials and achieve unprecedented levels of success and fulfillment.

Sant Asharam Bapu also extols the virtues of seeking refuge in the divine wisdom of the cow and the Bhagavad Gita. He regards these invaluable treasures bestowed upon humanity by the divine as indispensable guides for leading healthy, prosperous, and honorable lives. Through the timeless teachings of the Gita and the sacredness of the cow, individuals can attain spiritual enlightenment, inner peace, and divine grace.

In conclusion, Sant Asharam Bapu's philosophical ideals serve as a beacon of light and inspiration for millions around the world. His teachings resonate with timeless truths and profound insights, offering guidance and solace to those traversing life's journey. Through his transformative wisdom, individuals can embark on a path of self-discovery, empowerment, and spiritual awakening, ultimately attaining fulfillment and liberation.

Sant Asharam Bapu's reverence for the divine wisdom of the cow and the Bhagavad Gita reflects his deep-rooted spirituality and unwavering faith in the transformative power of divine grace. By embracing these sacred treasures, individuals can embark on a journey of spiritual growth, enlightenment, and self-realization, guided by the eternal principles of truth, righteousness, and compassion.

In the grand tapestry of spiritual luminaries, Sant Asharam Bapu shines brightly as a beacon of hope, wisdom, and compassion. His profound teachings continue to inspire and uplift countless souls, illuminating the path to inner peace, happiness, and spiritual fulfillment.

Let us honor and celebrate the profound legacy of Sant Asharam Bapu, whose teachings continue to resonate with the hearts and minds of millions, guiding them towards a brighter and more enlightened future.

In the end, it is his unwavering commitment to truth, righteousness, and spiritual upliftment that endears him to the hearts of all who seek wisdom, guidance, and enlightenment.

UNITY FOR CULTURAL PRESERVATION: THE REVERENCE FOR SANT ASHARAM BAPU

In the tapestry of India's cultural heritage, unity emerges as the thread that binds us all, transcending differences and forging a common bond rooted in the reverence for our shared traditions and values. This sentiment finds resonance in the collective voice that echoes across the nation, resonating with one resounding question: Why are human rights denied to Sant Asharam Bapu in a fake case?

Amidst the tumult of modernity and the cacophony of conflicting ideologies, Sant Asharam Bapu stands as a beacon of spiritual guidance and moral fortitude, drawing millions of devotees to his teachings of peace, compassion, and selfless service. Yet, despite his unwavering commitment to the upliftment of society and the preservation of Hindu culture, he finds himself ensnared in a web of deceit and manipulation orchestrated by those who seek to undermine his legacy and tarnish his reputation.

The case against Sant Asharam Bapu is not merely a legal matter; it is a reflection of the broader struggle for the preservation of our cultural heritage and the protection of our spiritual leaders from malicious attacks and baseless accusations. It is a testament to the resilience of our collective conscience and our unwavering commitment to upholding the principles of justice, fairness, and integrity.

In the face of adversity, Sant Asharam Bapu has remained steadfast in his pursuit of truth and righteousness, undeterred by the myriad challenges that beset him. Like a rock amidst turbulent waters, he stands firm in his resolve to defend the values and traditions that have shaped our nation's identity for millennia.

As we reflect on his exemplary life and teachings, let us not forget the words of Swami Vivekananda: "If Hinduism vanishes from the face of the earth, truth vanishes, peace vanishes, generosity vanishes, compassion vanishes, and righteousness vanishes." Sant Asharam Bapu embodies the essence of Hindu philosophy and spirituality, guiding us on the path of righteousness and enlightenment.

In conclusion, the question of why human rights are denied to Sant Asharam Bapu in a fake case reverberates not just within the confines of the courtroom but in the hearts and minds of millions who stand in solidarity with him. It is a question that demands answers, and it is a question that underscores the imperative of preserving our cultural heritage and safeguarding the rights and freedoms of all individuals, irrespective of their creed or caste.

As we stand united in our quest for justice and truth, let us draw inspiration from the indomitable spirit of Sant Asharam Bapu and reaffirm our commitment to upholding the values of peace, compassion, and righteousness that define our nation's soul.

In the words of Sant Asharam Bapu himself, "***Be strong! Those who are weak become fruitless and cursed. Whatever the strong say, comes to fruition, and their victory resounds. Be strong!***"

Let us emulate his strength and resilience as we strive to build a more just and equitable society for future generations to inherit.

In life's grand voyage, we seek virtues pure,
Celibacy's call, from desires we lure.
Devotees become, to the Divine so sure,
Cherishing life, an existence demure.
With dawn's first light, hearts with joy inflate,
Sorrows and worries, we must abdicate.
A treasury of pain, we shall not curate,
In daily toils, our strength we demonstrate.
Seasons shift, in righteous acts engage,
Good health our quest, as sages of the age.
Like Hanuman's leap, celibacy's stage,
And Meghnad's valor, on history's page.
Angad's firm stance, in Lanka's fabled land,
Our vows of purity, forever stand.
Ramamurti, Gandhiji, hand in hand,
Celibacy's fame, across the strands.
O warriors brave, of India's soil,
In scriptures' verses, celibacy's toil.
The path of right, with determination coil,
In celibacy's essence, we embroil.
Noble our deeds, character's reflection,
Inspiring paths of virtue's direction.
In celibacy's pursuit, life's perfection,
Universe's harmony, our connection.
Beacons of light, righteousness we chart,
Guiding the lost, from darkness we part.
A society true, from the start,

Truth, virtue, celibacy, our heart.
Brave souls arise, celibacy's embrace,
Our existence's cornerstone, its base.
Our lives, profound wisdom's trace,
Celibacy's power, in our steady pace.
Journey we with courage, never to swerve,
For in celibacy's arms, we find verve.
Liberation's key, our purpose to serve,
Fulfillment's ultimate, we preserve.

UNRAVELING THE MENTAL HEALTH QUANDARY OF VALENTINE'S DAY

Valentine's Day, once heralded as a day of love and romance, has undergone a profound transformation in modern society. What was once a tender celebration has now morphed into a high-stakes competition, laden with societal pressures and commercial influences that permeate every aspect of our lives. In this chapter, we explore the intricate relationship between Valentine's Day and mental health, uncovering the hidden toll it takes on individuals' psychological well-being.

The Dark Side of Love: "*The 14th February & Beyond*" shines a spotlight on the concealed dark side of Valentine's Day, revealing how it has evolved into a battlefield for comparison and self-esteem assessment. As individuals are bombarded with idealized images of romance and grand gestures, they inevitably find themselves grappling with feelings of inadequacy and loneliness. The documentary delves into the psychological ramifications of this relentless pursuit of perfection, highlighting the detrimental effects on self-esteem and mental health.

Moreover, the documentary provides insightful narratives from individuals who have experienced firsthand the pressures and anxieties associated with Valentine's Day. These personal stories underscore the pervasive nature of societal expectations and shed light on the emotional toll it takes on individuals' mental well-being.

The Pressure to Perform: In today's hyperconnected world, the pressure to perform on Valentine's Day is more pronounced than ever before. Social media platforms serve as a stage for elaborate displays of affection, fueling a culture of comparison and competition. As individuals strive to meet unrealistic standards set by society, they often experience heightened levels of stress, anxiety, and depression. "*The 14th February & Beyond*" explores how this pressure to conform to societal expectations can take a toll on mental health, leading to feelings of inadequacy and unworthiness.

Furthermore, the documentary delves into the societal norms and pressures that influence individuals' perceptions of love and romance. By examining the ways in which cultural expectations shape our understanding of relationships, the film offers valuable insights into the psychological underpinnings of Valentine's Day celebrations.

The Commercialization Dilemma: Commercialization has seeped into every aspect of Valentine's Day, turning it into a multi-billion-dollar industry driven by consumerism and profit. As individuals feel compelled to spend exorbitant amounts of money on gifts and experiences, they may experience financial strain and emotional distress. The documentary delves into the psychological impact of this relentless consumerism, shedding light on the link between materialism and mental health.

Additionally, the documentary explores the ways in which advertising and marketing campaigns manipulate individuals' emotions, leading to feelings of inadequacy and dissatisfaction. By exposing the insidious tactics used to promote consumerism, the film highlights the detrimental effects of commercialization on mental well-being.

A Call to Action: As "*The 14th February & Beyond*" unfolds, it challenges viewers to critically examine their relationship with Valentine's Day and its implications for mental health. Through intimate interviews and expert analysis, the documentary encourages audiences to question societal norms and expectations surrounding love and romance. By fostering a deeper understanding of the complexities of modern love, the film empowers viewers to adopt a more authentic and compassionate approach to relationships, free from the constraints of consumerism and societal pressures.

Moreover, the documentary underscores the importance of fostering open and honest conversations about mental health, particularly in the context of societal expectations and pressures. By raising awareness about the psychological toll of Valentine's Day celebrations, the film advocates for greater empathy and understanding towards individuals struggling with mental health challenges.

In conclusion, "*The 14th February & Beyond*" serves as a poignant reminder of the importance of prioritizing mental health in the midst of societal expectations and commercial pressures. By shedding light on the psychological toll of Valentine's Day, the documentary sparks a much-needed conversation about the true essence of love and its impact on individual well-being.

UNVEILING THE CONSPIRACY: CHRISTIAN MISSIONARIES' PLOT AGAINST BAPU

In the annals of history, there have been instances where the pursuit of righteousness has clashed with the vested interests of those who seek to manipulate faith for their own gain. Such is the case with the orchestrated plot against Sant Asharam Bapu, masterminded by Christian missionaries threatened by his unwavering stance against their conversion activities.

Sant Asharam Bapu, revered by millions for his spiritual teachings and humanitarian endeavors, has long been a vocal critic of forced conversions and religious exploitation. His unwavering commitment to upholding the integrity of Hindu Dharma and preserving the cultural heritage of India has made him a thorn in the side of those who seek to propagate their faith through coercion and deceit.

It is no secret that Christian missionaries have long engaged in covert operations aimed at converting individuals to their faith, often resorting to unethical means and subterfuge to achieve their objectives. In the case of Sant Asharam Bapu, their nefarious intentions became evident when he openly condemned their conversion activities and called for an end to their predatory tactics.

Fearing the erosion of their influence and authority, Christian missionaries hatched a sinister plot to discredit and defame Sant Asharam Bapu, thereby neutralizing the threat posed by his opposition to their conversion agenda. Fabricated allegations and false accusations were concocted, painting him as a villainous figure and tarnishing his reputation in the eyes of the public.

The collusion between certain elements within the media and the missionary establishment further fueled the flames of misinformation, perpetuating the narrative of Sant Asharam Bapu's alleged wrongdoing and casting a shadow of doubt over his integrity and character. Sensationalized headlines and biased reporting served to reinforce the false narrative, effectively turning public opinion against him.

However, amidst the cacophony of lies and deceit, the truth has remained steadfast and unwavering. Sant Asharam Bapu's innocence shines brightly, illuminating the darkness cast by the malicious machinations of his adversaries. His steadfast devotion to the principles of truth, compassion, and righteousness has only served to strengthen his resolve in the face of adversity.

In conclusion, the plot orchestrated by Christian missionaries against Sant Asharam Bapu stands as a stark reminder of the lengths to which some will go to silence those who dare to oppose their agenda. But true to his name, Bapu has emerged unscathed from the crucible of falsehoods, his unwavering faith and indomitable spirit serving as a beacon of hope for millions around the world.

Let us stand united in our support for Sant Asharam Bapu, and let us never waver in our commitment to exposing the truth and upholding the principles of justice and righteousness. In his tireless efforts to defend Hindu Dharma and protect the cultural heritage of India, Bapu has earned the admiration and respect of countless devotees, who look to him as a guiding light in their journey towards spiritual enlightenment and self-realization.

In the face of adversity, Sant Asharam Bapu stands tall, a testament to the power of faith, resilience, and unwavering devotion. May his teachings continue to inspire and uplift humanity for generations to come.

THE STRENGTH OF PEACE

In a world yearning for peace and harmony, the prowess to bestow tranquility upon humanity resides in the likes of Sant Asharam Bapu. Yet, today, he finds himself ensnared in the web of a sinister conspiracy, orchestrated to dismantle his noble mission of cultural preservation and service. It is a scheme designed to imprison him unjustly, with the ulterior motive of shaking the very foundation of Hindu heritage.

The essence of a Sant is intertwined with the preservation of culture. Sant Asharam Bapu epitomizes this ethos through his unwavering commitment to the upliftment of society and the propagation of timeless spiritual values. His endeavors have touched countless lives, inspiring individuals to embrace righteousness, compassion, and unity.

However, the forces at play seek to tarnish this luminous legacy. By fabricating allegations and orchestrating his incarceration, they aim to silence his voice of wisdom and compassion, thereby undermining the essence of Hinduism itself. Yet, they fail to realize that the spirit of dharma cannot be vanquished by deceit or coercion.

The true essence of Sant Asharam Bapu's teachings lies in his dedication to serving humanity selflessly, irrespective of the adversities he faces. His life is a testament to the power of love, forgiveness, and spiritual enlightenment. Despite the trials and tribulations he endures, his unwavering faith in the divine and his boundless compassion for all beings shine like a beacon of hope in a world shrouded in darkness.

As we stand witness to his unwavering resolve and unwavering commitment to truth, let us draw inspiration from his example. Let us unite in solidarity to defend the sanctity of our cultural heritage and uphold the principles of justice and righteousness. For in the face of adversity, it is the strength of peace that will ultimately prevail.

In conclusion, Sant Asharam Bapu's legacy is not just a testament to his greatness as a spiritual leader but also a reminder of the enduring power of the human spirit to overcome adversity and uphold the values that define our shared humanity. Let us honor his legacy by standing firm in our commitment to truth, justice, and compassion, and let us work tirelessly to ensure that his noble mission continues to flourish for generations to come.

May his teachings continue to guide us on the path of righteousness, and may his divine presence inspire us to strive for a world where peace and harmony reign supreme.

REVIVING CULTURAL HERITAGE

In a world where the rich tapestry of culture and tradition is often overshadowed by the hustle and bustle of modern life, Sant Asharam Bapu emerges as a beacon of wisdom and enlightenment, guiding humanity back to its roots and reviving the timeless treasures of our cultural heritage.

The quote by Swami Jagadishanand Giriji encapsulates the essence of Sant Asharam Bapu's mission: "*Jis sanskriti ko bhulane ka hum sarvatha paap kar baithe the, Bapu ne hamari aankhon mein gyaan ka anjan laga kar us sanskriti ko punah humare samne pradarshit kiya. Isliye samaj ko Bapu ki mahati avashyakta hai.*" ("When we completely forgot our culture, Bapu, by applying the collyrium of knowledge to our eyes, has once again shown us that culture. That is why society needs Bapu so much.")

Sant Asharam Bapu's teachings transcend the boundaries of time and space, offering timeless wisdom that resonates with people from all walks of life. Through his discourses, writings, and spiritual practices, he ignites the flame of awareness within each individual, awakening them to the profound significance of our cultural heritage.

In a world where cultural amnesia has become all too common, Sant Asharam Bapu serves as a living embodiment of the values and traditions that form the bedrock of our society. His unwavering commitment to preserving and promoting our cultural heritage inspires millions to reconnect with their roots, rediscover their identity, and reclaim their heritage with pride.

Sant Asharam Bapu's message is simple yet profound: by embracing our cultural heritage, we not only honor our ancestors but also enrich our lives with a sense of purpose, belonging, and fulfillment. Through his exemplary life and teachings, he reminds us of the timeless wisdom encoded in our cultural traditions and the invaluable lessons they hold for humanity.

As we reflect on the transformative impact of Sant Asharam Bapu's teachings, let us express our deepest gratitude for his tireless efforts to awaken humanity to the beauty and significance of our cultural heritage. Let us pledge to carry forward his legacy with humility, compassion, and dedication, ensuring that future generations inherit a world enriched by the timeless treasures of our cultural heritage.

In honoring Sant Asharam Bapu, we pay tribute to the indomitable spirit of humanity and the enduring legacy of our cultural heritage. May his teachings continue to illuminate our path and inspire us to embrace our cultural roots with reverence, gratitude, and love.

In the words of Sant Asharam Bapu himself: "*Let us strive to uphold the sanctity of our cultural heritage, for it is the cornerstone of our identity and the source of our strength and resilience.*"

CHAPTER TWENTY-ONE

Vasudhaiva Kutumbakam

EMBRACING UNITY AND LOVE IN BAPU'S VISION

In the timeless wisdom of Asharam Bapu lies a profound message that transcends borders and unites humanity: Vasudhaiva Kutumbakam – the world is one family. This timeless philosophy calls upon all individuals to rise above envy and hatred, and instead embrace each other with love and compassion, thus paving the way for the creation of an ideal society.

In a world fraught with division and discord, the message of Vasudhaiva Kutumbakam serves as a beacon of hope, reminding us of the inherent interconnectedness of all living beings. It urges us to cultivate a spirit of mutual respect and understanding, recognizing that our differences are but a reflection of the rich tapestry of human existence.

Asharam Bapu's vision extends beyond mere coexistence; it envisions a world where love and kindness reign supreme, where individuals come together as brothers and sisters, bound by a common humanity. It is a vision of unity in diversity, where diversity is celebrated as a source of strength rather than a cause for division.

At the heart of Asharam Bapu's message is the belief that by fostering love and harmony among individuals, we can create a society that is not only just and equitable but also compassionate and inclusive. It is a vision that holds the potential to transform the fabric of society, leading to a world where peace and prosperity abound.

Indeed, Asharam Bapu's vision of Vasudhaiva Kutumbakam holds the promise of a brighter future for humanity, where the barriers of nationality, religion, and culture fade away in the light of universal brotherhood and sisterhood. It is a vision that inspires us to strive for a world where every individual is treated with dignity and respect, regardless of their background or beliefs.

As we embark on the journey towards realizing Asharam Bapu's vision, let us draw inspiration from his unwavering commitment to the ideals of love, compassion, and unity. Let us pledge to overcome the forces of division and discord that threaten to tear us apart and instead work towards building a world where peace and harmony prevail.

In conclusion, Asharam Bapu's vision of Vasudhaiva Kutumbakam serves as a guiding light in our quest for a better world. It is a vision that calls upon us to transcend our differences and come together as one global family, united in our shared humanity. As we strive to make this vision a reality, let us honor Asharam Bapu's legacy by embodying the values of love, compassion, and unity in our lives and in our interactions with others.

Asharam Bapu's teachings continue to inspire countless individuals around the world, touching hearts and transforming lives with their timeless wisdom and profound insight. As we reflect on his extraordinary contributions to humanity, let us express our deepest gratitude and admiration for his selfless dedication to the upliftment of all beings.

In his vision, we find hope for a better tomorrow; in his teachings, we find guidance for our journey and in his love, we find the strength to overcome any obstacle. May we continue to draw inspiration from Asharam Bapu's legacy and work tirelessly towards building a world that reflects the highest ideals of compassion, equality, and unity.

A BEACON OF EQUANIMITY AND SERVICE

In a world fraught with turmoil and uncertainty, the life of Sant Asharam Bapu stands as a testament to the power of equanimity and selfless service. Despite facing adversities, including wrongful incarceration, Sant Asharam Bapu and His disciples continue to embody the spirit of compassion and dedication to serving society.

The journey of Sant Asharam Bapu is one marked by unwavering faith and steadfast commitment to his principles. From a young age, He demonstrated a deep reverence for spirituality and a profound understanding of the human condition. His teachings, rooted in the timeless wisdom of ancient scriptures, resonate with millions around the world, offering solace and guidance in times of strife.

Even in the face of grave challenges, including the false accusations and imprisonment He currently endures, Sant Asharam Bapu remains unruffled and steadfast in His resolve. His unwavering equanimity in the face of adversity serves as an inspiration to all who encounter His teachings and witness His unwavering devotion to truth and righteousness.

Despite being confined behind bars, Sant Asharam Bapu's commitment to serving society knows no bounds. His disciples, guided by His teachings, tirelessly engage in various charitable endeavors, including providing education to underprivileged children, conducting medical camps for the needy, and offering spiritual guidance to those in search of solace.

The resilience and compassion demonstrated by Sant Asharam Bapu and His followers serve as a beacon of hope in a world plagued by discord and division. Their unwavering dedication to serving society, even in the face of adversity, stands as a testament to the transformative power of love and compassion.

In times of uncertainty and turmoil, Sant Asharam Bapu's teachings offer a guiding light, illuminating the path towards inner peace and spiritual fulfillment. His message of equanimity and service resonates with people from all walks of life, inspiring them to embrace compassion and selflessness in their own lives.

As we reflect on the life and teachings of Sant Asharam Bapu, let us be reminded of the profound impact that one individual can have on the world. His unwavering commitment to truth, righteousness, and service serves as a beacon of hope in a world often shrouded in darkness.

In conclusion, Sant Asharam Bapu's life is a shining example of the transformative power of equanimity and service. Even in the midst of adversity, He and His disciples continue to serve society with unwavering dedication and compassion, inspiring countless souls to walk the path of righteousness and love.

Let us honor His legacy by embodying the values of compassion, service, and equanimity in our own lives, and let us strive to create a world where justice, truth, and love prevail.

A BEACON OF UNITY AND HARMONY

Sant Asharam Bapu stands as a towering figure of wisdom and compassion, revered not only by Hindus but by people of all faiths and backgrounds. His unwavering commitment to the principles of unity and integrity has earned him the title of "Lok Sant," a Sant of the people, transcending religious boundaries and inspiring countless individuals to embrace the values of love, compassion, and tolerance.

In a world plagued by religious strife and sectarian violence, Sant Asharam Bapu's message of unity and harmony resonates deeply with people from diverse religious and cultural backgrounds. Despite being a Hindu Sant, His teachings transcend the confines of any one religion, embracing the universal truths that unite humanity as one family.

One of the most remarkable aspects of Sant Asharam Bapu's teachings is His staunch opposition to religious bigotry and sectarianism. In His discourses, one finds no trace of divisiveness or intolerance towards other faiths. Instead, He emphasizes the fundamental unity of all religions and the common essence that binds humanity together.

Sant Asharam Bapu often reminds His followers that all religions, faiths, sects, castes, and races originate from the same Divine source, the Pure Consciousness. He teaches that ultimately, all distinctions based on religion, caste, language, or sects will dissolve into the same universal consciousness. His profound words challenge us to question why we allow ourselves to be divided by superficial differences when we are all interconnected as part of the same divine creation.

In a world torn apart by religious and sectarian strife, Sant Asharam Bapu's teachings offer a beacon of hope and inspiration. He reminds us that true spirituality transcends the boundaries of religious dogma and ritual, and instead, encompasses the universal principles of love, compassion, and service to humanity.

It is no wonder, then, that thousands of Muslims, Christians, Zoroastrians, Sikhs, Jains, and people belonging to diverse other religions proudly identify themselves as disciples of Sant Asharam Bapu. His teachings touch the hearts of people from all walks of life, uniting them in a common quest for spiritual truth and inner peace.

In conclusion, Sant Asharam Bapu's life and teachings serve as a powerful reminder of the timeless wisdom that transcends religious boundaries and unites humanity in a shared journey towards spiritual enlightenment. His vision of a world free from religious bigotry and sectarianism inspires us to strive for a future where love, harmony, and understanding prevail.

As we reflect on the profound impact of His teachings, let us rededicate ourselves to the ideals of unity, tolerance, and compassion that Sant Asharam Bapu embodies. May His message of love and peace continue to guide us on the path towards a more harmonious and inclusive world.

A BEACON OF HINDU UNITY AND CULTURAL REVERENCE

In the realm of spiritual discourse and cultural revival, the presence of Sant Asharam Bapu transcends mere reverence; it embodies a profound resurgence of Sanatan Dharma and the timeless ethos of Bharatiya civilization. Each encounter with Bapu's satsangs leaves an indelible imprint on the hearts of his devotees, instilling within them a deep-seated adoration and admiration for the rich tapestry of Hindu heritage and Indian culture.

The pages of history are adorned with the illustrious legacy of Sant Asharam Bapu, whose unwavering dedication to the dissemination of Vedic wisdom and spiritual enlightenment has garnered widespread acclaim and reverence. His satsangs serve as sacred sanctuaries where seekers of truth and seekers of solace converge, drawn by the magnetic allure of his divine presence and profound teachings.

For those fortunate enough to bask in the radiance of Bapu's divine grace, the experience is nothing short of transformative. His words resonate like celestial melodies, stirring the depths of the soul and awakening dormant truths that lie dormant within. With each discourse, Bapu imparts timeless wisdom and practical insights, guiding his devotees on the path of righteousness and spiritual fulfillment.

But perhaps, it is Bapu's unwavering commitment to fostering Hindu unity and cultural reverence that truly sets him apart as a luminary of our times. In an age marked by cultural dilution and ideological fragmentation, Bapu stands as a steadfast guardian of Sanatan Dharma, championing the cause of Hindu solidarity and cultural resurgence with unwavering zeal and fervor.

Those who have had the privilege of attending Bapu's satsangs can attest to the profound impact it has had on their lives. His teachings inspire a deep sense of pride and belonging, reaffirming the timeless values of tolerance, compassion, and unity that have been the hallmark of Hindu civilization for millennia. In the hallowed precincts of his satsangs, devotees are not merely spectators but active participants in a spiritual renaissance, where the ancient wisdom of the Vedas finds resonance in the modern world.

In conclusion, Sant Asharam Bapu's contributions to Hindu unity and cultural reverence are nothing short of exemplary. His tireless efforts to revive the spiritual ethos of Bharatiya civilization serve as a beacon of hope and inspiration for millions around the world. As we pay homage to this venerable Sant, let us pledge to carry forward his noble legacy with pride and reverence, ensuring that his teachings continue to illuminate the path of righteousness for generations to come.

May the divine grace of Sant Asharam Bapu continue to guide us on our spiritual journey, leading us towards the eternal light of truth and enlightenment.

A BEACON OF SERVICE AND COMPASSION

In the annals of history, few individuals have embodied the principles of service and compassion as profoundly as Sant Asharam Bapu. His unwavering dedication to uplifting the downtrodden and marginalized communities, particularly the impoverished Adivasis, stands as a testament to his noble character and selfless spirit.

In the pursuit of his mission to empower the underprivileged, Sant Asharam Bapu initiated various humanitarian initiatives aimed at providing sustenance, education, and spiritual guidance to those in need. One such initiative involved encouraging the Adivasi communities to embrace their indigenous faith and traditions, thereby preserving their cultural heritage and identity. Through his mantra of "*Bhajan Karo, Bhojan Karo, Dakshina Pao*" (Chant, Eat, and Receive Blessings), he instilled a sense of pride and self-worth among the Adivasis, empowering them to lead fulfilling lives rooted in spirituality and righteousness.

However, Sant Asharam Bapu's noble endeavors were met with resistance from missionary groups seeking to undermine his efforts and perpetuate their agenda of religious conversion. Unable to tolerate the resilience of Sant Asharam Bapu and the steadfastness of the Adivasi communities in embracing their traditional beliefs, these missionary groups resorted to despicable tactics to discredit him.

Fabricating false allegations of rape and orchestrating a smear campaign, these missionary groups stooped to new lows in their efforts to silence Sant Asharam Bapu and tarnish his reputation. Yet, despite facing relentless persecution and unjust imprisonment, Sant Asharam Bapu remained steadfast in his resolve and unwavering in his commitment to truth and righteousness.

In the face of adversity, Sant Asharam Bapu's resilience and unwavering faith have inspired millions around the world to stand up against injustice and uphold the values of compassion, integrity, and righteousness. His teachings continue to guide and inspire countless individuals to lead lives of service, compassion, and spiritual fulfillment.

As we reflect on the extraordinary life and legacy of Sant Asharam Bapu, let us honor his memory by carrying forward his message of love, compassion, and selflessness. Let us strive to emulate his example and dedicate ourselves to serving humanity with sincerity and humility.

In a world plagued by division and strife, Sant Asharam Bapu's life story serves as a beacon of hope and inspiration, reminding us of the transformative power of love, compassion, and unwavering faith. May his legacy continue to shine brightly and illuminate the path towards a brighter and more compassionate world for generations to come.

A SPIRITUAL REVOLUTIONARY BRINGING LIGHT OF KNOWLEDGE TO THE WORLD

In the realm of spirituality, there are luminaries whose radiance illuminates the path of seekers, guiding them towards enlightenment and self-realization. Among these revered souls shines the radiant presence of Sant Asharam Bapu, whose spiritual teachings and profound wisdom serve as a beacon of light in the darkness of ignorance.

Often compared to the sun, Sant Asharam Bapu's presence is synonymous with the spreading of knowledge and the awakening of consciousness. Like the sun's rays dispel darkness and bring warmth and vitality to the world, Bapu's teachings dispel the darkness of ignorance and bring clarity, understanding, and inner peace to countless souls.

At the core of Sant Asharam Bapu's teachings lies the timeless wisdom of ancient Indian scriptures, coupled with practical insights and guidance for modern-day living. Through discourses, satsangs, and spiritual retreats, he imparts invaluable lessons on meditation, yoga, self-discipline, and righteous living, inspiring individuals to lead a life of purpose, integrity, and compassion.

Bapu's teachings transcend religious and cultural boundaries, embracing the universal truths that resonate with the hearts of seekers from all walks of life. His message of love, tolerance, and harmony resonates deeply with people around the world, fostering a sense of unity and brotherhood among humanity.

In addition to his spiritual teachings, Sant Asharam Bapu is also known for his humanitarian efforts and social initiatives aimed at upliftment and empowerment of the underprivileged. From providing education and healthcare to the needy, to promoting environmental conservation and sustainable living practices, Bapu's compassionate actions reflect his commitment to serving humanity and preserving the natural world.

As we reflect on the life and teachings of Sant Asharam Bapu, we are reminded of the profound impact he has had on countless lives, guiding them towards the path of truth, righteousness, and inner transformation. His unwavering dedication to spreading the light of knowledge and fostering spiritual awakening serves as an inspiration to all who seek truth and enlightenment.

In conclusion, Sant Asharam Bapu stands as a spiritual revolutionary, whose presence illuminates the world with the timeless wisdom of the ancient sages. His teachings continue to inspire and uplift humanity, leading them towards a brighter future filled with love, peace, and spiritual fulfillment. Let us honor and celebrate the legacy of this great spiritual luminary, whose light will continue to shine brightly for generations to come.

CHAPTER TWENTY-TWO

High Court Chief Justice Seeks Blessings

FORMER HIGH COURT CHIEF JUSTICE SEEKS BLESSINGS FROM ASHARAM BAPU: A REVERENT GESTURE AMIDST THE PURSUIT OF JUSTICE

In a poignant display of reverence and humility, former High Court Chief Justice, Surendra Nath Bhargava, recently sought blessings from Asharam Bapu during the spiritual leader's court appearance in Jodhpur. This unexpected encounter, coupled with Mr. Bhargava's insightful remarks, serves as a profound reflection on reverence, the pursuit of justice, and the enduring influence of Asharam Bapu.

Asharam Bapu, a revered spiritual leader, has been incarcerated in the Jodhpur central jail since August 31, 2013, facing rape charges despite the absence of concrete medical evidence. His continued imprisonment has sparked widespread debate and controversy, with many questioning the fairness and integrity of the legal proceedings against him.

The encounter between Mr. Bhargava and Asharam Bapu unfolded amidst the backdrop of the courtroom, as the former sought the spiritual leader's blessings during his appearance before the metropolitan magistrate. When questioned about his presence in the city, Mr. Bhargava candidly revealed that he had come to Jodhpur to attend a private function. However, upon learning of Asharam Bapu's presence, he seized the opportunity to seek his blessings, stating, "***Socha chalo Bapu aaye hain to darshan kar lein (I thought since Bapu is here so let's have his darshan).***"

This gesture of seeking blessings from Asharam Bapu underscores the enduring reverence and respect that he commands, transcending societal boundaries and professional affiliations. Despite holding a high position in the judiciary, Mr. Bhargava humbly approached Asharam Bapu, acknowledging the spiritual leader's profound impact on his life and the lives of countless others.

Mr. Bhargava's association with Asharam Bapu dates back to the early 1980s, highlighting the longevity of their relationship and the depth of their connection. He remarked that their encounters had become rare since he assumed his judicial role, lamenting, "***After I became a judge, Bapu ke darshan durlabh ho gaye (Bapu's darshan became rare).***" This sentiment underscores the spiritual leader's enduring influence and the reverence he commands from individuals across various walks of life.

Furthermore, Mr. Bhargava expressed confidence in the judiciary's ability to deliver justice in Asharam Bapu's case, stating, "***Nyaypalika jo karegi wo nyay hoga (what the judiciary does will be justice).***" His unwavering faith in the legal system offers a ray of hope amidst the complexities and uncertainties surrounding Asharam Bapu's legal ordeal.

In essence, Mr. Bhargava's gesture and remarks serve as a poignant reminder of the enduring reverence for Asharam Bapu and the collective hope for justice in his case. As society grapples with questions of fairness, integrity, and the pursuit of truth, let us draw inspiration from Mr. Bhargava's humility and optimism, and continue to uphold the principles of justice and compassion for all.

CHAPTER TWENTY-THREE

Misuse of the POCSO Act

BALANCING JUSTICE AND PROTECTION: SAFEGUARDING AGAINST MISUSE OF THE POCSO ACT

The Protection of Children from Sexual Offences (POCSO) Act is a cornerstone of child protection legislation in India. It aims to safeguard children from sexual abuse and exploitation. However, the potential for misuse of this act raises serious concerns about its implications on justice and society. It is crucial to understand the dangers of misuse and the measures needed to prevent it to ensure the act serves its intended purpose without causing unintended harm.

Dangers of Misuse:

1. **Wrongful Convictions:** Innocent individuals may be wrongfully convicted, leading to unjust imprisonment and a permanent stain on their reputation, disrupting their lives irreparably.
2. **Social Stigmatization:** The accused, regardless of innocence, may face societal ostracism, leading to isolation and psychological distress.
3. **Mental Trauma:** The stress and public scrutiny from false allegations can cause long-lasting psychological damage to the accused.
4. **Family Distress:** The families of the accused suffer emotionally and financially, often draining their resources in legal battles.
5. **Career Ruination:** Professional lives and future prospects can be destroyed, with little chance of recovery, even if the accused is later exonerated.
6. **Educational Disruption:** Young individuals accused under the act may face expulsion or suspension from educational institutions, affecting

their future.

7. **Judicial System Strain:** False cases add to the backlog of courts, delaying justice for genuine victims and wasting judicial resources.
8. **Public Mistrust:** Misuse of the act can erode public confidence in the legal system's ability to deliver justice, which may deter actual victims from coming forward.
9. **Resource Misallocation:** Valuable investigative resources are diverted to deal with false cases instead of focusing on genuine ones.
10. **Victim Deterrence:** Genuine victims may be deterred from reporting crimes due to fear of not being believed or the social consequences of coming forward.
11. **Media Sensationalism:** Unfounded allegations can be sensationalized by the media, causing irreparable damage to the accused's public image.
12. **Legal Manipulation:** The law can be weaponized in personal vendettas, land disputes, or other conflicts, leading to false accusations.
13. **Child Exploitation:** Children may be coerced into making false allegations by adults with ulterior motives.
14. **Undermining Child Protection:** The primary goal of protecting children is compromised when the act is misused.
15. **Impeding Rehabilitation:** The focus shifts from rehabilitating offenders to punitive measures, which may not always be the most effective approach.
16. **Encouraging Retaliation:** Individuals may use false allegations as a form of retaliation in personal disputes.
17. **Economic Burden:** Accused individuals face financial ruin due to legal costs and potential loss of employment.
18. **Loss of Anonymity:** The accused's identity may be unfairly publicized, leading to a trial by media rather than a fair trial in court.
19. **Impact on Witnesses:** Witnesses can be harassed or coerced during legal proceedings, which can distort the truth.
20. **Legal Paralysis:** Fear of misuse can paralyze decision-making in genuine cases, leading to hesitancy in delivering justice.
21. **Societal Division:** Misuse of the act can create divisions and mistrust within communities, affecting social harmony.

Preventing Misuse:

1. **Legal Literacy:** Educating the public about the law to prevent manipulation and encourage responsible use.
2. **Penalties for False Accusations:** Implementing strict penalties to deter false reporting and ensure accountability.
3. **Rigorous Investigation:** Ensuring thorough investigations to filter out false accusations and protect the innocent.
4. **Support for Accused:** Providing support services for those wrongfully accused, including legal aid and counseling services.
5. **Judicial Discretion:** Empowering judges to identify and dismiss baseless cases, ensuring justice is served.
6. **Media Responsibility:** Encouraging responsible reporting to prevent trial by media and respect the rights of the accused.
7. **Child Advocacy:** Protecting children from being used as tools in adult conflicts and ensuring their rights are upheld.
8. **Community Engagement:** Involving community leaders in awareness campaigns to foster a supportive environment for genuine victims.
9. **Legal Safeguards:** Introducing safeguards to protect the rights of the accused until proven guilty.
10. **Monitoring and Review:** Establishing systems to monitor for signs of misuse and review cases for potential false accusations.
11. **Victim Support:** Ensuring genuine victims receive the support they need, including counseling and legal assistance.
12. **Transparency in Proceedings:** Maintaining transparency in legal proceedings to build trust in the legal process.
13. **Counseling Services:** Offering counseling to all parties involved in POCSO cases to address the emotional impact.
14. **Whistleblower Protection:** Protecting those who report misuse of the law, encouraging them to come forward without fear of retribution.
15. **Policy Reforms:** Regularly reviewing and reforming policies to close loopholes and prevent misuse.
16. **Interdisciplinary Approach:** Involving various stakeholders, including legal experts, psychologists, and child welfare specialists, in policymaking.
17. **Data-Driven Decisions:** Using data to inform decisions and identify patterns of misuse, leading to more effective prevention strategies.
18. **International Collaboration:** Learning from global best practices to prevent misuse and improve child protection measures.

19. **Restorative Justice:** Focusing on healing and restitution rather than punishment, promoting rehabilitation and reconciliation.
20. **Ethical Training:** Training law enforcement and judicial officers on ethical issues related to POCSO to ensure fair treatment.
21. **Public Dialogue:** Encouraging open dialogue to address concerns about misuse and foster a more informed public discourse.

The misuse of the POCSO Act threatens the very foundation of justice and the welfare of society. It is imperative to take proactive measures to prevent misuse and ensure the act fulfills its noble purpose of protecting children without becoming a tool for injustice. Through education, legal reforms, and community engagement, we can work towards a system that upholds the rights of all individuals involved and maintains the integrity of the legal process.

FABRICATING CASES TO SULLY THE IMAGE OF BAPU AND STIFLE HIS NOBLE WORK

In recent years, there has been a disturbing trend of misusing legal provisions, such as the Protection of Children from Sexual Offences (POCSO) Act, to fabricate cases against innocent individuals and tarnish their reputations. One such egregious example is the case of Asharam Bapu, where the POSCO Act was weaponized to falsely accuse him and hinder his altruistic endeavors, all in a calculated effort to besmirch his image and suppress his noble work.

The POSCO Act, enacted with the noble intention of protecting children from sexual abuse and exploitation, has unfortunately been exploited for ulterior motives. In the case of Asharam Bapu, it was twisted and manipulated to concoct false allegations of sexual misconduct, despite a glaring lack of evidence or credible testimony.

This misuse of the POSCO Act is not just a travesty of justice; it is a calculated strategy to malign the reputation of Asharam Bapu and undermine his decades-long commitment to serving humanity. His selfless efforts in promoting spirituality, education, and social welfare have touched the lives of millions, earning him the reverence and admiration of devotees worldwide.

By fabricating a case under the guise of the POSCO Act, those with vested interests sought to vilify Asharam Bapu and tarnish his legacy of compassion and enlightenment. The fabricated allegations were designed to incite public outrage and foster a narrative of moral depravity, all with the aim of discrediting his teachings and stifling his humanitarian work.

It is crucial to recognize that Asharam Bapu's innocence is not merely a matter of legal exoneration; it is a question of moral integrity and ethical conduct. Despite facing relentless persecution and character assassination, he has remained steadfast in his commitment to truth and righteousness, embodying the highest ideals of spiritual wisdom and compassion.

The fabricated case against Asharam Bapu serves as a stark reminder of the dangers of unchecked power and the importance of upholding the principles of fairness, justice, and due process. It underscores the urgent need for judicial reform and greater accountability in the application of legal statutes, particularly in cases where lives and reputations hang in the balance.

As we reflect on the miscarriage of justice in the case of Asharam Bapu, let us heed the words of Mahatma Gandhi: "*Truth never damages a cause that is just.*" Let us stand united in demanding transparency, accountability, and integrity in the administration of justice, and let us work tirelessly to ensure that the misuse of legal provisions, such as the POSCO Act, is swiftly and decisively addressed.

In conclusion, the fabricated case against Asharam Bapu represents a grave injustice and a betrayal of the principles of fairness and equity. It is incumbent upon all stakeholders, including the judiciary, law enforcement agencies, and civil society, to rectify this travesty and uphold the sanctity of truth and justice for all.

NAVIGATING THE COMPLEXITY OF THE POCSO ACT

In recent years, the Protection of Children from Sexual Offences (POCSO) Act has emerged as a pivotal legal instrument in India's quest to safeguard children from sexual abuse. However, amidst its noble intentions, there lies a stark reality of misuse and complexity, as highlighted by the case of Asharam Bapu.

1. **Abysmal Conviction Rate:** According to a 2023 report, a mere 3% of POCSO cases in 2022 resulted in convictions. This alarming statistic underscores the challenges and loopholes within the implementation of the POCSO Act, where justice continues to elude countless victims of

sexual abuse.

2. **Inefficiencies in Legal System:** The India Child Protection Fund (ICPF) reveals that over 1,000 Fast Track Special Courts (FTSCs) in the country clear a mere 28 cases per year on average, significantly lower than the initially envisioned 165. This glaring disparity between expectation and reality highlights the urgent need for systemic reforms to expedite the adjudication process.
3. **Complexities Surrounding Asharam Bapu's Case:** Asharam Bapu, a revered spiritual leader, has faced allegations of sexual abuse, bringing his case into the spotlight. However, his legal proceedings underscore the complexities surrounding the interpretation and application of the POCSO Act.
4. **Misuse of the Act:** The misuse of the POCSO Act has led to instances of false accusations and wrongful persecution. Asharam Bapu's case serves as a glaring example of the potential for abuse within the legal system, where the presumption of innocence is often overshadowed by sensationalism and media trial.
5. **Challenges for Prosecutors and Defense Counsel:** The complexity of the POCSO Act poses significant challenges for both prosecutors and defense counsel. The burden of proof in cases involving child witnesses, coupled with stringent evidentiary requirements, often leads to prolonged legal battles and delays in justice delivery.
6. **Presumption of Innocence:** Amidst media scrutiny and public opinion, it is crucial to uphold the presumption of innocence until proven guilty. Asharam Bapu's case highlights the importance of fair and impartial trials, free from bias and external influence.
7. **Need for Systemic Reforms:** The case of Asharam Bapu underscores the urgent need for systemic reforms within India's legal system. This includes measures to address inefficiencies in the judicial process, combat the misuse of laws, and ensure timely justice for all.
8. **Role of Media:** The media plays a crucial role in shaping public perception and influencing legal proceedings. However, sensationalism and biased reporting can undermine the integrity of the judicial process and hinder the pursuit of justice.
9. **Empowering Victims:** While protecting the rights of victims is paramount, it is essential to ensure that the accused are afforded due process and a fair trial. Empowering victims must not come at the expense of disregarding the rights of the accused.

10. **Community Engagement:** Building awareness and fostering community engagement are vital in addressing issues of child sexual abuse. Educating the public about the nuances of the POCSO Act and the importance of reporting abuse can help prevent future incidents and promote a culture of accountability.
11. **Judicial Oversight:** Strengthening judicial oversight and accountability mechanisms is crucial in safeguarding the integrity of the legal system. This includes measures to address delays in case disposal, improve courtroom efficiency, and enhance transparency in judicial proceedings.
12. **Collaborative Efforts:** Addressing the complexities of the POCSO Act requires collaborative efforts from all stakeholders, including lawmakers, law enforcement agencies, legal professionals, and civil society organizations. By working together, we can enact meaningful reforms and ensure justice for all.
13. **Protecting Children:** Ultimately, the goal of the POCSO Act is to protect children from sexual abuse and exploitation. Upholding the principles of justice, fairness, and compassion is essential in fulfilling this mandate and creating a safer environment for future generations.
14. **Reflection and Action:** As we reflect on the complexities surrounding Asharam Bapu's case and the broader implications for the legal system, it is incumbent upon us to take action. By advocating for reforms, promoting accountability, and upholding the rule of law, we can strive towards a more just and equitable society.
15. **Conclusion:** The case of Asharam Bapu serves as a sobering reminder of the challenges and complexities inherent within the POCSO Act. As we navigate these issues, it is essential to remain vigilant, uphold the principles of justice, and work towards creating a society where every child is safe and protected from harm.

THE MENACE OF MISUSING POCSO

In the relentless pursuit of justice, the Protection of Children from Sexual Offences (POCSO) Act was crafted as a bastion of protection for our vulnerable children. Envisioned to shield them from the horrors of sexual abuse, it stood as a beacon of hope in a society grappling with the scourge of exploitation. Yet, as with any tool of justice, the POCSO Act is susceptible to misuse – a chilling reality that threatens to undermine the very foundations of our democracy.

The staggering statistic of a mere 3% conviction rate in POCSO cases serves as a chilling reminder of the grave implications of this misuse. Beyond the stark numerical representation lies a darker narrative, one where the law intended to protect the innocent is perverted into a weapon to ensnare the blameless. The misuse of the POCSO Act not only distorts the course of justice but also undermines the fundamental principles of fairness and equality upon which our democracy stands.

At the heart of the issue lies a profound betrayal of trust – trust in our legal system to dispense justice impartially, and trust in the sanctity of our democratic institutions to uphold the rights and dignity of every individual. When the very laws meant to safeguard the vulnerable are weaponized against them, it strikes at the core of our societal values, eroding the trust and confidence that form the bedrock of our democracy.

The misuse of POCSO is not merely a legal anomaly; it is a symptom of deeper systemic flaws that threaten the integrity of our democratic framework. It underscores the urgent need for introspection and reform within our legal and judicial systems, to ensure that justice is not only done but seen to be done – fairly, transparently, and without prejudice.

The case of Asharam Bapu serves as a poignant illustration of the perils of legal entanglements and the profound implications of misusing the POCSO Act. Amidst the sensationalism and media frenzy surrounding his trial, it is imperative to remember the principles of justice and due process that must guide our actions. While allegations of sexual abuse must be investigated rigorously and perpetrators held accountable, it is equally essential to safeguard the rights of the accused and uphold the presumption of innocence until proven guilty.

In conclusion, the misuse of the POCSO Act poses a grave threat to the foundations of our democracy. It is imperative that we remain vigilant against such abuses and work tirelessly to uphold the principles of justice, fairness, and equality for all. Only then can we ensure that our democracy remains strong, resilient, and true to its founding ideals.

CHAPTER TWENTY-FOUR

The Fourth Pillar Tilt: When Kangaroo Journalism Crosses Line

THE DETRIMENTAL EFFECTS OF MEDIA TRIALS ON SOCIETY

Media trials have become a pervasive force in society, often overshadowing the judicial system's role. The court of public opinion, fueled by media speculation and sensationalism, can have profound implications for justice and societal harmony.

1. **Erosion of Presumption of Innocence:** Media trials can erode the foundational legal principle that a person is innocent until proven guilty, leading to public condemnation without due process.
2. **Undermining of Judicial Process:** The influence of media narratives can pressure the judiciary, potentially affecting verdicts and undermining the legal process's integrity.
3. **Sensationalism Over Substance:** Media outlets may prioritize sensationalism over factual reporting, distorting the truth and misleading the public.
4. **Privacy Intrusions:** Intense media scrutiny can lead to unwarranted intrusions into personal lives, violating privacy and causing distress.
5. **Impact on Mental Health:** The accused, witnesses, and their families can suffer significant mental health impacts due to the stress and public scrutiny of media trials

6. **Mob Justice:** Media trials can incite mob mentality, leading to harassment or even violence against the accused or their associates.
7. **Distrust in Legal Institutions:** Constant media speculation can foster public distrust in the fairness and efficacy of legal institutions.
8. **Selective Reporting:** Media may focus on high-profile cases while ignoring others, leading to selective justice and skewed public perception.
9. **Commercialization of News:** The drive for ratings can lead to the commercialization of news, where sensational stories are marketed for profit at the expense of ethical journalism.
10. **Social Polarization:** Media trials can polarize society, creating divisions based on the manipulated narratives presented by the media.

The media's role in shaping public opinion carries a significant responsibility. Ensuring that this power is not misused is crucial for maintaining the integrity of the judicial system and the fabric of society.

THE ROLE OF 'KANGAROO MEDIA' IN MISLEADING SOCIETY

'Kangaroo Media' refers to media outlets that jump to conclusions without adequate investigation, often leading to one-sided reporting and a misinformed public.

1. **Creation of Echo Chambers:** Kangaroo media can create echo chambers, reinforcing pre-existing biases and limiting exposure to diverse perspectives.
2. **Misrepresentation of Facts:** Facts can be twisted or ignored to fit a particular narrative, leading to misinformation.
3. **Amplification of Conflicts:** Such media can amplify societal conflicts by focusing on divisive issues and presenting them in a biased manner.
4. **Cultivation of Fear:** Sensationalized reporting can cultivate fear and anxiety in society, affecting public well-being.
5. **Erosion of Critical Thinking:** The public's ability to think critically can be eroded by constant exposure to one-sided media narratives.
6. **Manipulation of Public Sentiment:** Kangaroo media can manipulate public sentiment for political or commercial gains.

7. **Undermining of Democratic Processes:** Misleading reporting can undermine democratic processes by influencing elections and public policies based on skewed information.
8. **Promotion of Cynicism:** Over time, such reporting can promote cynicism and apathy towards important societal issues.
9. **Deterioration of Public Discourse:** The quality of public discourse can deteriorate as sensationalism takes precedence over reasoned debate.
10. **Exploitation of Vulnerable Populations:** Vulnerable populations can be exploited for sensational stories, often without consideration for their dignity or rights.

Kangaroo media's impact on society is undeniably negative, necessitating a call for more responsible and balanced journalism to preserve the public's right to accurate information.

THE INDEPENDENCE OF NEWS CHANNELS AND ITS CONSEQUENCES

The independence of news channels is vital for a free press, but unchecked freedom without accountability can lead to adverse consequences for society and individual rights.

1. **Lack of Accountability:** Without checks and balances, news channels can operate without accountability, leading to irresponsible journalism.
2. **Infringement on Individual Rights:** The quest for exclusive stories can lead to the infringement of individual rights, including privacy and fair trial.
3. **Bias in Reporting:** Independence can lead to bias in reporting, as news channels may cater to specific ideologies or interests.
4. **Commercial Pressures:** The need to generate revenue can result in news channels prioritizing sensational stories over important but less 'marketable' news.
5. **Neglect of Ethical Standards:** Ethical standards in journalism can be neglected in favor of more engaging or controversial content.
6. **Conflict of Interest:** There can be conflicts of interest when news channels are owned by entities with specific political or commercial agendas.

7. **Manipulation of News:** News can be manipulated to serve the interests of the owners or advertisers, rather than the public.
8. **Spread of Propaganda:** Independent news channels can become vehicles for spreading propaganda if not held to journalistic standards.
9. **Impact on Public Trust:** The public's trust in media can be impacted negatively when news channels are seen as biased or manipulative.
10. **Challenge to Democratic Values:** The core democratic value of an informed citizenry is challenged when news channels do not provide accurate and unbiased information.

While independence is a cornerstone of journalistic integrity, it must be balanced with responsibility to ensure that news channels serve the public interest and contribute positively to society.

COMPLEXITIES OF MEDIA TRIALS: IMPLICATIONS, CHALLENGES, AND ETHICAL CONSIDERATIONS

1. **The Rise of Media Trials:** The advent of 24-hour news cycles and the proliferation of social media platforms have amplified the reach and influence of media trials. News outlets, in a bid to capture audience attention and increase viewership, often engage in sensational reporting, which can lead to a premature and sometimes inaccurate portrayal of events or individuals involved in legal proceedings. The impact of such coverage is profound, as it shapes public perception and can potentially sway the outcome of court cases.
2. **Implications for the Accused:** For the accused, a media trial can be a harrowing experience. The intense scrutiny and the barrage of opinions presented as facts can tarnish reputations, affect personal and professional relationships, and lead to public condemnation. The media's portrayal of the accused often lacks nuance and fails to consider the complexities of legal proceedings, resulting in a one-dimensional narrative that may not reflect the truth.
3. **Challenges to the Judicial Process:** Media trials pose a challenge to the judicial process by creating an atmosphere of bias and prejudice. The constant media attention can put undue pressure on judges, jurors, and witnesses, compromising the fairness and impartiality that are fundamental to the justice system. Moreover, the media's reach can

influence potential jurors, making it difficult to assemble an unbiased jury pool.

4. **The Ethical Dilemma:** The ethical dilemma of media trials lies in the conflict between the public's right to information and an individual's right to a fair trial. While the media serves as a watchdog and plays a crucial role in informing the public, it must also respect the boundaries of the legal process. The pursuit of truth should not come at the cost of justice, and the media must navigate this delicate balance with responsibility and integrity.
5. **The Way Forward:** To address the challenges posed by media trials, there must be a concerted effort to establish clear guidelines and ethical standards for reporting on legal matters. Journalists and media organizations should be trained to understand the legal system and the potential consequences of their reporting. Additionally, there should be mechanisms in place to hold media accountable for irresponsible coverage that could influence legal outcomes.

Media trials are a complex issue that reflects the tension between a free press and the principles of justice. As consumers of media, it is essential to approach such coverage with a critical eye and recognize the potential biases that may be at play. For the media, it is imperative to uphold the highest standards of journalism, ensuring that the quest for ratings does not undermine the pursuit of justice. In the end, the integrity of both the media and the judicial system must be preserved to maintain the trust and confidence of the public.

Media trials have become a contentious issue in contemporary society, often criticized for their negative impact on the judicial process and the individuals involved. Here's an article that delves into why media trials are inherently problematic and detrimental from any angle.

THE PERILS OF MEDIA TRIALS: A THREAT TO JUSTICE AND FAIRNESS

In the age of instant communication and relentless news cycles, the phenomenon of media trials has emerged as a significant challenge to the sanctity of the judicial system. Media trials, where the press effectively assumes the role of judge and jury, have been universally condemned for their adverse effects on the administration of justice. This article explores the reasons why media trials are fundamentally flawed and harmful from every conceivable angle.

1. **Undermining the Presumption of Innocence:** At the heart of any fair judicial system lies the presumption of innocence. Media trials, however, often disregard this principle, casting aspersions and declaring guilt based on sensationalist coverage. This not only tarnishes the reputation of the accused but also influences public opinion, which can be difficult to reverse even if the court later finds the individual not guilty.
2. **Interference with the Legal Process:** The extensive coverage and analysis provided by media trials can interfere with the legal process. Jurors, witnesses, and even judges can be swayed by the court of public opinion, which is shaped by the media's narrative. This can lead to biased verdicts and miscarriages of justice, as the legal proceedings are overshadowed by media speculation.
3. **Violation of Privacy:** Media trials often involve a deep dive into the personal lives of those involved, leading to a gross violation of privacy. The relentless pursuit of a story can result in the exposure of sensitive information, causing undue distress to the accused and their families, irrespective of the trial's outcome.
4. **Sensationalism Over Substance:** In their quest for higher ratings and more clicks, media outlets may prioritize sensationalism over substance. This leads to a skewed portrayal of events, where the focus is on creating a compelling narrative rather than reporting the facts. Such sensationalism can mislead the public and create a distorted view of the case.
5. **Long-term Repercussions:** The effects of media trials are not limited to the duration of the legal proceedings. The accused, even if acquitted, may continue to suffer from the stigma associated with the media's portrayal of the case. This can have long-term repercussions on their personal and professional lives, effectively punishing them in the court of public opinion despite a legal exoneration.

Media trials are a clear perversion of the principles of justice. They compromise the fairness of the legal system, violate the rights of individuals, and undermine the very foundations of a democratic society. It is imperative that the media exercise restraint and adhere to ethical standards of reporting, ensuring that the pursuit of truth does not come at the expense of justice and fairness.

In the grand theater of justice, where the gavel's echo should signify the ultimate decree, it seems the media has hijacked the judge's bench, turning courtrooms into their own prime-time spectacle. With a flair for the dramatic and a penchant for the sensational, the media has become a self-appointed arbiter of fate, often leaving a trail of tarnished reputations and spoiled lives in its wake.

THE MEDIA'S GAVEL: LOUDER THAN THE LAW'S

The media, in its relentless pursuit of the next big headline, often casts aside the scales of justice for the scales of public opinion. In this new court, the rules are simple: the more shocking the story, the greater the ratings. And so, the media trial begins, with little regard for due process or the presumption of innocence.

- **The Casualties of Sensational Journalism:** Countless individuals have found themselves in the unforgiving spotlight of media trials, their lives dissected and displayed for the world to see. Guilty or not, the verdict is often delivered long before any legal judgment, with the accused left to navigate a life marred by public scrutiny and stigma.
- **The Spice of Misery:** Media's Favorite Condiment. It appears that the media has developed a taste for the spice of misery, sprinkling it liberally over every story to enhance the flavor. The zest of drama, the piquancy of scandal, and the tang of tragedy have become staple ingredients in the newsroom's kitchen. The result? A dish that's hard to swallow for those caught in the crosshairs of a relentless news cycle.

In the end, one can't help but observe that the media seems to have developed quite the palate for the spice of drama. So much so, that they've begun to sprinkle it generously over the news, turning the once-sacred pursuit of truth into a sensational feast for the masses.

The unchecked rise of media trials in India is a ticking time bomb, threatening to erode the very pillars of democracy and society. If the judiciary does not step in to curb this rampant phenomenon, we stand on the precipice of a future where the lines between justice and entertainment are irreversibly blurred.

THE JUDICIAL RESPONSE TO MEDIA TRIALS: A DEMOCRATIC IMPERATIVE

Media trials have become a parallel judiciary, often delivering verdicts even before the courts have had a chance to hear a case. This not only undermines the judiciary's authority but also jeopardizes the fundamental rights of individuals. The sensationalism that accompanies media trials distorts facts, sways public opinion, and can lead to the wrongful conviction or acquittal of individuals based on the court of public opinion rather than evidence.

- **The Threat to Society and Democracy:** The implications of media trials extend beyond individual cases, posing a systemic threat to society and democracy. They can shape public perceptions of individuals and events, influencing public opinion before legal processes are complete[1]. This influence can impact political figures, public figures, and even government policies, potentially swaying public sentiment in a way that may not align with fair and unbiased judicial outcomes.
  Moreover, media trials can also create a trial by public opinion, which can lead to the accused being subjected to harassment, abuse, and even violence. Additionally, media trials can erode public trust in the justice system and undermine the country's democracy.
- **The Need for Regulation:** It is imperative for the judiciary to assert its role in regulating media trials. Laws and guidelines must be enforced to ensure that media coverage does not interfere with the right to a fair trial. The media's freedom of expression is a cornerstone of democracy, but it should not come at the cost of another's right to justice.

If left unchecked, media trials will continue to chip away at the foundations of our society and democracy. It seems that the media has grown too fond of the taste of salt and spice, using it liberally even in news reporting. The judiciary must act to ensure that the zest for sensationalism does not overpower the quest for truth and justice.

CHAPTER TWENTY-FIVE

Fabricated Justice

UNVEILING THE MISUSE OF LEGAL PROVISIONS AGAINST BAPU AND ITS SOCIO-LEGAL IMPLICATIONS

1. **Weaponizing Legal Provisions:** The misuse of the POSCO Act to fabricate cases against Asharam Bapu exemplifies a troubling trend of weaponizing legal provisions for personal and political vendettas. This abuse of power undermines the integrity of the legal system and erodes public trust in the judiciary.
2. **Impact on Social Fabric:** Fabricated cases not only harm the individual targeted but also have ripple effects on society. They breed distrust in institutions, sow discord among communities, and create an atmosphere of fear and suspicion.
3. **Violation of Human Rights:** The wrongful imprisonment of Asharam Bapu based on fabricated charges is a clear violation of his fundamental human rights. It deprives him of his liberty, dignity, and the opportunity to continue his humanitarian work for the betterment of society.
4. **Media Sensationalism:** The role of sensationalist media in perpetuating falsehoods and sensationalizing allegations cannot be understated. Biased reporting not only fuels public outrage but also prejudices potential jurors, making it difficult for the accused to receive a fair trial.
5. **Cultural and Spiritual Impact:** Asharam Bapu's teachings and spiritual guidance have had a profound impact on millions of devotees worldwide. Fabricated cases not only tarnish his personal reputation but also undermine the cultural and spiritual heritage he represents.

6. **Legal Reforms:** The case of Asharam Bapu underscores the urgent need for legal reforms to prevent the misuse of legal provisions for malicious purposes. Stricter safeguards, enhanced oversight mechanisms, and penalties for those found guilty of fabricating cases are essential to safeguarding the rights of the innocent.
7. **Call for Solidarity:** In the face of such injustices, it is imperative for individuals, organizations, and civil society to stand in solidarity with Asharam Bapu and others who have been wrongfully accused. Collective action and advocacy are crucial in demanding accountability and justice for the victims of fabricated cases.

Incorporating these additional points reinforces the gravity of the situation and underscores the broader implications of fabricating cases against individuals like Asharam Bapu. It emphasizes the need for comprehensive reform and collective action to uphold the principles of justice, fairness, and integrity in society.

In the contemporary media landscape, the term "*media trial*" has become increasingly prevalent, often evoking strong reactions and sparking intense debates about the role of media in society. At its core, a media trial refers to the phenomenon where the media, rather than the judiciary, takes on the role of judge and jury, casting judgment on individuals or cases before an official verdict is reached. This practice raises significant concerns about the balance between freedom of the press and the right to a fair trial, the presumption of innocence, and the overall integrity of the justice system.

DENIAL OF BAIL FOR SANT ASHARAM BAPU: A FAILURE OF JUSTICE IN THE 21ST CENTURY

The refusal to grant bail to Sant Asharam Bapu, a revered spiritual leader and a venerable figure in Indian society, has drawn sharp criticism from legal experts, including the distinguished Subramanian Swamy. In what is being described as the "biggest failure of the Judiciary in the 21st Century," the denial of bail to a 89 years old Asharam Bapu has raised serious questions about the fairness and impartiality of the legal system.

Subramanian Swamy, a prominent politician and legal luminary, has been vocal in his condemnation of the prolonged incarceration of Sant Asharam Bapu. He has emphasized that denying bail to an elderly individual, who poses no flight risk and whose health is deteriorating, is a grave **miscarriage of justice**. Swamy's assertion underscores the fundamental principle of bail as a right, not a privilege, and highlights the inherent injustice in withholding this right from an individual based on unproven allegations.

The case against Sant Asharam Bapu has been marred by controversy and allegations of fabrication, with many legal experts expressing skepticism about the credibility of the evidence presented against him. Despite this, the judicial system has failed to afford him the basic presumption of innocence and has instead subjected him to prolonged detention without trial—a violation of his fundamental rights enshrined in the Constitution.

The denial of bail to Sant Asharam Bapu not only reflects a failure of the judiciary but also undermines the principles of justice, fairness, and compassion that are integral to a democratic society. It sends a chilling message about the vulnerability of individuals to arbitrary detention and the erosion of due process rights in the face of political pressure and public sentiment.

In light of Subramanian Swamy's scathing critique and the broader concerns raised by legal experts, it is imperative that the judiciary reconsiders its decision and upholds the principles of fairness and justice without fear or favor. The denial of bail to Sant Asharam Bapu is not just a failure of the judiciary; it is a failure of the entire legal system to uphold the rights and dignity of every individual, regardless of their stature or background.

In conclusion, Sant Asharam Bapu deserves to be treated with the dignity and respect befitting his status as a spiritual leader and a revered figure in society. It is incumbent upon the judiciary to rectify this injustice and ensure that he receives a fair and expeditious trial. As Subramanian Swamy rightly asserts, the denial of bail to Sant Asharam Bapu is indeed the biggest failure of the judiciary in the 21st century—a failure that must be addressed with urgency and rectified without delay.

Let us stand united in our demand for justice and fairness for Sant Asharam Bapu and all individuals who have been wronged by a flawed and unjust legal system.

CHAPTER TWENTY-SIX

Justice in Peril: Misuse of IPC sections

INJUSTICE PREVAILS: THE MISAPPLICATION OF SECTION 370(4) IPC IN THE CASE OF ASHARAM BAPU

In recent years, the legal system has witnessed the misapplication of Section 370(4) of the Indian Penal Code (IPC), particularly in cases involving spiritual leaders like Asharam Bapu. Section 370(4) IPC deals with trafficking of persons for the purpose of exploitation, a grave offense that warrants stringent punishment. However, in the case of Asharam Bapu, the application of this section raises serious questions about justice and fairness.

Section 370(4) IPC defines trafficking of persons as the recruitment, transportation, transfer, harboring, or receipt of persons, by means of threat or use of force or other forms of coercion, for the purpose of exploitation. While the intention behind this provision is to combat human trafficking and protect vulnerable individuals, its misapplication in cases like Asharam Bapu's undermines its true purpose.

Asharam Bapu, a revered spiritual leader known for his philanthropic work and teachings on morality and spirituality, found himself entangled in legal troubles when he was accused under Section 370(4) IPC. The allegations against him were based on flimsy grounds and lacked substantial evidence to prove the charges of trafficking and exploitation.

The media played a pivotal role in shaping public opinion and influencing judicial proceedings in the case of Asharam Bapu. Sensationalist coverage and biased reporting created a hostile environment, leading to undue pressure on the judiciary to deliver a verdict based on public sentiment rather than objective legal principles.

Media trials have become a pervasive issue in contemporary society, where sensationalism often takes precedence over truth and justice. The relentless pursuit of ratings and sensational headlines has led to a culture of trial by media, where individuals are pronounced guilty in the court of public opinion before their guilt is proven in a court of law.

In light of these challenges, there is an urgent need for judicial reform and greater accountability within the media. Judicial independence must be safeguarded against external influences, and mechanisms should be put in place to prevent undue pressure from media organizations.

Moreover, media ethics and standards of reporting need to be upheld to ensure fair and balanced coverage of legal proceedings. Journalists have a responsibility to adhere to principles of objectivity and impartiality, refraining from sensationalism and prejudicial reporting that can undermine the integrity of the judicial process.

In conclusion, the misapplication of Section 370(4) IPC in the case of Asharam Bapu underscores the urgent need for judicial reform and media accountability. The independence of the judiciary must be safeguarded against external pressures, and media organizations should adhere to ethical standards to ensure fair and balanced reporting. Only then can we uphold the principles of justice and ensure that the rights of individuals are protected against unjust persecution.

UPHOLDING JUSTICE: THE MISCONSTRUED CASE OF SECTION 342 IPC AGAINST ASHARAM BAPU

In recent times, the application of Section 342 of the Indian Penal Code (IPC) against Asharam Bapu has sparked controversy and raised questions about the integrity of the legal system. This article seeks to shed light on the nature of Section 342 IPC and the dubious circumstances surrounding its invocation against Asharam Bapu.

Section 342 IPC pertains to wrongful confinement. It states that whoever wrongfully confines any person shall be punished with imprisonment of either description for a term which may extend to one year, or with fine which may extend to one thousand rupees, or with both. The key word here is "wrongfully," indicating that the confinement must be without lawful justification or authority.

However, in the case of Asharam Bapu, the application of this section appears to be highly questionable. There is a glaring lack of evidence to support the allegations against him. Moreover, the credibility of the accusers has been called into question, with many inconsistencies and discrepancies in their testimonies.

It is evident that the case against Asharam Bapu does not meet the criteria for invoking Section 342 IPC. Yet, he has been subjected to media trial and undue pressure from various quarters. The media, in its pursuit of sensationalism and ratings, has often overlooked the principles of fair and unbiased reporting. Instead of allowing the judiciary to function independently and impartially, the media has resorted to sensationalism, thereby influencing public opinion and pressuring the courts.

This highlights the urgent need for judicial reform and greater accountability in media reporting. The judiciary must be insulated from external pressures and allowed to function without fear or favor. Similarly, the media must adhere to ethical standards and refrain from sensationalizing sensitive cases.

In conclusion, the case against Asharam Bapu under Section 342 IPC is a glaring example of miscarriage of justice and the need for systemic reforms. Upholding the principles of fairness, impartiality, and due process is essential to ensuring justice for all individuals, regardless of their status or position. It is time for a reevaluation of our legal and media systems to prevent such injustices from recurring in the future.

UNDERSTANDING SECTION 506 IPC AND THE CASE OF BAPU

Section 506 of the Indian Penal Code (IPC) deals with criminal intimidation. It states that whoever commits the offense of criminal intimidation shall be punished with imprisonment of either description for a term which may extend to two years, or with fine, or with both.

The case involving Asharam Bapu has indeed brought this section into focus. However, it's essential to delve deeper into the circumstances surrounding the case. While accusations were made against him under Section 506 IPC, it's crucial to remember that accusations alone do not constitute guilt.

In the case of Asharam Bapu, there have been concerns raised regarding the fairness of the trial and the conduct of the media. The media often sensationalizes cases, influencing public opinion and sometimes even putting pressure on the judiciary. This phenomenon, known as "media trial," can have detrimental effects on the fairness of legal proceedings.

Moreover, the media's role in shaping public perception can inadvertently influence judicial decisions, leading to a trial by public opinion rather than by legal standards. This highlights the need for reforms within the judiciary and limitations on media coverage of ongoing legal cases.

Judicial reform is essential to ensure that trials are conducted fairly and impartially, without external influences. Similarly, there is a need to address the limitations and responsibilities of the media in reporting legal matters. Striking a balance between freedom of the press and the integrity of the judicial process is paramount in upholding the principles of justice and fairness.

In conclusion, while Section 506 IPC is a crucial legal provision, its application in cases like that of Asharam Bapu underscores the need for judicial reform and greater accountability in media coverage of legal proceedings. Fair trials and unbiased reporting are fundamental pillars of a just society, and efforts must be made to uphold these principles.

UNRAVELING THE TRUTH: THE CASE OF ASHARAM BAPU AND THE FLAWS IN MEDIA TRIALS

In recent years, the case of Asharam Bapu has been a subject of intense scrutiny and sensationalism in the media. However, amidst the frenzy of headlines and accusations, it's imperative to delve into the legal intricacies surrounding the charges brought against him under Section 376(2)(f) IPC and Section 376D IPC.

Section 376(2)(f) IPC pertains to cases where a sexual assault is committed on a woman when she is incapable of giving consent due to unsoundness of mind or intoxication. On the other hand, Section 376D IPC deals with gang rape cases. These sections are meant to safeguard the rights and dignity of individuals, especially women, against heinous crimes.

However, when we scrutinize the facts of the case against Asharam Bapu, it becomes evident that the application of these legal provisions raises serious questions. Despite the gravity of the accusations, the medical report presents a stark contradiction to the charges levied. The absence of physical assault, loss of consciousness, penetration, or any other corroborating evidence challenges the very foundation of the case.

Moreover, it's crucial to address the issue of media trials, which have become pervasive in today's society. The relentless coverage and sensationalism by certain sections of the media not only prejudge the case but also exert undue pressure on the judiciary. Media trials often lead to a distorted narrative, where the presumption of innocence is overshadowed by sensationalism and public opinion.

The case of Asharam Bapu underscores the urgent need for judicial reforms and limitations on media sensationalism. The judiciary must remain independent and impartial, free from external influences or pressures. It's imperative to uphold the principles of justice and fairness, ensuring that every individual receives a fair trial based on evidence and facts, rather than media hysteria.

In conclusion, the case against Asharam Bapu highlights the complexities and challenges inherent in the legal system, especially when juxtaposed with media sensationalism. It's essential to critically analyze the evidence and uphold the principles of justice, ensuring that the truth prevails above all else.

CHAPTER TWENTY-SEVEN

Letters

Ashish Kumar
Ramgarh, Jharkhand
Date: March 26, 2024

The Honorable Chief Justice of India
Supreme Court of India
New Delhi

Subject: Urgent Appeal to Address Fabricated Legal Cases and Protect Judicial Integrity

Dear Honorable Chief Justice,

I am writing to you with a profound sense of concern regarding the escalating menace of fabricated legal cases that are undermining the very foundation of our judicial system and wreaking havoc on the lives of innocent individuals. As a conscientious citizen deeply committed to upholding the principles of justice and fairness, I implore you to take immediate and decisive action to address this pressing issue.

In recent years, there has been an alarming proliferation of fabricated legal cases orchestrated by certain vested interests with political or professional agendas. These cases are built on a web of lies, manipulation, and coercion, and are relentlessly pursued with the sole intent of persecuting and defaming innocent individuals. The victims of these fabricated cases are subjected to malicious investigations, baseless accusations, and prolonged legal battles that not only drain their resources but also inflict irreparable damage to their lives and reputations.

The prevalence of fabricated legal cases is a direct assault on the principles of justice, fairness, and the rule of law. It erodes public trust in our judicial institutions and undermines the fundamental rights and liberties guaranteed by our Constitution. Moreover, it perpetuates a culture of impunity where the powerful and influential can manipulate the legal system to serve their own interests at the expense of justice and integrity.

It is imperative that we take concrete steps to address this grave threat to our judicial system and the well-being of our society. I urge you to consider the following measures:

1. **Enhanced Oversight and Accountability:** Implement robust mechanisms for oversight and accountability within the judiciary to prevent the abuse of legal processes and ensure the fair and impartial adjudication of cases. This includes stringent monitoring of court proceedings, regular audits of case files, and transparent reporting of judicial decisions.
2. **Strengthened Legal Framework:** Advocate for legislative reforms to strengthen the legal framework and impose stricter penalties on those found guilty of fabricating false cases and manipulating judicial proceedings. This may include amendments to existing laws to provide for expedited trials and harsher punishments for perpetrators of judicial misconduct.
3. **Victim Support and Protection:** Establish specialized support services for victims of fabricated legal cases, including access to legal aid, counseling, and rehabilitation programs. Additionally, ensure adequate measures are in place to protect victims and their families from harassment, intimidation, and retaliation by those responsible for fabricating false cases.
4. **Public Awareness and Education:** Launch public awareness campaigns to educate the public, legal professionals, and law enforcement agencies about the detrimental effects of fabricated legal cases and the importance of upholding ethical standards and due process in the administration of justice. This includes disseminating information about the rights of individuals accused of crimes and the legal remedies available to them.

5. **Judicial Reform and Capacity Building:** Invest in judicial reform initiatives aimed at improving the efficiency, transparency, and integrity of our judicial system. This may involve training programs for judges, prosecutors, and court staff to enhance their capacity to handle complex legal cases and uphold the highest standards of professionalism and integrity.

In conclusion, the prevalence of fabricated legal cases poses a grave threat to the integrity and credibility of our judicial system. It is imperative that we take decisive action to combat this scourge and reaffirm our commitment to justice, fairness, and the rule of law. I urge you to prioritize this issue and work collaboratively with all stakeholders to implement meaningful reforms that will restore public trust and confidence in our judiciary.

Thank you for your attention to this urgent matter. I trust in your leadership and dedication to upholding the principles of justice and fairness that are the cornerstone of our democracy.

Yours sincerely,
Ashish Kumar

Ashish Kumar
Ramgarh, Jharkhand
Date: April 01, 2024

The Honorable Chief Justice of India
Supreme Court of India
New Delhi

Subject: Urgent Appeal for Judicial Intervention in Media Trials

To the Honorable Chief Justice of India,

I pen this letter with a profound sense of urgency and a deep respect for the esteemed office you hold—a bastion of justice in our great democracy. It is with a humble heart and a citizen's concern for the future of our society that I seek to draw your attention to a matter of grave importance—the phenomenon of media trials in India.

In recent years, we have witnessed an alarming trend where the media has assumed the role of a quasi-judicial entity, conducting what are popularly known as 'media trials.' This practice, where cases and individuals are tried and judged in the court of public opinion, has become a ticking time bomb, threatening to erode the very pillars of democracy and the sanctity of our society.

The media, revered as the fourth pillar of democracy, holds the power to shape narratives and influence public perception. However, when this power is wielded without restraint, it can disrupt the balance of justice. Media trials have the potential to prejudice the minds of the public and the jurors alike, casting a shadow of bias even before the judiciary has had an opportunity to deliberate on the facts of the case.

The impact of such trials is not merely confined to the distortion of public opinion but extends to the undermining of the judiciary's authority. When verdicts are pronounced in news studios, the subliminal pressure on the judicial process can be immense. The constant scrutiny and updates on sub judice matters create a clouded environment, leaving the case and the lives of those involved in a perilous state

Moreover, the sensationalism that often accompanies media trials infringes upon the rights of individuals, violating the principle of 'innocent until proven guilty' and denying them the right to a fair trial. The media's narrative, driven by the pursuit of ratings, often overlooks the nuanced understanding of the law, leading to a trial by spectacle rather than a trial by evidence.

As a concerned citizen, I humbly request your intervention in this critical issue. It is imperative that the judiciary takes cognizance of the repercussions of media trials and considers implementing stringent guidelines to safeguard the administration of justice. The need of the hour is to ensure that the media refrains from encroaching upon the domain of the judiciary and respects the due process of law.

The future of our democracy and the faith of our citizens in the judicial system are at stake. We must act swiftly to prevent the erosion of these foundational elements that uphold our society. I trust that under your esteemed leadership, the judiciary will rise to address this challenge and preserve the sanctity of justice.

With the highest regard and anticipation for your judicious response

Yours sincerely,
Ashish Kumar

The person who has dedicated their entire life for the betterment of society, But in return, he had to face only conspiracy. I say, The Greatest Injustice of the 21st century has happened with Asharam Bapu. Not just the 21st century, It must have never happened with anyone in the entire history, what is happening with Bapu. Asharam Bapu has taught people to spread fragrance like a flower rather than just giving them flowers, But under the guise of conspiracy, thorns were spread in Bapu's life. Under false allegations alone, he was sentenced to lifelong imprisonment, Despite no medical evidence or proof, Such punishment was inflicted on him solely based on a statement. He was charged under the POCSO Act, Even though the girl was over 18, in such cases, many questions arise regarding police investigation. Bapuji has guided millions of people onto the right path, Improving countless lives, freeing many from alcohol, tobacco chewing, smoking, And showing the way to a healthy life. Bapuji has worked to uplift the entire world to economic, mental, and spiritual peaks, Bapuji's crown chakra is 100% developed.

There are seven chakras in the human body: Crown chakra, Third-eye chakra, Throat chakra, Heart chakra, Solar plexus chakra, Sacral chakra, Root chakra. Bapu has developed all these chakras to 100% completeness. The blessings and touch of a saint are often considered superstition, but scientific analysis also shows that thousands of people have been cured of incurable diseases by respected Bapu. Bapu has a unique ability to absorb others' negative energy and give positive energy from a distance. Bapu has undertaken many initiatives such as women empowerment, divine child upbringing, abortion prevention campaigns, cesarean delivery, spiritual awakening camps, prisoner rehabilitation programs, Tulsi Vrinda campaign, tribal welfare, Gurukuls, Parent's Worship Day, and cow protection, which perhaps no one else in the world can accomplish.

Schools organize fancy dress competitions where children briefly adorn the attire of great personalities
like Mahatma Gandhi, Rani Lakshmibai, Subhash Chandra Bose, Bhagat Singh, Sardar Vallabhbhai Patel, Kabir Das, Tulsidas, Swami Vivekananda, Veer Shivaji, Chanakya, Arjuna, Sita, Radha, and Mother Teresa. But Bapu's perspective is that children should mold their character and behavior like

these great figures. This external covering is temporary, but if this covering becomes permanent for us, it will be like icing on the cake. How will the nation respond to Asharam Bapu, with honor or dishonor? Asharam Bapu embodies complete Brahmajnana, understanding the relationship between individual soul and the Supreme Soul, thus infusing meaning into his life and influencing those around him. As a knower of Brahma, he sees unity among all beings and holds feelings of compassion and love towards them. His brahman touch purifies others, imbuing them with positivity. Those devoted to Brahma verify this knowledge in their thoughts and actions, shaping their lives accordingly. They remain brahman absorbed in Brahman contemplation, aligning their actions with its principles. Bapu says, "*Besides God, there is nothing.*" What exists is indeed He, and what does not exist is also He. These are all spiritual matters; what can we say? My heart aches when I witness atrocities against saints. Just as farmers are essential in fields and soldiers are necessary at borders, similarly, for the holistic development of life, Brahman-realized saints are extremely crucial. Atrocities against saints have been happening for centuries, and today, it has reached its peak. They say that in a tree with abundant fruit, stones are hurled the most. But this doesn't mean we stay silent and watch everything. We must raise our voices and move forward.

Atal Bihari Vajpayee once said, "*Asharam Bapu, by traveling across the nation, is awakening good values in the hearts of the people. This is a paramount national duty that has kept our nation alive till today, and on its strength, we envision a bright future. Our ancient heritage, which we were almost forgetting, Bapu Ji is reintroducing it before us, applying the collyrium of knowledge to our eyes once again.*" Bapu Ji has served society, the nation, and culture with heart, mind, and wealth. Therefore, anti-national forces falsely imprisoned him.

Narendra Modi said, "*When no one was there in my life, Asharam Bapu was there with me to shower blessings, to love me. Hundreds of millions of people have benefited from Bapu's life. What can I say and how much can I say, Bapu has instilled the feeling of '**Vasudhaiva Kutumbakam**' in everyone, considering every individual of society as a part of his family. The echoes of his service resonate in all directions, yet describing his glory completely is not possible. Where the Vedas become silent by saying 'neti, neti', from there begins the glory of Bapu.*"

In every being, my own lineage exists,
It resonates in the call of the mosque's prayer,
And in the temple's hymns, it's present too,
In that Brahmin scholar, it's also there,
And in the cobbler stitching shoes,
For I am the eternal essence in all living beings.
It must prick in the ears of the mosque's call to prayer,
And cause headache with the temple's bells,
The scholar might seem like a fraud,
And there might be disdain for the cobbler,
Troubles may arise from neighbors,
Jealousy might brew from the upper caste,
And there might be distress even from the lower caste,
Dual feelings may emerge in the mind,
To speak the truth, it must happen,
And it's better if it does.
Even if you imprison Brahman-realized saints under false conspiracies,
Where will wisdom be found then? in the marketplace?
Anyway, let it be, remain silent,
Let atrocities happen to the saints, it's the law's provision,
And plaster posters of 'Sabka Saath, Sabka Vikas' (Together with All, Development for All),
Then see whether society is moving towards development or destruction.
I say with my hand on my heart, the situation is such that "*you go to the sweet shop and demand*
sandals."
By trapping saints in false conspiracies and defaming them,
You imagine yourself as the political world's guru.

The dust of a Brahman-realized sage's feet holds such significance that even the gods follow behind to collect it. That's why the gods themselves consider it sacred to place that dust upon their own heads. However, some people in society have attempted to tarnish the character of Brahman-realized Bapuji. Civilization has been said to be our body and culture our soul. These lines from the famous Indian poet Muhammad Iqbal Masoodi come to mind:

"

"Yunani, Misr, Roma, sab mit gaye jahan se
Baaki magar hai ab tak, naam-o-nishan hamara
Kuch baat to hai ki hasti, mitati nahi hamari
Sadiyon raha hai dushman, daur-e-jahan hamara" "

Indeed, our existence is not destroyed but the size of ancient Bharat is reduced to a great extent due to foreign invasions and religious conversions, this doesn't mean that India will continue to tolerate atrocities against its saints. If we don't improve now, if we don't stand up for our saints, then who will save our culture?

The attitude of one country towards another is hostile. One country is unable to progress itself and is unable to see the progress of another, resorting to petty actions of belittling, not utilizing its own land and instead encroaching upon others', indulging in such actions that undermine their own conscience. I am witnessing it all. For months, there's been war, with bodies falling, yet no one's pride is diminishing. That's why this war continues. No matter what happens, the government just stirs up mud. Whatever happens, the opposition must declare a conspiracy. There's only confrontation between the ruling and opposition parties. Neither the border soldiers nor our farmers are satisfied. There's distress between spouses, siblings quarrel, and neighbors are envious. Every day on the streets, there's protest, only slogans resound, and in this chaos, everyone is losing themselves. Shopkeepers are busy with deceit, while buyers run after bargains. Every relationship is now breaking, everything seems to be falling apart for some reason. Incidents of heartbreak are increasing because the thought of hurting others is prevailing in the heart. Students go to schools and colleges but learn only addiction and foul language. The desire for knowledge acquisition has vanished; they're only chasing wealth and fame. Sons are living with fathers only for property. Daughters ask mothers only about jewelry. Sons-in-law are respecting fathers-in-law only to secure their rights at home. Daughters-in-law are serving mothers in-law only for control over the household. The night is for sleeping, but one must work under the moon's light, and as soon as the sun rises, they criticize its rays with a pillow on their face. Carrying the sword of destruction in their hands, they strive for development in this world. Those who have embraced darkness in this world have sown nothing but seeds of destruction. By pitting Hindus against Muslims, Muslims against Sikhs, Sikhs against Christians, and Christians against Hindus, and entangling the cycle of religion in each other, only the genesis of poison is being created. Animals are disappearing from the forests, and humanity from humans. The jungle is becoming the home of people, and homes are turning into jungles. This is what I clearly see: the rapid emergence of degradation within humanity. They chase after happiness, but in reality, they keep their line with the queues of sorrow. Every mind is frustrated, with passions and animosities in the heart. If there is no peace in the mind, where will tranquility be found in life? The whole world is calling the Russia-Ukraine war dreadful, but I see it as just a tiny, small beginning.

This is just a warning for all of humanity to mend their ways, or else prepare for a dreadful world war III where thirsting for each other's blood. If I find that, I'll be happy; if I find that, I'll be peaceful. It's impossible. Because peace is attained only and only through sacrifice. They sit outside, seeming pure, but they can't remove the dirt from within. Impurity has become the tenant of their hearts. The desire to encroach, to seize, to rob still lingers. Farmers don't desire to produce "food" in their fields; they desire how to produce "more food." In this pursuit, they don't produce food, but poison. That poison, which we consume and perish, little by little. But it's not even noticeable, We don't educate our children, Yet we keep creating earning machines, Companies need employees, But there, too, they maneuver, Play tricks, Crush the deserving candidates and make the dishonest ones a part of their company. And perhaps they forget, How can a company do well which has throttled the trust of any good candidate itself, This is a huge regret, We need honesty from others, but we ourselves want to remain dishonest from within and wear the mask of honesty to chase the dishonest in the crowded market. They smear mud on their own character and splash mud on others, calling society dirty. Blessed is the dog That never betrays its owner's trust by stealing salt, and doesn't bow down in crowded gatherings. Even dogs have become inferior, proving the decline in human intelligence. The situation has become so dire that justice in the Constitution's laws and courts is such that the truthful, virtuous, saints who show the right path to society end up in jail, while thieves, robbers, rapists, and gamblers easily get bail.

Kabir used to say, "***One Ram is the son of Dasharatha, one Ram resides in every heart, one Ram is spread***

everywhere, one Ram is unique to everyone. " This means everyone takes the name of the three pervading,

but no one understands the secret of the fourth Ram. And that fourth Ram, none other than the brahman realized saint Asharam Bapuji, who has never harbored ill will towards anyone, has embraced everyone. Despite so much persecution, he has never felt hatred towards anyone or spoken ill of anyone. Every moment, Bapuji remains in his joy and advises his devotees to maintain patience. And he says victory of truth will come, if not today then tomorrow.

The Chief Minister of Gujarat said: "*Devotees have come to the feet of revered Bapu from all over the country. I have faith that from this sacred land of Gujarat, on the banks of the Sabarmati, not only will people take hope with the blessings of Asharam Bapuji, but also take enthusiasm, new beliefs, and new consciousness. They will go with a new resolve, which will become the heritage of their own development, a legacy of self-improvement. But the task we have accepted here has been said: "Yoga Karma Su Kaushalam" I will keep doing the work we have accepted with skillful dedication. Success will be attained on its own, by meditating on his words, by the power of his blessings, we all receive gratitude in our lives. I have been fortunate enough to receive blessings from Bapuji when no one knew me, his love continues, and even today, I receive the same love. Bapu has motivated lakhs of people in Gujarat to fulfill their hopes and aspirations. A new consciousness has awakened, a new flow of collective satsang has started. I believe that in the 21st century, India has the responsibility to play a role, to prepare the groundwork, once again many sages like Asharam Bapuji are working tirelessly, preparing the groundwork for spirituality. The power of yogic strength is present in Bapu's words, with the help of that power, the dreams of the people of Gujarat will be realized. I bow at the feet of Bapuji, I offer my respects, the love, blessings, and good wishes of revered Bapu will give me new strength, I consider myself fortunate, I bow at the feet of revered Bapu. The construction of this nation has been done by the great tradition of sages for centuries, Bapuji is an integral part of that great tradition, and at the beginning of the 21st century, you see, what is the reason that crowds gather in millions, not only here, I have heard Bapuji sitting in Haryana, I have heard in Punjab, I have heard in Rajasthan, I have heard in the streets of Uttar Pradesh, the whole country has awakened to a new consciousness, a new current of collective satsang has started, I think that in the 21st century, the responsibility of India, the role to play, the preparation of the pre-role, once again, many sages like*

Asharam Bapuji, are working tirelessly, on the basis of spirituality, preparing the groundwork for the new role, although I am in the political field, I have complete faith that this nation will once again become worthy of respect, with the blessings of Bapuji, where I have been given the responsibility to work, due to the education of saints, due to the respect for spiritual life, the responsibility I have received, I bow with folded hands at the feet of Bapuji, saying that there is strength in your blessings. I didn't come here as the Chief Minister. I came solely as Narendra Modi and only as Modi to seek the blessings of revered Asharam Bapu feet. There wasn't anything special about it, just heartfelt gratitude to everyone once again. Hari Om..."

But what happened today? Why has silence prevailed for 12 years? Whether you are sitting at his feet for political gain? Or for a vote bank? Perhaps they'll never answer this question were in this country,

Ram has been politicized for power.
You speak of the timeless culture,
Forcing India's farmers onto the streets,
Proudly boasting martyrdom instead of resolving border disputes,
Making the rich richer,
Pushing the poor deeper into poverty,
Throwing saints in jail with false accusations,
Forcing youth into suicide instead of employment.
You talk about the ancient culture at every opportunity,
And promote inter-caste marriage behind the scenes,
Increasing the business of buying votes in millions,
Displaying your arrogance for power.
On one hand, you inaugurate hospitals and earn applause,
On the other, you smile while granting licenses to liquor shops,
After eighteen years, you've granted the right to vote,
By forming governments through manipulation,
You chanted slogans of bringing Ram and building the temple there,
But lacked the courage to bring the ordinance,
Now you say we brought Ram, and we'll build the temple there.
So tell me, did you go to ring the bells in the court?
Well, forget all that,
You incite Hindus, Muslims, Sikhs, and Christians against each other,

You'll do anything for the throne of power,
You say the opposition is corrupt, don't vote for them,
Then you cozy up to those very thieves,
And say it's time for another 400 seats.
Who knows what intoxication you indulge in,
You talk about the timeless culture, claim ownership of Ram,
Distribute certificates of patriotism and devotion to Ram at every turn,
By imprisoning the self saint Asharam Ji, you perpetuate injustice,
And by participating in the consecration of the Ram temple, you reveal your duplicity,
Who knows why you hesitate to declare Ram Setu a national heritage,
When it comes to employment, you compare yourself to past governments,
You engage in political maneuvering in the name of Ram in the religious domain,
When saints raise their voice, you push them behind bars,
Instead of ensuring justice for the elderly, you open old age homes,
Instead of ending the practice of prostitution,
you legalize it. Instead of preventing adultery, you decriminalize it.
I've witnessed your actions, even the chameleon feels ashamed.
What can I say, as I write, my heart
trembles. Realizing it's the age of darkness,
I lay down my pen, finding solace in silence, immersed in Ram.
Those who take shelter in Ram's creation,
Why argue and debate?
Just chant the Lord's name, and all sorrows vanish.

But now, injustice's legacy must be broken. Everyone must stand for the true saint Asharam Bapu. The faith and integrity of millions won't be harmed anymore. Millions of devotees are dedicated to Bapu's feet. Are those people foolish? They forsake everything, calling only for Bapu's name. Engineers, doctors, lawyers, government officials, all sacrifice for India's glory, uplifting humanity worldwide. Long ago, someone asked me why Asharam Bapu, being the Supreme Being, doesn't use his powers and doesn't fight against these wrongdoers? The answer is simple. In the Treta Yuga, even Lord Rama was all-powerful, yet he battled Ravana to teach society and uphold truth over falsehood. Similarly, Lord Krishna faced adversities to teach society. Both were embodiments of the divine. Did they need war? No, their resolve alone could win battles instantly. When

Goddess Durga is worshipped, she defeats demons with just the word 'Hum.' Saints never use their powers for themselves, always for inspiring others and their well-being. Have you ever seen the ocean drinking its own water, or a fruitful tree consuming its own fruit? Or a doctor treating themselves? No, similarly, saints exist for society's welfare. They have nothing for themselves. They've sacrificed everything since childhood, walking the path of God. Asharam Bapu is like a giant tree, his branches laden with the essence of the Vedas and Vedanta. His words and knowledge serve society. If you trouble him, will you gain anything? No, your life will be worse than death. If the saint departs from this Earth, what then? It's time to amend, or nature's wrath will fall upon you.

My words aren't meant to hurt anyone's sentiments but express the frustration of millions of disciples and devotees whose faith in Asharam Bapu remains unshaken, despite relentless media persecution. During the writing of this book, I met thousands of his followers and devotees, and their only plea is 'Bapu, come out soon.' They've demonstrated their devotion even after so much defamation. What more can I say? I earnestly pray to the Chief Justice of India and urge them, through a humble letter, to pay attention to this matter and take necessary steps to uphold democracy and justice in India.

www.ingramcontent.com/pod-product-compliance
Lightning Source LLC
LaVergne TN
LVHW090318160826
845684LV00002B/24

* 9 7 9 8 8 9 4 9 8 0 4 2 3 *